American National Security and Civil Liberties in an Era of Terrorism

Edited by
David B. Cohen
and
John W. Wells

palgrave
macmillan

AMERICAN NATIONAL SECURITY AND CIVIL LIBERTIES IN
AN ERA OF TERRORISM

First published 2004 by
PALGRAVE MACMILLAN™
175 Fifth Avenue, New York, N.Y. 10010 and
Houndmills, Basingstoke, Hampshire, England RG21 6XS.
Companies and representatives throughout the world.

PALGRAVE MACMILLAN is the global academic imprint of the Palgrave
Macmillan division of St. Martin's Press, LLC and of Palgrave Macmillan Ltd.
Macmillan® is a registered trademark in the United States, United Kingdom and
other countries. Palgrave is a registered trademark in the European Union and
other countries.

ISBN 1–4039-6199–9 hardback
ISBN 1–4039-6200–6 paperback

Library of Congress Cataloging-in-Publication Data

American national security and civil liberties in an era of terrorism / edited by
David B. Cohen and John W. Wells.
     p. cm.
  Includes bibliographical references and index
  ISBN 1–4039-6199–9 (hc) — 1–4039-6200–6 (pbk.)
     1. Civil rights—United States. 2. September 11 Terrorist Attacks, 2001- 3.
War on Terrorism, 2001- 4. Terrorism—United States—Prevention. 5. United
States—Politics and government—2001- I. Cohen, David B., 1967- II. Wells,
John Wilson, 1969-

JC599.U5A4985 2004
323'.0973—dc22
                                                            2003065607

A catalogue record for this book is available from the British Library.

Design by Autobookcomp

First edition: April 2004
10 9 8 7 6 5 4 3 2 1

Printed in the United States of America.

DATE DUE

JUL 0 2 2009	
JUL 1 5 2009	
JUL 2 9 2009	
NOV 1 7 2010	
APR 0 4 2014	

To those who pit Americans against immigrants, and
citizens against non-citizens; to those who scare peace-
loving people with phantoms of lost liberty; my
message is this: Your tactics only aid terrorists—for
they erode our national unity and diminish our resolve.
They give ammunition to America's enemies, and pause
to America's friends. They encourage people of good
will to remain silent in the face of evil.

> —*U.S. Attorney General John Ashcroft,*
> *December 6, 2001*

Preserving our freedom is one of the main reasons we
are now engaged in this new war on terrorism. We will
lose that war without firing a shot if we sacrifice the
liberties of the American people.

> —*U.S. Senator Russell Feingold (D-WI),*
> *October 25, 2001*

Contents

List of Tables

Preface

From its inception, the United States has been viewed as an experiment. Initially, it was an experiment to see if a nation so geographically diffuse could possibly be forged into a cohesive nation-state. Another early question was whether a nation that lacked the traditional foundations of legitimacy, a state church, and a crowned monarch could possibly remain stable. Since then, other ways of viewing America as an experiment, such as Abraham Lincoln's question as to whether or not a nation of, for, and by the people could possibly endure, have been presented. As important as all of these questions have been, and indeed as salient as they have been in framing much of the history of American political thought, another question has been foisted into the realm of debate. *To what extent can a nation that takes great pride in viewing itself as the paradigmatic example of an open society combat terrorism and still maintain its steadfast commitment to civil liberties?*

The issues at stake run considerably deeper than is at first apparent. What is at stake is nothing less than whether the ideas associated with the modern period of political philosophy—the freedom of conscience, the inviolable rights of the individual to privacy, the constitutionally limited state, as well as the more recent emergence of a truly multicultural society—can survive the potentially threatening effects of modernity itself. Modernity has brought with it many of the blessings of contemporary life, but the conveniences have come with a price. Indeed, improvements in communications and transportation systems have brought the world closer together and spawned a whole new way of conceptualizing human community—the global village. But, as has been pointed out by a number of scholars, the increasing availability of the commodities of modernity has not necessarily meant the triumph of modern ideas over traditional ones.[1] Neither has the trend toward globalization or the lack of military conflict between the world powers since the end of the cold war. In fact, as was evidenced in the events of September 11, 2001, modern technology can be employed to advance decidedly antimodern philosophies.

The essays in this book will examine the intricacies of this experiment, which pits the assumptions of liberalism against the ramifications of a world brought closer together. What is the response of the liberal state to the difficulties posed by those who would use terrorism to threaten it? Can the modern liberal state use illiberal means for self-defense and yet still be regarded as liberal? Will the curtailing of civil liberties in the aftermath of September 11 be a temporary response or is the truly open society fading?

While there is little doubt that such perplexing questions will be difficult to answer, there is room for optimism. This is due to the fact that in contrast to closed societies, liberal democracies have always found ways to adapt to changing circumstances. This vitality is directly based upon the availability of open dialogue in the setting of national priorities. Thus, the very topic at hand—the preservation of civil liberties in the face of the pressing need to secure the nation's defense—will be addressed effectively only to the extent to which the public square is open to dissenting views and civil liberties are vigorously maintained. This is not to deny that there will be a need to make hard choices. Further, there are likely to be tradeoffs that necessitate a renewed conception of rights in the face of changing international realities. The good news is that such balancing acts have always been the mainstay of democratic politics. In this sense, the road ahead should not be seen as a departure from normal politics; rather, it should be viewed as the kind of challenge that democracy is designed to accommodate.

Notes

1. In Benjamin R. Barber's celebrated work, *Jihad vs. McWorld* (New York: Times Books, 1995), he explores how modernity's expanding reach may actually be contributing to the vitality of the antimodern philosophies, theologies, and ideologies that are emerging as a backlash. Another key book in this area, Thomas L. Friedman's *The Lexus and the Olive Tree* (New York: Farrar, Straus, Giroux, 1999), also identifies this dynamic. However, like Francis Fukuyama's *The End of History and the Last Man* (New York: Free Press, 1992), Friedman is far more sanguine about the long-term prospects of liberalism. Finally, one of the most pessimistic accounts is Samuel P. Huntington's *The Clash of Civilizations and the Remaking of World Order* (New York: Simon and Schuster, 1996). According to Huntington, the West should not be deceived into thinking that its ideas really represent the triumph of irresistible universal truths. In fact, liberalism's fate cannot be separated from its connection to the economic, cultural, and military strength of the core Western states. Accordingly, Huntington advocates a return to an unapologetic defense of liberal Western values in the face of mounting multiculturalism and global integration.

Introduction

American National Security and Civil Liberties in an Era of Terrorism

John W. Wells

David B. Cohen

*The choice between liberty and safety is too often a false one. The abuse of power
is never a substitute for effective police work.*

—*U.S. Representative Jerrold Nadler (D-NY), May 20, 2003*

Few would contest the claim that the terrorist attacks of September 11, 2001
marked a significant point in American history. For the first time in nearly
two centuries, American cities were burning due to the actions of foreign
agents. Americans used to the protection afforded by two oceans and
friendly nations along the borders were compelled to give second thought to
homeland security and what it means to live in a global world. The initial
shock had scarcely begun to abate when politicians and scholars began a
debate regarding the nature of civil liberties—a debate that promises to
continue well into the new millennium.

The purpose of this collection of essays is to contribute to that debate and
offer policy and theoretical insight regarding the effects that September 11 is
likely to have. The essays are eclectic and offer a broad range of perspectives.
Institutions, political culture, and public policy are all addressed as far as
they relate to the maintenance of a robust regime of civil rights and liberties.
The essays are timely and recognize the need to balance the imperatives of
civil liberties and national security. Central to all of the essays, however, is
how such a balance might be struck that does not unnecessarily proscribe
one or the other.

Americans have grown accustomed to linking national security to civil
liberties. Throughout much of the twentieth century, a steady ebbing and
flowing of debate and accusation have marked the agonistic struggle
between civil libertarians and advocates of increased police powers. Civil
libertarians have stressed the liberal nature of American democracy.[1] Individuals bring their rights into the political order and do not surrender them
under any condition. Those rights are, in fact, "inalienable." Freedom is the
paramount concern among such thinkers and efforts to proscribe rights,
regardless of justifications based upon the need for national security, are
viewed with a healthy amount of skepticism.

From the very outset of the republic, the impulse toward protecting the citizen from the encroaching powers of the federal government was a defining feature. Constitutional debates between Federalists and anti-Federalists routinely included heated exchanges over the relative importance of liberty versus the need to maintain stability. The Constitutional Convention itself was called, at least in part, to ensure a stable federal government in the wake of domestic disturbances.[2] Anti-Federalists, fearing the unwarranted concentration of power in the hands of a centralized government, sounded the warning that freedom would be the inevitable casualty of any attempt to further strengthen the constitutional powers of the federal government.[3]

Thomas Jefferson, along with his political ally James Madison, expressed outrage toward the John Adams administration due to its support for the Alien and Sedition Acts.[4] From the perspective of both Virginians, the Adams administration's circumscribing of free speech amounted to nothing more than an abrogation of the terms of the social contract. Echoes of this sentiment would resound throughout the nineteenth century as civil libertarians like Henry David Thoreau would respond with outrage toward what they considered to be a populace too willing to part with their right to express their conscience.

The twentieth century, however, marked an even greater tension between the competing claims of civil libertarians and national security advocates. With America's entrance onto the world stage during World War I and its exposure to anarchist and socialist thought, nativists shrilly proclaimed the need to regulate the public realm more vigorously. Led by Attorney General A. Mitchell Palmer, national security advocates proclaimed the need to purge the country from the unsavory influences of "anti-Americanism."[5] Eugene Debs is perhaps the most salient symbol of the era. He was jailed for his public opposition to America's involvement in the war.[6] Following the end of hostilities, the fervent attack on dissent only gained more strength before finally abating during the economic prosperity of the 1920s. This first "Red Scare" is still regarded by civil libertarians as a defining example of what happens when the nation relaxes its commitment to civil liberties.

Civil liberties were again under attack as the United States entered World War II decades later. Beginning with the Franklin D. Roosevelt administration's approval of the forcible relocation and internment of Japanese Americans and culminating in the rise of Joseph McCarthy's assault on Harry Truman's State Department, the period of the mid-twentieth century continues to cast a long shadow over the debate. Individuals of high reputation, such as Secretary of State George Marshall, found themselves the target of public accusation. A chill fell across free speech as would-be dissenters self-censored themselves to avoid being labeled as "pink."

The strong emphasis on free speech during the sixties was a direct reaction to the McCarthy era. Buoyed by the Warren Court's determination to expand the space for public dissent, civil libertarians reveled in the willingness of countless Americans to express their opinions on issues ranging from civil rights to the Vietnam War. The tradition from the sixties, as evidenced by reaction of opponents to the second Gulf War, has still not entirely run its course even though nearly four decades have elapsed. This is indicative of the extent to which the protest culture of the sixties continues to exert some influence on contemporary culture.

Also persistent is the reaction that many middle Americans had to the movements of the 1960s. The efforts on the part of supporters of Operation Iraqi Freedom to portray protestors as anti-American harkens back to the days of Vietnam. What supporters of the current George W. Bush administration have that Johnson and Nixon supporters lacked a generation ago, however, are the searing images of the crumbling World Trade Center. It is impossible to overemphasize the impact of the repeated broadcast of those images on the minds of many Americans. With this brief historical backdrop in place, we may now turn to a discussion of the specific entries in this volume.

In chapter 1, Jerel Rosati reviews in more detail the history of America's commitment to civil liberties and concludes that it is far too early to determine whether or not the events of September 11 have actually made a long-term impact on the nation's civil liberties regime. The disappearance of communism at the end of the cold war was greeted with great anticipation by civil libertarians. The putative logic behind the national security state was no longer relevant given the collapse of America's archenemy. Much like the "peace dividend" that was to have swollen the nation's financial coffers, a civil liberties dividend was expected. Over the course of the four decades of cold war the nation's national defense bureaucracy had grown substantially. Reform was to be the logical outgrowth of the end of the standoff. Time will tell if September 11 fatally interrupted the process of change toward greater openness and tolerance of dissenting opinion.

The centerpiece of the federal government's response to the terrorist attacks of September 11 is the USA PATRIOT Act. Passed in the immediate aftermath of the attacks, the PATRIOT Act grants increased powers to the federal government and its investigative agencies. According to Chris Banks in chapter 2, this concentration of power merits careful attention in that civil liberties are decidedly diminished in the state's determination to wage war on terror. He begins with an overview of the federal government's historical response to civil disturbance. Banks points out that governmental powers have often been expanded to meet past threats and the PATRIOT Act is but the latest in a long line of such congressionally sanctioned expansions of federal police power.

In what is clearly an attempt to respond to the revolution in communications technology, the PATRIOT Act grants far more latitude to the state when it comes to the gathering of information—particularly e-mail records and phone conversations of would-be terrorist threats. In addition, the right to expel noncitizens and to detain them is also discussed. Banks raises concerns as to how such provisions alter the meaning of the Fourth Amendment and dilute its prohibition on unreasonable searches and seizures. By situating the conversation against the backdrop of constitutional law, Banks points to the long-term ramifications of the PATRIOT Act and how its provisions may in fact be altering the nation's long-established commitment to restraining the state's police power.

Few issues have raised as much concern among defenders of civil liberties as the question of detainees and the use of military tribunals. For obvious reasons, including the suspension of rights that might otherwise be available for defendants, military tribunals are problematic. Otis Stephens, Jr., explores some of the issues raised by their use in chapter 3. The chapter reviews the historical record of military tribunals, focusing in particular on their usage during the administrations of Abraham Lincoln and Franklin Roosevelt. Stephens points out that during times of war extraordinary means have been taken to ensure that those who might pose special risks to the nation's security are dealt with in ways that circumvent normal legal procedures. While perhaps troubling to many, the use of tribunals is not a novelty and the Bush administration does have ample statutory and case law histories upon which to defend the use of tribunals during the War on Terror. The issue is complicated, however, by the ambiguous nature of the current war inasmuch as a specific and foreseeable terminus for the conflict defies prediction.

In chapter 4, John Blakeman brings the complexities of the War on Terror into stark relief. One of the most important questions regarding terrorism is the extent to which its effects are at all addressable via judicial remedy. In effect, can states that support terrorism be held financially accountable for the loss of life and property that their support helps to make possible? Blakeman points out that such an approach poses numerous difficulties. For one thing, the prospect of actually collecting funds from a state that is found guilty of supporting terrorism is itself highly problematic. What is to be the enforcement mechanism? Thus far, Congress has resorted to a myriad of means that actually have the effect of redressing jury verdicts without penalizing the particular states that are found guilty of supporting terrorism. Blakeman contends that this demonstrates a flaw in this strategy inasmuch as it fails to hold the rogue states themselves accountable for their terrorist support.

Dave Cohen, Alethia Cook, and Dave Louscher examine the threat to civil liberties posed by biological terrorism in chapter 5. Unlike other weapons of mass destruction (such as nuclear weapons), biological weapons have been used frequently by states and terrorist groups throughout the centuries. The authors argue that the anthrax attacks of autumn 2001 demonstrate that the threat to the U.S. from bioterrorism is imminent. Complicating matters is the fact that the wide variety and availability of biological agents and forms of delivery make response planning and disease containment a very difficult task. Among the instruments for mitigating such a biological attack are traditional disease-containment methods of isolation, quarantine, and vaccination; however, these tools can be problematic when considering American notions of individual civil liberties. The authors illuminate the challenges of bioterrorism faced by policymakers through an exploration of the responses of various countries to severe acute respiratory syndrome (SARS).

Cohen, Cook, and Louscher ultimately conclude that in the event of a bioterrorist incident, especially one involving a communicable agent, public health officials will move quickly to control its spread through the use of isolation, quarantine, and/or vaccination. However, according to the authors, "there is no one-size-fits-all instruction manual on how to respond to a biological attack." "Rather," they argue, "response needs to be tailored in a disease-specific fashion and planning should be made in such a way that response to a biological weapons attack be flexible enough to adapt to changing and unforeseen circumstances. In some cases, large-scale isolation, quarantine, and vaccination may be appropriate; in others, it may do more harm than good."

Taking as their point of departure the Republican emphasis on devolution, Ed Sharkey and Kendra Stewart provide an analysis of public policy responses to terrorism at the state level in chapter 6. This is a new area for states. Issues of security and national defense have traditionally been the purview of the federal government, but in an era when the new federalism meets globalization, states must find the resources and the know-how to combat international terrorism. This is made particularly difficult in the wake of the return of austerity budgets in many state capitals. The decade of the nineties was a good time to be a governor as many states found their state budgets swollen by the tax revenue created from booming economies. The first decade of the twenty-first century, however, has been a different story. Many states find that they must make painful choices when determining how to spend public money. With the added burden of providing for the homeland defense of vital targets and planning civil emergency contingency plans, many states are severely strained.

Sharkey and Stewart point out that this has led to a myriad of approaches to dealing with the issue of homeland security. Much as the states became the testing grounds for domestic policy in the nineties, they are now fulfilling that role in the areas of homeland defense and civil liberties. The multiple approaches employed by the states have created a kind of collage effect on civil liberties. Depending upon where one lives in the United States, civil liberties policies are different. This poses additional problems to those wishing to maintain a uniform policy of civil liberties across the country.

In chapter 7, Brian Gerber and Chris Dolan contend that the 9/11 attacks have brought about a revival of the centralizing trend in governmental power. Since the nomination of Barry Goldwater in 1964, the movement away from centralization has steadily gained ground. Talk of a new federalism, premised on the idea of returning to the states many functions heretofore executed by the government in Washington, has been a defining feature of the nation's move to the right over the course of the last generation. Using the debate over whether or not to federalize the employees used to screen traveler baggage as their point of departure, Gerber and Dolan contend that the ideological air is beginning to blow in a different direction. Private screeners tend to be undertrained and underpaid, and their ranks are prone to high rates of turnover. Presumably, using governmental employees will lead to a safer situation for passengers as the army of screeners will become professionalized. Gerber and Dolan argue that airline security policy illuminates a demonstrable area where governmental support may very well be preferable to the outcome of a free market.

In chapter 8, Kendra Stewart and Christian Marlin examine what they regard as the government's conscious effort to elevate the value of stability over that of liberty in its handling of the issue of censorship. Operating from the old principle that the first casualty of war is the truth, Stewart and Marlin point to the diminished effectiveness of the press during the War on Terror. Although the chapter is not a catalogue of various attempts to muzzle the press, it does list several potentially disturbing instances where U.S. military raids have gone relatively unreported, trial records have been sealed, and hearings have been conducted well out of range of the nation's media. In what is perhaps the most unsettling contention of the chapter, Stewart and Marlin raise the prospect that the press itself is complicit in restricting the flow of information to the public. In a time of high approval ratings for the president and the lingering effects of the "rally-round-the-flag" response of the American public, the press has become increasingly wary of raising those issues that cast in doubt various policies being implemented by the administration.

In chapter 9, Susan Tabrizi provides a closer examination of American public opinion in the wake of the September 11 attacks. Recognizing the importance of a strong level of public support for civil liberties, Tabrizi examines the changing nature of that support. In the initial aftermath of the attacks, the public became less supportive of viewing civil liberties as automatically deserving of deference. The fear instigated by the attacks led many citizens to conclude that security had moved into a more paramount position. As time has passed, however, the older attachments to privacy and individual liberty have steadily gained ground in public opinion polls. Tabrizi concludes by suggesting that this is a hopeful sign inasmuch as it points to the long-term health of the nation's commitment to civil liberties.

On the crucial issue of political culture, Dan Tokaji offers compelling insight into the true health of the nation's civil liberties commitments in chapter 10. Operating with the dichotomy of negative and positive dissent, Tokaji argues that America has failed to create what amounts to a fully functioning liberal polity. From the standpoint of state power, the various constitutional restraints have functioned effectively in that they have prevented the government from stifling opposition altogether. The problem, reminiscent of Isaiah Berlin's famous distinction between positive and negative freedom, is that the failure to actively create space for dissent has the effect of guaranteeing a quietistic polity. Tokaji reaches into America's philosophical past to produce two primary voices for a renewed commitment to a revitalized public square, Martin Luther King, Jr., and Henry David Thoreau. Neither man was content to accept the status quo as fair or just. They therefore used their influence to open up new spaces for dissent and protest in hopes of changing governmental policy and public opinion. In the absence of such space, how can dissent really function? Tokaji contends that the extent to which dissent and discussion do occur, the discourse itself is impoverished. Without a renewed interest in providing the space for citizen deliberation, the nation's dedication to civil liberties is incomplete. Tokaji proposes expanded government funding for nonprofit agencies in an effort to create the loci for public discussion and dissent. Only by availing individuals to existing outlets for their input can true citizens be created and a robust democratic order be instituted.

Finally, the volume concludes with an examination by John Wells of the nation's changing political culture. He concludes that America is truly in a new era. Globalization has taken place and is deepening its effects in many aspects of national life. As such, Americans used to the traditional feelings of security brought about by relative geographic isolation from the world's trouble spots now find themselves having to confront the reality of domestic terror. Among the questions posed in the final chapter is the extent to which the dissipation of this feeling of security will have a long-term impact on the civil liberties regime in America. In addition, the feeling that the country has finally been plunged into the world runs counter to the open-endedness that has characterized American political culture. Based on the experience of the frontier, Americans have traditionally seen their options as being open. The presence of so much space afforded the nation's citizens a safety valve for difference and individual experimentation. Does the sense that the country has run up against the boundaries of the world itself necessarily undermine the willingness of Americans to be tolerant of difference?

.The chapter concludes with speculation as to how the post–September 11 America will ultimately appear. The analysis relies on a reading of John Locke and Thomas Hobbes. Locke's political theory was born in optimism that largely benign individuals are capable of governing themselves with only minimal governmental intrusion. The Hobbesian alternative, however, posits the hopelessly violent aspects of the state of nature. The only solution is to exchange freedom for security. The choice, however, does not emerge so starkly inasmuch as the American people are already retreating to their private realm, having largely abandoned public spaces in favor of pursuing the largely consumer-driven society of late mass consumer capitalism. What this portends is a waning belief in the efficacy of public protest and dissent but a stronger-than-ever insistence on privacy. This dual sense both adds to and detracts from the health of the nation's civil liberties regime.

The volume is diverse in its approach to the delicate problem of balancing civil liberties and the need to maintain national security. This is a deliberate reflection of the fact that the issue will require extensive debate, in both the political realm and in the scholarly community. As demonstrated by the West's ability to prevail at the end of the cold war, democracy possesses many resources for dealing with the issues that the current crisis raises. While this fact should provide a sense of optimism to those who wish to see the persistence of a robust civil liberties regime, it should not obscure the fact that liberty requires vigilance. It is with that in mind that the current collection of essays seeks to contribute to the dialogue concerning the need to restrain our zeal at home even as we continue to guard our borders from threats emanating from abroad.

Introduction

1. Champions of the liberal idea include such Supreme Court justices as William Brennan, Louis Brandeis, and Hugo Black. In addition, figures from the American political tradition such as John Dewey and Henry David Thoreau are also considered to be spokespersons for the tradition of free expression and civil liberties.
2. The rebellion of Daniel Shays in 1786 apparently frightened many of the nation's elites. Concern over such outbreaks of violence precipitated a belief in the minds of some of the nation's elites that a stronger government was needed if chaos was to be avoided. See Stanley Elkins and Eric McKitrick, *The Age of Federalism* (New York: Oxford University Press, 1993).
3. Saul Cornell, *The Other Founders: Anti-Federalism and the Dissenting Tradition in America, 1788–1828* (Chapel Hill, NC: University of North Carolina Press, 1999).
4. During John Adams's tenure as president, a Federalist-controlled Congress passed four laws, collectively known as the Alien and Sedition Acts, as a means to undercut its critics, led by Thomas Jefferson. In so doing, the First Amendment to the Constitution suffered a serious blow in what was nothing more than a political power struggle. Among others, the 1798 legislation consisted of the Enemy Alien Act, a law which is still in effect, which grants the president the authority during a declared war to imprison, deport, or detain individuals fourteen years of age and older who are citizens of nations at war with the United States. The Enemy Alien Act requires no evidence of criminal or harmful conduct. The Sedition Act is the most infamous of the 1798 legislation perhaps because it was the most zealously enforced. Among other things, the Sedition Act allowed for a monetary fine and imprisonment for the printing or publication of "any false, scandalous and malicious writing" against the U.S. government (or officials of) "with intent to defame . . . or to bring them . . . into contempt or disrepute; or to excite against them, or either or any of them, the hatred of the good people of the United States." See Martin E. Halstuk, "Policy of Secrecy—Pattern of Deception: What Federalist Leaders Thought about a Public Right to Know, 1794–98," *Communication Law and Policy* 7, no. 51 (winter 2002) and David Cole, "The New McCarthyism: Repeating History in the War on Terrorism," *Harvard Civil Rights-Civil Liberties Law Review* 38, no. 1 (winter 2003).
5. See Cole, "The New McCarthyism."
6. See *Debs v. U.S.*, 249 U.S. 211 (1919).

Chapter 1

At Odds with One Another:

The Tension between Civil Liberties and National Security in Twentieth-Century America*

Jerel A. Rosati

The September 11 tragedy and the War on Terror have clearly demonstrated the tension between the demands of national security and the demands of democracy in the making of U.S. foreign policy. Democracy requires an open political process and high levels of civil rights and liberties in order for its citizens to politically participate. The demands of national security usually require a much less open political process with limitations on civil rights and liberties. The demands of democracy and the demands of national security inherently have contradictory implications for political participation within a democratic society.

This chapter examines the exercise of civil liberties throughout American history, especially in relation to the ebb and flow of the politics of national security during the twentieth century. Not only does a focus on the evolution of the exercise of civil liberties provide a richer understanding of the significance of the historical contradictions between the demands of national security and democracy in the making of U.S. foreign policy, but it deepens an understanding of continuity and change in the politics of U.S. foreign policy and the president's ability to govern.

Historical Background and Developments

Political participation is guaranteed not under the Constitution of the United States as originally written but within its first ten amendments. After delegates from the various states produced a new constitution in Philadelphia in 1787, a controversial ratification process ensued. It is worth remembering "the vast majority of the Framers flatly repudiated the entire idea of a federal bill of rights, on philosophical as well as political grounds [as represented by *The Federalist Papers*]. It is also worth remembering that James Madison, the 'father' of the Bill of Rights, had to be dragged into fatherhood largely by forces outside his control."[1]

A bill of rights was promised to allay the fears widespread among Americans that the new constitution would create a central government that would restrict personal and state freedoms. Therefore, in order to guarantee approval by the states, ten amendments to the Constitution were eventually passed and took effect in 1791—three years after the Constitution was initially ratified. These ten amendments, which restrain the national government from limiting personal freedoms, have come to be known as the Bill of Rights.

According to the First Amendment of the Bill of Rights, "Congress shall make no law . . . abridging the freedom of speech, or of the press; or the right of the people peaceably to assemble, and to petition the Government for a redress of grievances." Such civil rights and the exercise of such liberties were considered essential to prevent the majority from tyrannizing the minority and to prevent minority factions from controlling the majority. These rights and liberties allowed people to participate and speak without fear of persecution or political repression—a necessary core requirement of democratic politics. The Declaration of Independence, written by Thomas Jefferson and signed by many of America's founding fathers in 1776, went so far as to argue "that whenever any form of government becomes destructive to these ends [life, liberty, and the pursuit of happiness], it is the right of the people to alter or to abolish it, and to institute new government."[2]

Although citizen participation and a broad exercise of civil liberties represented an "ideal" of the American Revolution and the U.S. Constitution, the historical record has varied over time. Three contradictory patterns in civil rights and liberties have predominated.[3] First, the right to participate and exercise civil liberties—that is, American civil rights—was extremely limited throughout much of American history.

Second, civil rights and liberties have expanded throughout American history. Even though women and minorities were initially denied civil rights and liberties, they fought for and eventually achieved them. Yet, it is important to remember that the successful expansion of civil rights and liberties was accomplished at the price of considerable blood, sweat, and tears: A "tradition of speech—and struggle to obtain the right to speak—did develop. Courageous, often rebellious Americans—including, most prominently, opponents of slavery and advocates of civil rights, women's rights and union's rights—fought for and shaped our system of free expression, often at considerable personal risk."[4]

Finally, while civil rights and liberties have expanded throughout history, there also have been times of contraction in the exercise of civil liberties. Historically, large numbers of individuals have experienced political discrimination and have had great difficulty in exercising their civil liberties, especially because of their class, gender, race (particularly new immigrants and minority ethnic groups), and their political beliefs (especially those who challenge government policy, established groups, and the status quo). Times of contraction in the exercise of civil liberties tend to occur particularly in response to events that generate political instability and fear, such as the rise of industrialization and efforts to unionize, economic depressions and downturns, large waves of immigration to the states, and, most importantly, periods of national emergency and war.[5]

The Preoccupation with National Security Versus Democratic Liberties

Under conditions of war, American civil liberties and political participation are often curtailed and violated in a systematic way by the government, usually with the active support of groups and people throughout society. This typically occurs because the demands of national security take precedence over the demands of democracy during war, where most segments of society tend to rally behind the president and the government in order to fight the enemy abroad. It is in the context of this political environment that the government's and, in particular, the president's ability to dominate the politics of U.S. foreign policy is maximized. This is because wars and national emergencies, in particular, tend to be times when little tolerance exists for individuals and groups that politically criticize or challenge the government's foreign policy or the status quo within society.

The general American tendency toward conformity, as stated by political scientist Seymour Martin Lipset, "has been noted as a major aspect of American culture from Tocqueville in the 1830s to [David] Riesman [in *The Lonely Crowd*] in the 1950s."[6] In fact, times of perceived threats to national security are often accompanied by what historian Richard Hofstadter has called "the paranoid style in American politics."[7] In other words, war often produces a preoccupation with internal threats to national security, and certain groups within society are targeted as security risks because of their ethnicity or political beliefs.

The net result is that the ability to politically participate and exercise civil liberties tends to be limited during periods of conflict because the government's war effort, combined with American nationalism and superpatriotism, tolerates little dissent and encourages political repression. Witness, for example, the furor surrounding the country band the Dixie Chicks when in March 2003, on the eve of the Iraq War, lead singer Natalie Maines told her London concertgoers that "we're ashamed the president of the United States is from Texas."[8] The remark was followed by scores of radio stations boycotting their music as well as publicity events in which their albums were destroyed.[9] The band later apologized for the comment after being pressured by their recording label.[10] This episode represents the "underside" of American history that is too often ignored, yet it has been part of American history and is important to know in order to understand the evolution of political participation and the politics of U.S. foreign policy.

There have been three major periods in the twentieth century when the demands of national security have prevailed over the demands of democracy and the exercise of civil liberties in domestic politics has been severely curtailed: 1) World War I; 2) World War II; and 3) the cold war. Each of these periods has been accompanied by the supremacy of the president in the making of U.S. foreign policy.[11]

The years after the Vietnam War, however, have been characterized by a decline in the demands of national security throughout American society, creating an uneasy tension between national security and democracy. This development has led to a corresponding rise in the liberty of Americans to fully exercise their civil rights in electoral and group politics in order to influence the future of U.S. foreign policy. The net result is that presidents have had to operate in a political environment where they have had greater difficulty exercising power in the politics of U.S. foreign policy. The terrorist attacks of September 11, 2001, and the war on terrorism may have again altered the tense dynamics between the demands of national security and democracy and its corresponding implications for exercising presidential power in foreign policy at the beginning of the twenty-first century despite the collapse of the cold war.

World War I

Civil liberties were heavily curtailed and circumscribed as a result of developments during World War I. Strong antiwar sentiment existed as President Woodrow Wilson asked Congress to declare war on Germany. Convinced that he had done everything humanly possible to keep America out of the war, Woodrow Wilson demanded uncritical public support. The government thus decided to clamp down on civil liberties, a move which was reinforced by intolerance and bigotry throughout much of the public. Not surprisingly, the power of President Wilson and the executive branch grew dramatically during the war.

The administration instituted one of the earliest modern and systematic uses of mass communications for propaganda purposes—that is, the propaganda campaign was intended to convince Americans that the United States was fighting to make the world safe for democracy. On April 14, 1917, eight days after the formal declaration of war, President Wilson established the Committee on Public Information (CPI) to promote the Allied war aims. The CPI consisted of the secretary of state, the secretary of war, the secretary of the navy, and was directed by a journalist from Denver, George Creel, who advised President Wilson that propaganda was more powerful than censorship in promoting public support. Throughout the war, the CPI distributed over 75 million pieces of printed material, including posters, pamphlets and books, as well as short movies. It also created 75,000 "4-Minute Men" who gave speeches throughout the country supporting food conservation and other issues important to the war economy. In the beginning, the CPI emphasized facts, but with time they promoted the cartoonish, exaggerated image of the "savage" Germans. The CPI geared their propaganda not only toward Americans but also toward their enemies, especially Germans. They tried to prompt Germans to rebel, citing inflated figures of the size of U.S. forces and a promise for peace.[12]

One of the main results of the propaganda office was the growth of major anti-German sentiment throughout the country. Much of this occurred because most of the press, and the public, accepted voluntary censorship and actively promoted the war effort. With the fear of the "Hun" increasing, German Americans became the target of political attacks and hostility. Popular prejudices equated most anything German—names, language, and culture—with disloyalty.

Members of the Socialist party and the political Left also were targets of the narrowing and violation of civil liberties. This came at a time when the Socialist party, launched in 1901, was growing in popularity and making remarkable gains as a political force throughout American society. In 1912 Socialist party leader Eugene V. Debs received over 900,000 votes for president, about 6 percent of the total. "No fewer than 1,200 municipal officials—including 56 socialist mayors and many more aldermen and city councilmen—were elected, and there were [at that time] socialist police chiefs as well as state legislators."[13] In 1917, socialist candidates received 21 percent of the vote in New York City, 25 percent in Buffalo, 34 percent in Chicago, and 44 percent in Dayton, Ohio.

But the Socialist party and the Left experienced a rapid decline with the rise of political repression imposed by the government in the name of national security, which was reinforced by the rise of the progressive movement represented by Woodrow Wilson and Theodore Roosevelt as well as factional infighting among socialists and the Left. In order to squash political dissent and opposition, the government ultimately passed the Espionage Act in 1917, forbidding any action that helped the enemy or interference with the draft. This move was followed shortly by the Sedition Act of 1918, which virtually eliminated free speech in the United States. The Sedition Act forbade Americans to "utter, print, or publish disloyal, profane, scurrilous, or abusive language about the form of government, the Constitution, soldiers and sailors, the flag, or uniform of the armed forces . . . or by word or act oppose the cause of the United States."[14]

By the end of the war, as many as 200,000 Americans were accused or indicted for remarks heard in public; those found guilty were fined heavily or imprisoned. Eugene Debs, the Socialist party leader, received a twenty-year sentence in a federal prison for speaking out publicly against American participation in the war (and in 1920, while still in jail, he polled nearly 1 million votes for president).[15]

With the Bolshevik revolution in 1917, a wave of anti-Bolshevism and antiradicalism hit the country. The U.S. government, led by the Justice Department and the Federal Bureau of Investigation (FBI), initiated a Red Scare campaign that completely destroyed socialist and other left-wing organizations. Numerous radicals and hundreds of innocent immigrants were deported back to Russia, while thousands of U.S. citizens were incarcerated by the government without charges. By the early 1920s, the FBI had secretly labeled a half million Americans as dangerous.

These government actions violated the civil rights and liberties of numerous people, many of whom were American citizens. Nevertheless, the actions were supported by nativist and conservative groups that promoted what was referred to as "100 percent Americanism." They saw eastern and southern European immigrants, the Jewish and Catholic religions, and different cultures and views as threats to their image of small-town, Protestant America. These discriminatory actions were reinforced by big business, which welcomed the influx of immigrants as a cheap source of labor but bitterly fought against the rise of unionization, liberal reform, and socialism. Thus, World War I was instrumental in the widespread violation and curtailment of civil rights and liberties that virtually destroyed the political Left—pacifists as well as socialists—who were the major challengers to the politics of the status quo.

World War II

During World War II, the government censored the press and the FBI became more active in investigating fascist and communist subversive activity at home. The Smith Act was passed in 1940, making it illegal to advocate the overthrow of the U.S. government by force or to organize or belong to a group with such a goal. The House Un-American Activities Committee engaged in antiradical investigations that focused on the threat of communism. Yet, overall, the civil liberties of Americans were curtailed to a lesser degree during World War II than during World War I.

Germans and the political Left were not severely targeted by discriminatory and repressive measures. This may be explained in part by the assimilation of most German Americans, and other Europeans, within society (especially after World War I), the rise of liberalism under President Franklin Roosevelt, the fact that the Soviet Union was allied with the United States against fascism, and the existence of only minimal dissent in the face of the clear national security threat posed by the Axis powers.

Nevertheless, many American citizens and immigrants of European descent who were associated with the fascist countries were victims of wartime fears. This was especially the case for Italian immigrants and Italian Americans: Over 600,000 Italian citizens who were "legal" immigrants within the United States were classified as "enemy aliens" during the war and had to face travel restrictions and curfews; many Italians lost their jobs; about 1,600 Italian immigrants were interned, which cost them their livelihoods, possessions, and freedom; and about 10,000 Italian American citizens were forced to move from their houses in California coastal communities to inland homes. Italian cultural organizations, language schools, and newspapers were often closed. Italian Americans represented the largest group of foreign-born residents—over 5 million, of whom about 500,000 Italian American men served in the United States armed forces. At Fort Missoula in Montana—an old frontier Army post that served as one of the nation's largest internment camps—along with Italians, about 11,000 Germans and German Americans as well as some Bulgarians, Czechs, Hungarians, and Romanians were interned during the war.[16]

A much more grave situation, however, faced those Americans who were not of European heritage, especially following the attack of Pearl Harbor. The fear of enemy sabotage or a Japanese attack on the West Coast led to such hysteria among Americans that the U.S. government had the military collect all individuals of Japanese descent, most of whom were naturalized American citizens, and hold them in concentration camps throughout the war.

On February 19, 1942, President Franklin D. Roosevelt signed Executive Order 9066, ordering that individuals of Japanese descent living within the continental United States be moved to internment camps in an effort to ensure the internal security of the country. Those affected had only forty-eight hours to dispose of their homes and businesses, they had to forfeit all bank accounts and investments, and they were permitted to take only personal belongings that could be carried in hand luggage. Over 110,000 individuals of Japanese descent, including men, women, and children—mostly American citizens—were rounded up and spent the next three years of their lives in camps located in desolate locations throughout the western United States.

Although the constitutional rights of Japanese Americans were ruthlessly violated, the Supreme Court actually upheld the executive order in *Korematsu v. U.S.* (1944), thus reflecting the politics of the times and the preoccupation with national security over the demands of democracy. Yet, American fears and paranoia proved to be completely unfounded. The Japanese proved to be very patriotic Americans. The executive order did not apply to the Hawaiian Islands, where over 150,000 Japanese Americans remained free and where no charges of sabotage were ever reported. The Japanese were model citizens during their stay in the camps. In fact, over 17,000 Japanese Americans volunteered in the U.S. military to fight in the war once they were allowed to join in 1944. No Japanese American soldier ever deserted the U.S. military, even though they were kept in segregated units, and their wartime exploits became legendary. After the war, Japanese Americans were released from the camps and given only $25 and transportation to make their way back into American society.[17]

This was one of the most blatant examples of political repression in American history. Such was the power of the president and the government, with much societal support, during World War II. So sad was the episode, in fact, that the American government eventually apologized to Japanese Americans and gave reparations to those (few) internees who were alive forty years later.

The Cold War

Even with the end of World War II, the civil liberties of Americans were again attacked with the onset of the cold war. The strong anticommunist legacy in American history and the growth of McCarthyism as a political force made communism an enemy to be feared and fought both abroad and at home. McCarthyism represented a broad political coalition of conservative and nativist groups throughout American society. Nothing was immune to their attack, for communists and un-Americanism seemed to be everywhere—within the Truman administration, the government, the Democratic party, in academia and local schools, in Hollywood and the media, and all other walks of life. The anticommunist hysteria, or Red Scare II, became so intense, and the demands of national security overwhelmed the demands of democracy so thoroughly, that even defending the constitutional rights and liberties of Americans was considered evidence of disloyalty—of aiding and abetting the enemy. The domestic politics of anticommunism curtailed the exercise of civil liberties and contributed to the liberal-conservative consensus that provided the foundation for the president's ability to exercise prerogative government in the making of U.S. foreign policy.

It is true that there were some individuals who engaged in espionage for the Soviet Union. It is also true that there were individuals who were members of the Communist Party, USA.[18] "Of course, not all Communists attacked their adversaries and only a handful received direct orders from Moscow. The rank and file included many who were engaged in work similar to that of other political activists—attending meetings, distributing leaflets, demonstrating, organizing workers" to promote equality, opportunity, and peace, especially within the United States.[19] Furthermore, communists and sympathizers of the Soviet Union were small in numbers. An overwhelming number of Americans formed the basis of the anticommunist consensus throughout the United States, composition of which contained elites and masses, Democrats and Republicans, liberals and conservatives.

Nevertheless, under the warlike conditions of the cold war many Americans became paranoid and preoccupied with the threat of communism. Criticizing the status quo exposed one to charges of being "unpatriotic," "un-American," and "disloyal." Given this environment, it is easy to see why most liberals moderated their beliefs and behavior to become part of the liberal-conservative consensus. Most Americans learned to go along and "shut up" in public even if they did not fully agree with the dominant beliefs and institutions. This resignation also helps to explain why the cold war years were a period of mass apathy and declining political participation. Clearly, it was a time of great conformity and intolerance in American politics, and these sentiments were driven largely by McCarthyism and the politics of anticommunism. Those who did not conform to the anticommunist norm were often silenced by political repression or lost their legitimacy and credibility.

Government employees were compelled to take "loyalty oaths"; a "secrecy system" was erected to protect classified information; and personnel involved in national security affairs were given lie-detector tests and had their backgrounds investigated. It has been estimated that during the McCarthy era, of a total work force of 65 million, 13 million people were affected by loyalty and security programs. In the name of national security, the government even restricted the number of Americans traveling to communist countries.[20]

All these actions were originally intended to protect U.S. national security and respond to congressional investigations of communism in government. However, the "national security ethos" that arose was quickly abused in order to keep information from the public domain and to maximize support throughout society for the government's policies.

Yet the real abuse during the cold war years involved attempts by the government and allied groups throughout society to weed out communists and stifle public dissent in the name of national security. Congressional committees engaged in one investigation after another in an effort to identify and destroy communist influence, and this directly affected people's lives and careers. The attorney general kept a list of hundreds of subversive organizations, making individuals vulnerable to charges of disloyalty if they were affiliated with any of these groups, even if their membership was before or during World War II—and not during the cold war.[21]

David Caute, in *The Great Fear: The Anti-Communist Purge Under Truman and Eisenhower,* documents how thousands of government employees, teachers, labor leaders, journalists, librarians, scientists, writers, and entertainers at national, state, and local levels—virtually all innocent of charges of disloyalty—lost jobs, careers, and reputations as a result of wild accusations and guilt by association. The most celebrated cases, for example, involved people in the movie business that were dismissed and "blacklisted" from working in major Hollywood studios. Yet, "every segment of society was involved. From General Motors, General Electric, and CBS to the *New York Times,* the New York City Board of Education, and the United Auto Workers."[22]

Even academia, with its commitment to academic freedom, failed to fight McCarthyism. Nearly one-half of the social science professors teaching in universities at the time expressed medium or high apprehension about possible adverse repercussions to them as a result of their political beliefs and activities. In fact, Ellen Schrecker, in *No Ivory Tower: McCarthyism and the Universities,* found that academia contributed to McCarthyism. "The dismissals, the blacklists, and above all the almost universal acceptance of the legitimacy of what the congressional committees and other official investigators were doing conferred respectability upon the most repressive elements of the anti-Communist crusade. In its collaboration with McCarthyism, the academic community behaved just like every other major institution in American life."[23]

As Caute has shown, by 1949 twenty-two states required teachers to sign loyalty oaths as a condition of employment, twenty-one forbade "seditious" classroom instruction, and thirty-one considered membership in subversive organizations as defined by the Department of Justice a sufficient cause for dismissal. In California, twenty-eight public and private colleges, including Stanford University and the University of California at Berkeley, installed security officers—usually former FBI agents—to compile information on the political beliefs and affiliations of professors for state officials. Caute has calculated that as a consequence of these anticommunist laws and practices, more than 600 public school teachers and professors lost their jobs. Throughout the University of California system alone, twenty-six professors were dismissed who refused to sign the loyalty oath, thirty-seven others resigned in protest, forty-seven professors from other institutions turned down offers of appointment in California, and fifty-five courses from the university curriculum were eliminated.[24] In *Compromised Campus: The Collaboration of Universities with the Intelligence Community,* Sigmund Desmond demonstrates that university officials, including the presidents of Yale and Harvard, secretly cooperated with the FBI while publicly portraying their institutions as bastions of academic freedom.[25] Such draconian measures by the government and university administrators would trigger the "free speech movement" that began at the University of California, Berkeley and activate students on campuses throughout the nation, leading to the rise of the New Left and antiwar movements.

Perhaps most important, McCarthyism had a "chilling" effect throughout society; millions of Americans were intimidated by these repressive actions, for they sent clear messages to the public about what constituted proper political thought and behavior in American politics. As early as 1947 in response to the House Un-American Activities Committee's investigation of the Hollywood Ten—referring to ten top filmmakers and actors—Martha Gellhorn, a former leftist and one-time wife of Ernest Hemingway, sarcastically referred to it as "a little terror, calculated to frighten little people." But "it works"; under such pressure "a man can be well and truly destroyed." Her comments were prophetic. Someone "with a family will think many times before speaking his mind fearlessly and critically when there lies ahead the threat of an Un-Americans' investigation, a publicized branding, and his job gone." For if you could destroy the Hollywood Ten, "pretty soon you can ruin a painter and a teacher and a writer and a lawyer and an actor and a scientist; and presently you have made a silent place."[26]

During this time the FBI maintained a widespread network of informants to weed out subversives and covertly instituted Operation Cointelpro to target the Communist Party, USA. One of the "informants" was Ronald Reagan who, while serving as the president of the Screen Actors Guild, was secretly reporting to the FBI on suspect members of the union he was elected to represent. Under Director J. Edgar Hoover this counterintelligence program soon broadened to include the civil rights movement and then the antiwar movement during the 1960s.[27]

The FBI ended up carrying out over 500,000 investigations of so-called subversives without a single court conviction and created files on over one million Americans. Hoover stated the goals of the activities of the "Disruption of the New Left" Internal Security Counter Intelligence Program to the FBI's Albany, New York, office in the following manner:

> The purpose of this program is to expose, disrupt, and otherwise neutralize the activities of the various new left organizations, their leadership and their

adherents. It is imperative that activities of those groups be followed on a continuous basis so we may take advantage of all opportunities for counter intelligence and also inspire action where circumstances warrant. . . . We must frustrate every effort of these groups and individuals to consolidate their forces or to recruit new or youthful adherents. In every instance, consideration should be given to disrupting organized activity of these groups and no opportunity should be missed to capitalize on organizational or personal conflicts of their leadership. [Emphasis in original.][28]

These steps, which violated the ability of Americans to exercise their liberties in accordance with the Constitution, were legitimate in the minds of Hoover and many American conservatives, for they believed that the civil rights movement and the New Left, including people like Martin Luther King, Jr., and Students for a Democratic Society leader Tom Hayden, were too radical, too un-American, and too threatening to the status quo, if not downright communist directed.

More moderate political leaders, including cold war liberals such as Lyndon Johnson and Hubert Humphrey, tended to support these counterintelligence actions because they were unsure about the influence of communism, their governmental legitimacy and power were being challenged, and they were repulsed by such nonconformist political behavior—especially since they were accustomed to a relatively politically supportive and passive population, especially when it came to foreign policy. As David Halberstam described LBJ's increasingly "bunker" mentality in the White House by 1966: "So instead of leading, he was immobilized, surrounded, seeing critics everywhere. Critics became enemies; enemies became traitors."[29]

Although most Americans remained unaware of these covert actions at home, American nationalism believed in anticommunism and tolerated little dissent from the norm. This was, after all, the height of presidential power in exercising prerogative government in support of foreign policy in the name of national security. The right of political dissent and even a concern for public health were not allowed to get in the way of the war on communism—such was the primacy of the national security ethos throughout government.

For example, over 100,000 people who lived downwind from the Nevada Test Site felt the nuclear blasts and, more importantly, were exposed to the resulting radioactive fallout during the 1950s. These people were predominantly Mormons, very patriotic believers in God and country, who lived in small towns in Nevada and Utah. In addition, islanders have been exposed to radioactive fallout from nuclear tests in the Pacific; military troops have been exposed to radioactive fallout while engaged in war exercises following nuclear tests in the Pacific and the Nevada Test Site; civilians have been exposed to dangerous bacteria as a result of the army's germ warfare tests over populated areas; civilians were injected with radioactive substances in experiments to determine the effects of radiation; workers and local residents have been exposed to radiation from the government's nuclear weapons production facilities located throughout the country; miners and nearby residents have been exposed to radioactive material from uranium mines; Vietnam veterans (and countless local Vietnamese) have been exposed to dioxin in the chemical defoliant "Agent Orange"; and military personnel and civilians are exposed to military toxic wastes while they work and live near toxic waste dumps on military bases. Overall, it is estimated that millions of Americans, military and civilian, have been exposed to radioactive and toxic substances used by the U.S. government and the military in the name of national security.[30]

The politics of the cold war was serious business. Political instability was typically portrayed by supporters of the cold war and the Vietnam War as a function of communists or so-called "outside agitators" who were trying to stir up trouble. Cold War proponents simply could not understand that growing numbers of Americans were sincerely speaking out against them and their policies. Therefore, the FBI's programs were complemented by similar covert counterintelligence activities conducted throughout the national security bureaucracy. The Central Intelligence Agency opened the mail of American citizens, kept over 1.5 million names on file, and infiltrated religious, media, and academic groups. The National Security Agency monitored all cables sent overseas or received by Americans from 1947 to 1975. Army Intelligence investigated over 100,000 American citizens during the Vietnam War era. The Internal Revenue Service allowed tax information to be misused by intelligence agencies for political purposes.

The U.S. government, moreover, worked closely with local leaders, relying on the police and the National Guard, to prevent demonstrations and officially restore law and order.[31] The criminal justice system, for example, was used to arrest, try, and, in some cases, convict demonstrators as a means of preventing and deterring the exercise of their civil liberties, thus producing "political prisoners." These efforts to repress dissent resulted in dozens of Americans being fatally shot by the police and the militia during the turbulent years of the 1960s, including four individuals at Kent State University in Ohio and two students at Jackson State University in Mississippi. Finally, President Nixon attempted to take things into his own hands by allowing White House operatives to destroy his enemies and guarantee the reelection of the president, leading to the Watergate crisis.

In almost every situation during the cold war years, the political dynamics were the same. The government and its conservative allies in virtually all levels of society resisted those who attempted to peacefully exercise their civil liberties through the political system and change the status quo from a liberal or leftist perspective. While the civil rights and antiwar movements were overwhelmingly involved in political acts of nonviolence and civil disobedience, among both leaders and followers, the government was engaged in a massive campaign to limit and stifle the exercise of civil rights and liberties. Acts by the police to disrupt demonstrations often resulted in violence, radicalization, increased repression, and more violence until American society seemed to be at war with itself. Ultimately, these efforts to restrict and neutralize the civil rights and liberties of Americans failed to contain the growth of massive political dissent against the Vietnam War during the 1960s and early 1970s.

The Post–Vietnam War Resurgence of Civil Liberties

Two major patterns involving civil liberties have prevailed in the post-Vietnam years until the September 11 attacks. On the one hand, the breakdown of the liberal-conservative and anticommunist consensus has allowed Americans to exercise their civil liberties as never before. The civil rights and antiwar movements that arose during the late fifties and sixties fundamentally challenged the conformity and passivity that prevailed during the height of the cold war and were highly responsible for expanding the world of group and participatory politics by the late sixties and seventies. The events surrounding civil rights and Vietnam produced greater ideological, electoral, and political diversity. Clearly, individuals and groups throughout American society have greater opportunities to exercise their civil liberties and participate in politics then previously. Furthermore, one of the offshoots of the social movements of the 1960s and 1970s is that, although participation in elections has decreased, more Americans actively participate in group politics than before.

On the other hand, some cold war patterns prevail where threats to national security still take precedence over the ability of Americans to exercise their democratic rights. This continues to be the case because a large military and intelligence community continues to exist and engage in counterintelligence activities, a national security ethos still pervades the government and the military-industrial-scientific support infrastructure, and many Americans have a more conservative internationalist view of the world. Therefore, presidents have experienced a paradox of power in the post–Vietnam War political environment.

The Iran-Contra affair demonstrates both of these patterns. Many of the Iran-Contra activities of the Reagan administration involved efforts to stifle legitimate dissent to its policies. According to Robert Parry and Pete Kornbluh, in "Iran-Contra's Untold Story": "The White House deployed secretly funded private-sector surrogates to attack anti-Contra [congressional] lawmakers through television and newspaper advertisements and to promote the Contra cause through organizations with hidden funding ties to the administration. The FBI mounted intrusive and intimidating investigations of groups opposed to Reagan's Central American policies. . . . administration officials sought to manipulate criminal probes to protect their operations from exposure."[32]

Activities of the FBI, as part of its international terrorism counterintelligence program, included the investigation of over 18,000 individuals and 1,300 groups opposed to President Reagan's Central American policies, including the National Council of Churches, the Maryknoll Sisters, the United Automobile Workers, and the National Education Association, even though no criminal activity was ever uncovered. Of these, the U.S. General Accounting Office found that the FBI investigated 6,985 U.S. citizens and permanent resident aliens, over 2,000 cases were selected simply because the individuals were from foreign countries that sponsored terrorism, and that the FBI "monitored First Amendment-type activities" in more than two thousand other cases.[33]

Although these efforts to silence the exercise of civil rights and liberties occurred throughout the 1980s, this cold war and national security orientation operated in a post–Vietnam War domestic political environment, where such views and activities were much more likely to be exposed and criticized. Although Congress, the media, and the public were very slow to initially respond to the Reagan administration's involvement in Iran-Contra, many of these activities, nevertheless, were eventually challenged, exposed, and stopped when the Iran-Contra affair became the issue on the political agenda beginning in the fall of 1986. Such a political and constitutional crisis for President Reagan and the nation could only have occurred in a post–Vietnam War environment following the decline of the cold war. This also helps to explain the greater toleration for dissent and opposition experienced during the Persian Gulf crisis and war, even though some individuals were harassed for their beliefs and Arab Americans were placed under FBI surveillance.[34]

Thus, contradictory patterns of continuity and change have created a new and uneasy tension between the demands of national security and the demands of democracy. With increasing numbers of Americans exercising their civil liberties, constraints on the president's ability to govern and potential opposition to his policies have grown. At the same time, if a president tries to limit dissent by violating civil rights and liberties in the name of national security, he risks political scandal, constitutional crisis, and disaster. Such was the fate of Richard Nixon and Ronald Reagan with Watergate and Iran-Contra. Only in less intrusive ways can a president rely on the cold war patterns of the past in governing foreign policy, such as denying the public information through use of the secrecy system or involving the intelligence community in much more limited counterintelligence operations. By doing anything more, the president risks great political uncertainty, especially if the actions become public knowledge and find their way onto the political agenda.

It also means that the foreign policy bureaucracy is also more likely to be challenged in such a political environment as well. For example, in the late eighties the government tried to build a Special Isotope Separation Project, a plutonium purifying plant, at the Idaho National Engineering Laboratory in eastern Idaho. An important reason this site was chosen was because it was thought the plan would face little resistance in rural Idaho. The George H. W. Bush administration miscalculated, however, as a number of interest groups as well as local newspapers feverishly opposed the project. Despite the promise of jobs, the local population was swayed in opposition to the plutonium plant and the project was dropped, demonstrating that concern for public safety and civil liberties can prevail over the needs of national security, as least since Vietnam and the end of the cold war.[35]

The End of the Cold War: Placing the Tension in Perspective

With the collapse of the Soviet Union and communism in Eastern Europe, the end of the cold war has had important implications for the exercise of civil liberties and the future of American politics. First, Americans can rest assured that communism will likely have almost no appeal within the United States any longer. Therefore, Americans should have little reason to fear the threat of communism in the foreseeable future. Second, the decline of international communism means that anticommunism should fade as an important political issue (among liberals and especially conservatives), although the most extreme groups may continue to see the communist bogeyman on the march. In other words, where the threat of Bolshevism and communism has been used throughout the twentieth century by conservatives and the political Right to resist change and promote their policies, it should no longer have the symbolic value for uniting conservatives and attracting the support of Americans it had in the past, especially during the red scares of World War I and the cold war years.[36]

The collapse of communism, in other words, has further expanded the ability of Americans to exercise their civil liberties in American politics. Americans can choose to participate in electoral and group politics with little fear for their civil liberties, personal standing, and livelihood, especially in comparison to the cold war years. This suggests that ideological diversity will continue to increase among the mass and elite public, while new foreign policy issues may generate more political involvement in electoral politics, social movements, and interest groups. This is probably best illustrated by the existence of a divided public and country before the actual initiation of hostilities in the Persian Gulf War. It also suggests the need and potential for the reduction, and possible reform, of the immense national security bureaucracy and the prevalence of the national security ethos.[37]

However, even with the decline of communism, international conflict and new issues—such as drugs and terrorism—will continue to plague the world, bureaucratic institutions created to protect national security will continue to exist, and American nationalism will continue to promote conformity in response to crises. A type of dualism of freedom and intolerance with respect to the exercise of civil liberties has existed in the practice of American politics. On the one hand, American civil rights and liberties have steadily expanded throughout American history. In the post–Vietnam War era, Americans on the whole have become freer and more tolerant than during any previous period. This tolerance and freedom is much more in accordance with the ideals set down by the Declaration of Independence and the Constitution of the United States. On the other hand, there also have been periods of contraction in the exercise of civil liberties within the United States. Americans have been vulnerable to streaks of intolerance and discriminatory practices usually accompanied by emotional appeals to

Americanism and nationalism, especially during times of war. These contradictory patterns in the exercise of civil liberties are reflected in the beliefs among both the mass and elite publics.[38]

Senate Foreign Relations Committee Chairman J. William Fulbright (D-AR) was quite aware of this contradiction between Americans belief in freedom and civil rights and civil liberties, and, at the same time, Americans low tolerance for criticism. Nevertheless, Fulbright was the first significant public official to publicly criticize the war in Vietnam at the height of the Americanization of the war and the liberal-conservative anticommunist consensus. Most members of Congress, from both parties, and the Johnson administration, especially Lyndon Johnson, considered his dissent to be an unpatriotic act of disloyalty. Yet, Fulbright believed that

> To criticize one's country is to do it a service and pay it a compliment. . . .
> Criticism, in short, is more than a right; it is an act of patriotism, a higher form
> of patriotism, I believe, than the familiar rituals of national adulation. . . .
> And, in so doing, in the words of Albert Camus, "if at times we seemed to
> prefer justice to our country, this is because we simply wanted to love our
> country in justice, as we wanted to love her in truth and in hope."[39]

It was a courageous act by Fulbright. Although he would lose reelection, he was crucial in helping to legitimize the growing antiwar movement throughout the country.

This dualism is important for understanding continuity and change in the politics of U.S. foreign policy over the years. It is not mere coincidence that a high point of presidential power in foreign policy occurred during a time when the demands of national security took precedence over the exercise of civil rights and liberties demanded by democratic practice. Likewise, as Americans came to enjoy a greater ability to exercise their constitutional rights and liberties since the Vietnam War, it should not be surprising that domestic politics had constrained the president's ability to govern foreign policy and for the bureaucracy to act with abandon—that is until the devastating attacks on the World Trade Center and Pentagon occurred, ushering in a new era of political repression in the name of national security.

The threat to civil liberties during this new war on terrorism is no doubt great. Whether or not the war on terrorism will be a sustained long-term conflict resulting in a permanent crackdown on individual liberties and expression has yet to be determined. Ultimately, much will depend on how the following questions are eventually addressed by the American political process: *Will the Bush administration's war on terrorism resonate in the long run within the domestic political environment and especially among the American people? Will Americans feel it's a time of war and national emergency?* If so, the result will likely be greater presidential power and greater ability to exercise prerogative government in the name of national security. Or, *will Americans feel that it is "war in a time of peace," with diminishing fears and concerns about the threat of terrorism?* If so, the chances increase that the demands of democracy will resurface, making violations of civil rights and liberties more politically controversial and damaging.

The answers are unclear; the future remains uncertain. Much will depend on events and reactions, especially concerning the frequency and intensity of future terrorist attacks by foreigners on Americans and on American soil. Such uncertainty means that there will be an uneasy, and changing, tension and balance between the demands of national security and the demands of democracy. The future of civil rights and liberties of many people hang in the balance.

Notes

*From *The Politics of the United States Foreign Policy* 2nd edition by ROSATI. © 1999. Reprinted with permission of Wadsworth, a division of Thomson Learning: www.thomsonrights.com. Fax 800–730-2215.

1. Sean Wilentz, "The Power of the Powerless: The Fierce and Forgotten Battle for the Bill of Rights," *New Republic,* no. 23 and 30 (December 1991): 32. See also Gordon S. Wood, *The Radicalism of the American Revolution* (New York: Knopf, 1992).

2. For some valuable context, see David Lowenthal, *Possessed by the Past: The Heritage Crusade and the Spoils of History* (New York: Free Press, 1996); Pauline Maier, *American Scripture: Making the Declaration of Independence* (New York: Knopf, 1997). As with various bills of rights, there were at least ninety different declarations of independence that Americans in the colonies (later states) and localities adopted between April and July of 1776, with many precedents in English history. See Maier, *American Scripture.*

3. For an overview, see James MacGregor Burns and Stewart Burns, *A People's Charter: The Pursuit of Rights in America* (New York: Knopf, 1991); Sara M. Evans, *Born for Liberty: A History of Women in America* (New York: Free Press, 1989); Leonard Dinnerstein, Roger L. Nichols, and David M. Reimers, *Natives and Strangers: Ethnic Groups and the Building of America* (New York: Oxford University Press, 1979); Alphonso Pinkney, *Black Americans* (Englewood Cliffs, NJ: Prentice-Hall, 1969); and Howard Zinn, *A People's History of the United States* (New York: Harper & Row, 1980).

4. David Kairys, "The Evolution of Free Speech," *In These Times,* 18–24 December 1991, p. 12.

5. See, for example, John H. Broesamle, *Reform and Reaction in Twentieth Century American Politics* (Westport, CT: Greenwood Press, 1990); James MacGregor Burns, *The Crosswinds of Freedom* (New York: Knopf, 1989); Arthur A. Stein and Bruce M. Russett, "Evaluating War: Outcomes and Consequences," in *Handbook of Political Conflict: Theory and Research,* edited by Ted R. Gurr (New York: Free Press, 1980), pp. 399–422.

6. Seymour Martin Lipset, *Political Man: The Social Bases of Politics* (Garden City, NY: Anchor, 1968), p. 448. See also David Riesman, Nathan Glazer, and Reuel Denney, *The Lonely Crowd: A Study of the Changing American Character* (Garden City, NY: Anchor, 1953).

7. Richard Hofstadter, *The Paranoid Style in American Politics and Other Essays* (New York: Alfred A. Knopf, 1965).

8. Louis B. Parks, Barbara Karkabi, and Marty Racine, "Chicks Face 'Landslide' of Anger after Remark," *Houston Chronicle*, 15 March 2003, p. A1.

9. David Segal, "Dixie Chicks Bare Their, Uh, Souls," *Washington Post*, 25 April 2003.

10. For articles examining American intolerance for dissent by celebrities in the wake of the Iraq War, see, e.g., Frank Rich, "Bowling for Kennebunkport," *New York Times*, 6 April 2003; Lloyd Sachs, "Freedom of Speech Comes at a Price—But Only for Some," *Chicago Sun-Times*, 30 March 2003; Warren St. John, "The Backlash Grows Against Celebrity Activists," *New York Times*, 23 March 2003.

11. For an overview, see William H. Chafe, *The Unfinished Journey: America Since World War II* (New York: Oxford University Press, 1986); Frank J. Donner, *The Age of Surveillance* (New York: Vintage, 1981); Robert J. Goldstein, *Political Repression in Modern America: From 1870 to the Present* (Cambridge, MA: Schenkman, 1977); M. J. Heale, *American Anticommunism: Combating the Enemy Within, 1930–1970* (Baltimore: Johns Hopkins University Press, 1990); Michael Linfield, *Freedom Under Fire: U.S. Civil Liberties in Times of War* (Boston: South End Press, 1990); Richard Gid Powers, *Secrecy and Power: The Life of J. Edgar Hoover* (New York: Free Press, 1987); George Brown Tindall, *America: A Narrative History* (New York: W.W. Norton, 1988); and Zinn, *A People's History*.

12. Alan Brinkley, *The Unfinished Nation* (New York: McGraw Hill, 1993), p. 617; George B. Tindall, *America: A Narrative History* (New York: Norton, 1988), pp. 1003–1005.

13. Milton Cantor, *The Divided Left: American Radicalism, 1900–1975* (New York: Hill and Wang, 1978), p. 31. See also James MacGregor Burns, *The Workshop of Democracy* (New York: Alfred A. Knopf, 1985), and Tindall, *America*.

14. In Paul Goodman and Frank Otto Gatell, *USA: An American Record,* vol. 2 (Hinsdale, IL: Dryden Press, 1972), p. 380.

15. The Supreme Court, in fact, upheld Debs's imprisonment. See *Debs v. U.S.*, 249 U.S. 211 (1919).

16. James Brooke, "After Silence, Italians Recall the Internment," *New York Times*, 13 August 13 1997, p. A8. See also Arnold Krammer, *Undue Process: The Untold Story of America's German Alien Internees* (Boulder, CO: Rowman and Littlefield, 1997).

17. See John W. Dower, *War without Mercy: Race and Power in the Pacific War* (New York: Pantheon, 1986); Audrie Girdner and Anne Loftis, *The Great Betrayal: The Evacuation of the Japanese-Americans During World War II* (New York: Macmillan, 1969); Peter Irons, *Justice at War: The Story of the Japanese-American Internment Cases* (New York: Oxford University Press, 1983); William Manchester, *The Glory and the Dream: A Narrative History of America, 1932–1972* (New York: Bantam, 1975); Jacobus TenBroek, Edward N. Barnhart, and Floyd W. Matson, *Prejudice, War and the Constitution* (Berkeley, CA: University of California Press, 1954); and Michi Weglyn, *Years of Infamy: The Untold Story of America's Concentration Camps* (New York: Morrow, 1976).

18. See, e.g., Harvey Klehr, John Earl Haynes, and Kyrill M. Anderson, *The Secret World of American Communism* (New Haven: Yale University Press, 1998).

19. Sam Tanenhaus, "Keeping the Faith," *New York Review of Books*, 25 June 1998, p. 48.

20. Ralph S. Brown, *Loyalty and Security* (New Haven, CT: Yale University Press, 1958). See also Stephen J. Whitfield, *The Culture of the Cold War* (Baltimore: Johns Hopkins University Press, 1991).

21. Even the courts ruled in favor of national security over individual civil liberties as illustrated by the 1951 *Dennis v. United States* case in which the Supreme Court ruled that advocating or teaching revolutionary philosophy constituted a crime. See Stanley I. Kutler, *The American Inquisition: Justice and Injustice in the Cold War* (New York: Hill and Wang, 1982).

22. Ellen W. Schrecker, *No Ivory Tower: McCarthyism and the Universities* (New York: Oxford University Press, 1986), pp. 10–11. See David Caute, *The Great Fear: The Anti-Communist Purge under Truman and Eisenhower* (New York: Simon and Schuster, 1978); and Victor S. Navasky, *Naming Names* (New York: Penguin, 1980).

23. Schrecker, *No Ivory Tower,* p. 340. See also Lionel S. Lewis, *Cold War on Campus: A Study of the Politics of Organizational Control* (New Brunswick, NJ: Transaction, 1988); and Paul Lazarsfeld and Wagner Thielens, Jr., *The Academic Mind* (Glencoe, IL: Free Press, 1958).

24. Caute, *The Great Fear,* pp. 406–24. See also David Caute, *The Fellow Travelers: A Postscript to the Enlightenment* (London: Weidenfeld and Nicolson, 1973).

25. Sigmund Desmond, *Compromised Campus: The Collaboration of Universities with the Intelligence Community, 1945–1955* (New York: Oxford University Press, 1992).

26. Martha Gellhorn, "Cry Shame . . . !" *New Republic* (October 6, 1947): 21.

27. See Gary Wills, *Reagan's America* (New York: Penguin, 1988), pp. 295–97; and James Kirkpatrick Davis, *Spying on America: The FBI's Domestic Counterintelligence Program* (New York: Praeger, 1992).

28. Cited in Tom Hayden, *Reunion: A Memoir* (New York: Collier, 1988), p. 283.

29. David Halberstam, *The Best and the Brightest* (New York: Random House, 1969), p. 623.

30. See, e.g., Howard Ball, *Justice Downwind: America's Atomic Testing Program in the 1950s* (New York: Oxford University Press, 1986); Leonard A. Cole, *Clouds of Secrecy: The Army's Germ Warfare Tests over Populated Areas* (Totowa, NJ: Rowman & Littlefield, 1988); Michael D'Antonio, *Atomic Harvest: Hanford and the Lethal Toll of America's Nuclear Arsenal* (New York: Crown, 1993); Carole Gallagher, *American Ground Zero: The Secret Nuclear War* (Cambridge: MIT Press, 1993); Clifford T. Honicker, "America's Radiation Victims: The Hidden Files," *New York Times Magazine,* 19 November 1989, pp. 38–41, 98–103, 120; Thomas H. Saffer and Orville E. Kelly, *Countdown Zero: GI Victims of U.S. Atomic Testing* (Middlesex, England: Penguin, 1982); U.S. Congress, General Accounting Office, *Nuclear Waste: DOE's Program to Prepare High-Level Radioactive Waste for Final Disposal* (November 1989); Eileen Welsome, *The Plutonium Files: America's Secret Medical Experiments in the Cold War* (New York: Random House, 1999).

31. See Frank J. Donner, *Protectors of Privilege: Red Squads and Police Repression in Urban America* (Berkeley: University of California Press, 1990).

32. Robert Parry and Peter Kornbluh, "Iran-Contra's Untold Story," *Foreign Policy* (fall 1988): 5.

33. U.S. Congress, General Accounting Office, *International Terrorism: FBI Investigates Domestic Activities to Identify Terrorists* (September 1990). See also Richard O. Curry, ed., *Freedom at Risk: Secrecy, Censorship, and Repression in the 1980s* (Philadelphia: Temple University Press, 1988).

34. See, for example, Lisa Belkin, "For Many Arab Americans, FBI Scrutiny Renews Fears," *New York Times,* 12 January 1991, p. 1A.

35. Keith Schneider, "Idaho Says No," *New York Times Magazine,* 11 March 1990, pp. 57–61.

36. Throughout twentieth-century American history, threats to the democratic exercise of civil rights and liberties have tended to come predominantly from the political Right for two reasons: Conservatives and the political Right have traditionally been most intolerant of civil liberties and concerned with combating the threat of alien ideas, such as communism and socialism; and they have been powerful forces in government and have successfully generated political support throughout society by using the strong symbolic appeals of nationalism and Americanism. See David H. Bennett, *The Party of Fear: From Nativist Movements to the New Right in American History* (Chapel Hill: University of North Carolina Press, 1988); Michael Paul Rogin, *The Intellectuals and McCarthy: The Radical Specter* (Cambridge, MA: MIT Press, 1967); and Herbert McClosky and Alida Brill, *Dimensions of Tolerance: What Americans Believe about Civil Liberties* (New York: Russell Sage Foundation, 1983). It must be recognized, however, that the far Right has no monopoly on intolerance and repression. Elements of the far Left, such as Marxist-Leninist groups, are also quite dogmatic and authoritarian—although they never had more than a minute following within American society and have never been influential within the government. Furthermore, liberals have been guilty of initiating violations of civil liberties, as with the internment of Japanese Americans under California Governor Earl Warren and President Franklin Roosevelt, and of feeding and appeasing the political Right, such as the internal security measures instituted by the Truman administration following World War II that fanned the flames of anticommunism and McCarthyism during the cold war years. See also Richard M. Freeland, *The Truman Doctrine and the Origins of McCarthyism: Foreign Policy, Domestic Politics, and Internal Security, 1946–1948* (New York: Alfred A. Knopf, 1972); James L. Gibson, "Political Intolerance and Political Repression during the McCarthy Red Scare," *American Political Science Review* 82 (June 1988): 511–29; William Keller, *The Liberals and J. Edgar Hoover: Rise and Fall of a Domestic Intelligence State* (Princeton, NJ: Princeton University Press, 1989); and Richard H. Pells, *The Liberal Mind in a Conservative Age: American Intellectuals in the 1940s and 1950s* (New York: Harper & Row, 1965).

37. See Kate Doyle, "The End of Secrecy: U.S. National Security and the Imperative for Openness," *World Policy Journal* (spring 1999): 34–51; Morton H. Halperin and Jeanne M. Woods, "Ending the Cold War at Home," *Foreign Policy* 81 (winter 1990–1991): 128–43.

38. See, for example, James L. Gibson, "The Political Consequences of Intolerance: Cultural Conformity and Political Freedom," *American Political Science Review* (June 1992): 338–56; McCloskey and Brill, *Dimensions of Tolerance.*

39. J. William Fulbright, *The Arrogance of Power* (New York: Vintage, 1966), pp. 27, 25, 65.

Chapter 2

Protecting (or Destroying) Freedom through Law:

The USA PATRIOT Act's Constitutional Implications

Christopher P. Banks

Those who won our independence believed that the final end of the State was to make men free to develop their faculties; and that in its government the deliberative forces should prevail over the arbitrary. They valued liberty both as an end and as a means. They believed liberty to be the secret of happiness and courage to be the secret of liberty. . . . They recognized the risks to which all human institutions are subject. But they knew that order cannot be secured merely through fear of punishment for its infraction; that it is hazardous to discourage thought, hope and imagination; that fear breeds repression; that repression breeds hate; that hate menaces stable government. . . .

—Justice Louis Brandeis, Whitney v. California (1927).

The American Constitution was originally designed as an experiment in republican liberty and limited government. Its founders envisioned an "energetic" executive who could meet foreign threats with great dispatch and necessity, sometimes even without congressional approval, if the circumstances warranted it. Also, but with some reluctance and at the insistence of the anti-Federalists, state governments agreed to ratify the Constitution if it included, as part of the governing framework, a separate Bill of Rights. In the new political system courts would ensure that citizens remain free by insisting that the rule of law, instead of the rule of men, governed human behavior whenever arbitrary governmental action threatens individual freedom. As Woodrow Wilson once put it, the "federal judiciary . . . is the only effectual balance-wheel of the whole system" and, concomitantly, "[b]y the word of the Supreme Court must all legislation stand or fall, so long as law is respected."[1]

A great test of these principles emerges from September 11 and the enactment of the USA PATRIOT Act. The act was signed into law on October 26, 2001, less than six weeks after the attack on the World Trade Center and the Pentagon. It emerged from the pressure applied to Congress

by the Bush administration and its attorney general, John Ashcroft, who
jointly proposed the comprehensive antiterrorism proposal only eight days
after the tragedy. A sense of how quickly Congress acted is provided by
Representative John Conyers (D-MI) who described the legislative process
leading up to its enactment as "shameful," especially concerning a law "of
such vital import and impact on our very liberties." Conyers's remarks were
recorded in May 2003 at a House Constitution subcommittee meeting
assessing the Fourth Amendment implications of the PATRIOT Act,
where he said:

> That legislation, [which] was drafted in secret over a weekend by representa-
> tives of the Department of Justice and the House leadership, was brought to
> the floor with no one having an opportunity to see it in advance. Members had
> to vote on a multi-hundred page bill with no one having had a chance to read
> the bill except for staffs. The bill was available an hour in advance. People had
> to vote based on summaries.[2]

Like other critics, he felt that "[Congress] legislated in hysteria in October of
2001," something "[it has] done . . . before in times of crisis."[3]

The lessons of history may have caused Congress to balk briefly at
instituting the sweeping reforms proposed by the attorney general. But, like
the ghosts of Congress's past, it ultimately bowed to mounting public
pressure for a quick and decisive answer to the terrorist threat by passing, in
great haste, a modified version of the Bush administration's proposal.
Notably, the final legislation was the product of intense negotiations
between the Bush administration, the Department of Justice (DOJ), and key
congressional leaders, but with little floor debate. While some legislators,
like Patrick Leahy (D-VT), expressed concern early on in the deliberations
that what the Bush administration envisioned was too much of a threat to
civil liberties, only one Senator, Russ Feingold (D-WI), cast a dissenting vote
on the final legislation. Hence, while some concessions were made (such as
the imposition of sunset provisions that curtail the length of time certain
provisions are supposed to remain in effect), for the most part the executive
branch got most of what it asked for from Congress.[4]

In spite of the haste, the PATRIOT Act had lofty aspirations, for it was
designed to correct five perceived weaknesses, or failures, of the national
government to prevent the 9/11 atrocity. It sought 1) to improve sharing of
information between law enforcement and foreign intelligence agencies; 2)
to gather antiterrorism intelligence by taking advantage of the flexible
warrants' requirement of the Foreign Intelligence Surveillance Act (FISA); 3)
to expand wiretap authority over electronic communications; 4) to seize
funding utilized in terrorist activities; and 5) to impose mandatory detention
and deportation of non-U.S. citizens who are suspected of having links to
terrorist organizations.[5] As with the 1996 Antiterrorism and Effective Death
Penalty Act (AEDPA), these emphases represent a radical shift away from
the policy of "consequence management" in dealing with the terrorist

threat. The law, in short, is proactive and attempts to prevent acts of aggression before they materialize.[6]

Unquestionably the law's pre-emptive quality represents a challenge for the Supreme Court (and the rest of the federal judiciary) in their balance-wheel capacity. This chapter suggests that the courts face a vexing challenge in trying to strike a reasonable balance between securing national security while maintaining public safety and individual freedom. Yet what they do—and in particular what the Supreme Court does in responding to legal challenges to antiterrorism legislation—will define whether Wilson's prophecy will be fulfilled. The pernicious problem at hand—to prevent terrorist acts before they happen in a twenty-first-century world—presents intractable problems of liberty with few simple constitutional, or pragmatic, solutions. All at once the PATRIOT Act is a criminal *and* military response to an undeclared war instituted by a faceless, unseen enemy whose only allegiance is not to, a country but a cause. As a legal solution, it is a preemptive strike against ephemeral terrorists but also real human beings who live, and would rather die, if they cannot remain free from governmental oppression. As applied, but also as a hasty political reaction to terror, the law implicates core issues of liberty, including rights under the First (associational and speech), Fourth (search and seizure), Fifth (due process, grand jury), Sixth (right to counsel), Eighth (cruel and unusual punishment), and Fourteenth Amendments (due process, privacy, and equal protection). In short, it is crucial to ask if the PATRIOT Act sacrifices too much when it attempts to protect, but not destroy, freedom through law. While the full scope of the law's constitutional impact cannot be addressed in a single essay, this chapter discusses a few issues by first summarizing the Act's main provisions and then analyzing some of the more pernicious Fourth Amendment issues the law is likely to generate when it is challenged in federal court. It concludes by observing that one of the unfortunate legacies of September 11 is the uncomfortable place the PATRIOT Act will inevitably occupy as an ill-conceived law that sweeps too broadly in trying to safeguard American citizens in the undeclared war on terrorism.[7]

The USA PATRIOT Act

The PATRIOT Act's key provisions include methods of facilitating exchange of foreign intelligence information obtained in law enforcement with officials responsible for internal security. In addition to enhancing enforcement techniques and increasing penalties to investigate, deter, and punish terrorists, it authorizes more sophisticated electronic surveillance with less judicial supervision, including roving wiretaps. The law also tightens restrictions on immigration by authorizing federal agencies to prevent foreign terrorists from entering the country while, at the same time, legalizing the detention and swift deportation of foreign terrorists. Finally, it strengthens existing financial controls to prevent or stop the funding of terrorist groups.[8]

The PATRIOT Act's most significant elements are summarized in their legal context under three general headings: information sharing and expanded surveillance capability; new immigration restrictions; and, antiterrorist money laundering provisions.

Information Sharing and Expanded Surveillance Capability

Congress did not write on a blank slate in crafting the PATRIOT Act's Title II ("Enhanced Surveillance Procedures") provisions.[9] While the legislators were sensitive to allaying the anxiety associated with the September 11, they also were mindful that the nation's pre-existing national security legislation was forged in large part by reforms brought on by past executive misfeasance, a pattern of abuse that frequently battered civil rights and liberties under the pretext of making the nation secure. The government's modern tendency to keep a secret but watchful eye on its potential enemies can be traced back to World War I, where the fear of communist (and socialist) subversion prompted the infamous "slacker" (to flush out draft dodgers) and "Palmer" (to ferret out Communists) raids.[10] Indeed, in implementing President Roosevelt's directive to monitor domestic subversive activity, the fledgling Federal Bureau of Investigation (FBI) began the practice of gathering intelligence on private citizens without any individualized suspicion that the citizens were engaging in any criminal activity.[11] Moreover, the Central Intelligence Agency (CIA), which was created in 1947 from the vestiges of the wartime Office of Strategic Services and statutorily barred from engaging in domestic law enforcement or internal security activities, gradually inserted its foreign intelligence activities into the domestic sphere, a traditional FBI realm. By the end of the cold war, the difference between what was foreign and domestic relative to the CIA and FBI blurred to the point where there was little separation between the agencies' respective prosecutorial and foreign investigation functions.[12] As a result, over the next four decades (which of course encompassed the cold war and the social upheaval associated with the civil rights movement and the Vietnam War) the executive branch seized the opportunity to exercise its largely unfettered discretion to combat threats posed by would-be communists and other perceived radicals or dissidents, often with Congress's implicit consent. Notably such dissents, or government targets of improper surveillance, included Dr. Martin Luther King, Jr.[13]

The 1970s, though, witnessed the Watergate scandal, the forced resignation of President Richard Nixon, and an ensuing, but unprecedented, reform movement to keep the people informed and the government accountable. Statutes, like the Freedom of Information Act, were passed to give citizens the chance to inquire about, and in the process question, the validity of conducting affairs of state under a cloak of secrecy. Increasingly, scrutiny was brought to bear on the intelligence community, first through the Commission on CIA Activities within the United States (the "Rockefeller Commission") and then by the Select Committee to Study Governmental

Operations with Respect to Intelligence Activities (the "Church Committee").[14] Whereas the Rockefeller Commission was significant in suggesting that the legality of CIA operations is a function of its purpose (whether it is engaging in foreign intelligence as opposed to domestic law enforcement), the input from the Church Committee was valuable because it recommended that Congress engage in increased oversight in monitoring how agencies conduct covert operations.[15] Among other things, the result was the creation of new committees that tied appropriations to intelligence gathering, along with the passage of the Freedom of Information Act, and related statutes safeguarding citizen privacy.[16] Most importantly, Congress isolated, through regulation, the CIA's covert operations from the FBI's domestic investigation duties.[17]

This latter reform, and its resultant lack of synergy between the CIA and FBI, dovetailed with evolving judicial doctrine and new legislation that fashioned the legal parameters of permissible electronic surveillance before September 11, 2001. In *Katz v. United States* (1967), the Supreme Court repudiated pre-existing property-based notions of the Fourth Amendment and recognized that an individual enjoys a reasonable expectation of privacy in government prosecutions that rely on incriminating evidence obtained through a surreptitious electronic means. There, the Court acknowledged, but did not resolve, the government's contention that there was a "national security" exception to the warrants requirement.[18] Also, in *Berger v. New York* (1967), New York's law authorizing an *ex parte* (but judicially approved) wiretap was nullified as a Fourth Amendment violation because it permitted a judge to grant a wiretap request if a law enforcement official's affidavit showed reasonable grounds to believe criminal activity was occurring. The ex parte procedure, the Court ruled, not only failed to comport with the Fourth Amendment's probable cause standard, but it also ran afoul of the warrant clause's requirement to describe sufficiently, and with particularity, the place to be searched or what might be uncovered by the wiretap.[19] Congress responded to *Katz* and *Berger* by enacting Title III of the Omnibus Crime and Control and Safe Streets Act of 1968, a law that generally bars electronic eavesdropping but also allows it in criminal investigations supported by probable cause (in which a serious "predicate" offense is being committed) and a warrant (secured with advance judicial approval).[20] Although Title III permitted warrantless surveillance in exceptional situations (e.g., if there is immediate harm to national security interests), a warrant application must nonetheless be filed within 48 hours of the time the intrusion began.[21]

In the post–cold war period, the line between domestic law enforcement and foreign intelligence gathering was blurred in a world defined by rapid technological change and global uncertainty. So *Katz, Berger,* and Title III raised, but did not completely resolve, the issue of whether it was constitutional for the executive to conduct warrantless electronic searches in order to protect national security. In *United States v. United States District Court* (1972), the Supreme Court rejected the attorney general's position that Title

III represented an inherent grant of presidential authority that absolved the executive from *all* Fourth Amendment constraints in national security investigations. In reasoning that the relevant Title III language was neutral in regard to the president's constitutional power to conduct electronic surveillance, the Court emphasized that the "warrant clause of the Fourth Amendment is not dead language" and, accordingly, "[p]rior review by a neutral and detached magistrate is the time-tested means of effectuating Fourth Amendment rights."[22] While the Court said that the "circumstances" of the case (involving information gathered about a bombing of the CIA building from a wiretap approved only by the attorney general) did not form an adequate basis for a complete exemption from the Bill of Rights, the Court reiterated that its holding only applied to "domestic aspects of national security."[23]

Hence, while it did not address whether the Fourth Amendment also limited foreign intelligence activities, *United States District Court* (otherwise known as the *Keith* case) specifically invited Congress to create a law authorizing a "specially designated court" to review affidavits on the basis of their unique facts and then, in turn, strike an appropriate balance between public safety and individual rights in "sensitive cases."[24] While the executive, and the lower federal courts, struggled with ways to comport with *Keith*'s implications,[25] Congress accepted the invitation a few years later by passing the Foreign Intelligence Surveillance Act of 1978 (FISA).[26] The statute, which also was inspired by the recommendations of the Church Committee, created the Foreign Intelligence Surveillance Court (FISC) in the District of Columbia, a court staffed on a rotating basis by seven district court judges appointed for seven-year terms by the chief justice of the Supreme Court.[27] The FISC's purpose is to review, in secret *(ex parte* and *in camera)*, applications for government surveillance of "foreign powers" (or their agents) that, in the attorney general's opinion, pose a national security threat.[28] Specifically, as originally constructed, a FISA application mandated certification that *"the* purpose" of the surveillance is to procure foreign intelligence information; but it was also expected that any evidence derived from the investigation might also be turned over to law enforcement personnel. It remained an open question, though, whether "the purpose" was synonymous with "the sole purpose," which in turn led to litigation battles that in time refined the standard's scope. Hence, while courts conceded that foreign surveillance might uncover facts concerning criminal behavior, they also established a rule indicating that the surveillance would cease (or a Title III order would be obtained) at the moment the purpose of the investigation began to center on an unrelated criminal prosecution.[29]

Although FISA technically pertains to counterintelligence investigations, its passage still reinforced the partition between law enforcement and foreign intelligence gathering by putting the latter activity under a different legal standard.[30] Whereas government agents with a criminal investigation purpose had to comply with the warrant requirement, agents (from the Department of Justice's Office of Intelligence Policy and Review) culling foreign intelligence could get approval from a secret, specially convened court that bases its surveillance application decisions on criteria that did not necessarily meet probable cause in the usual (i.e., law enforcement) sense.[31] For a non-FISA search warrant, there must be probable cause that a crime has been committed; but a FISA warrant must only demonstrate that there is probable cause that the subject of the search is a foreign power or agent of a foreign power.[32] By narrowing the scope of the search to foreign powers or their agents, FISA institutionalizes the perception, if not the reality, that agents could bypass the more stringent Title III requirements by using a FISA order as, in effect, a fishing expedition to get evidence of a crime.[33] On the other hand, FISA, in theory (but perhaps not in practice), offers slightly greater protection for American citizens if they are targets of the investigation, since any information derived from it must be a necessary element of (and not just relate to) the activities of a foreign power.[34] Consequently, a "quasi-criminal standard of probable cause" applies to American citizens: The government must prove that the target is acting in something that "may involve" a crime, or that the person is "knowingly" acting or helping a foreign power in illicit activity.[35] Furthermore, as an additional precaution that helps safeguard privacy, the attorney general is required to promulgate specific procedures that minimize the acquisition, retention, and dissemination of nonpublic information derived from the FISA search relating to an "unconsenting United States person."[36]

Accordingly, 1970s intelligence reform, and the legal wall of separation it created between relevant intelligence communities, affected the particular methods national security agencies used to electronically monitor foreign agents suspected of sedition and, potentially, criminal behavior by U.S. citizens that is unrelated to efforts to undermine the government. Hence, reform and the perceived need for separation impacted the development of the PATRIOT Act's Title II. Even though law could be manipulated to skirt constitutional requirements in intelligence investigations because of the separation between law enforcement and foreign surveillance, ironically, after 9/11 the disjunction between the counterintelligence agencies was identified as one of the major failures of the government in being unable to prevent the attacks. Shortly before the 9/11 tragedy, pertinent information was available, but not shared, between the various agencies that had national security responsibility. As a result, the PATRIOT Act sought to centralize power in the executive branch and mute judicial controls in the interest of streamlining bureaucratic reaction time.[37] Thus, Title II was specifically designed to reduce the legal barriers that would otherwise impede an effective antiterrorist response by enhancing the federal government's potential to monitor, track, and capture messages exchanged between hostile forces in the United States and elsewhere.[38]

Domestic Criminal Investigations

The PATRIOT Act affects each level of privacy protection afforded individuals under pre-existing federal law. In general, pre–PATRIOT Act law gave preference to safeguarding private telephone, face-to-face conversations, and electronic or computer messages in the Title III context by prohibiting eavesdropping unless a warrant could be obtained in a set of narrowly defined circumstances. At this highest level of privacy protection, the surveillance is subject to a number of detailed procedural steps (like, for example, minimizing the seizure and disclosure of innocent communications), including the requirement of giving notice (after the order expires) that the search took place and, of course, advance judicial approval. Telephone records and e-mail held by third parties in storage are given the next level of security, so a warrant or sometimes a subpoena can be used to gain access to them without fulfilling the more stringent requirements associated with a full-blown Title III search warrant. Information disclosing the identity of the source and destination of communications made from, and to, a particular place (through the use of pen registers and trap and trace devises) is given the least amount of privacy protection, so law enforcement can generally rely upon government certification (and not a court finding) that incriminating evidence is likely to be discovered, without the subjects of the investigation ever being notified.[39]

In addition to criminalizing cybercrime as a (predicate) Title III offense and authorizing the interception of illegal communications to select computer systems (i.e., those used by the federal government, banks, or those in interstate or foreign commerce),[40] the PATRIOT Act's Section 203 allows the disclosure, and sharing, of "foreign intelligence," "counterintelligence," or "foreign intelligence information" derived from grand jury investigations to "any federal law enforcement, intelligence, protective, immigration, national defense, or national security official" if it helps them discharge their duties.[41] While Section 203's final version is less invasive than what the Bush administration and the Justice Department originally proposed, it also mandates that within a "reasonable time after disclosure is made," a court must be notified, under seal, that the disclosure happened and to whom the disclosure was made.[42]

Apart from the new legislation's impact on grand juries, Section 209 of the PATRIOT Act allows judicial authorization (at a lesser, non–Title III standard) for obtaining government access to voicemail.[43] Sections 210 and 211 target the recovery of previously unrecoverable information from telephone or cable connections. The delay associated with getting a court order is obviated by expanding subpoena power to capture data transmitted through telephone lines and the Internet, such as credit card and bank account numbers, Internet protocol addresses, and Internet session times (Section 210).[44] Since cable operators sell telephone service and Internet access, Section 211 amends the Cable Communications Policy Act to subject them to the same rules governing the lawful interception of telephone and Internet communications for law enforcement purposes. Hence, instead of having an adversary hearing and a court order, government officials can get requisite evidence through "*ex parte* court orders under the no-notice procedures" pertaining to telephone or Internet service providers.[45]

The government's capacity to monitor pertinent data (i.e., source and addressee information) from computer systems is increased with Section 216 by establishing new procedures for using "trap and trace" (recording incoming telephone numbers) and "pen register" (recording outgoing telephone numbers) devises. Thus, Section 216 permits tracking of Internet e-mails and user information. Section 216 goes beyond existing law by allowing law enforcement officials the flexibility of getting "new pen trap orders" in multiple jurisdictions (i.e., nationwide), but without the corresponding need to get a court order for every affected district where the devise needs to be placed. The change, in theory, eliminates time that is wasted in trying to pursue a suspect in different geographic regions (and which, under prior law, would require a duplicative order be issued by a court). This is accomplished by letting the court issue the order without actually knowing the identity of the Internet service provider; thus, the law enforcement official working the case has discretion to insert the relevant ISP if a certification is made that the pen trap is relevant to an ongoing criminal investigation. However, to answer the objection that e-mail header information is more enlightening than the receipt of a telephone number, the law requires the agency using the device to file an *ex parte* (and under seal) report with the court within thirty days of the order's termination.[46]

Nationwide search warrants are also permitted in Sections 219 and 220.[47] But perhaps one of the most controversial amendments in regards to criminal law enforcement is the PATRIOT Act's revision of common law and procedural rules generally barring "no knock searches." If certain preconditions are met, Section 213's "sneak and peak" provision applies to *any* criminal investigation (not just terrorism prevention) and permits law enforcement to delay notification that a search and seizure has occurred until *after* it already happened.[48] Although notification is required "within a reasonable period of [the warrant's] execution," it can be prolonged if the court has "reasonable cause" to believe that immediate notice will have an "adverse result" (generally exigent circumstances, but also impeding an investigation or trial). Also, seizures of personal effects, records, electronic information and the like are sanctioned with delayed notice if the court finds a "reasonable necessity."[49] Apart from the changes in domestic law enforcement procedure, in other ways the PATRIOT Act relaxes extant law regarding foreign intelligence investigations.

Foreign Intelligence Investigations

The PATRIOT Act enhances intelligence gathering and law enforcement capability by amending the Foreign Intelligence Surveillance Act (1978) in several respects. It increases the size of the special court (FISC) by four judges (to a total of eleven), and mandates that at least three judges of the entire court live within a twenty-mile radius of the District of Columbia.[50] Under PATRIOT Act Section 206, a FISA "roving wiretap" is authorized if a court finds that "the actions of the target (of the investigation) of the application may have the effect of thwarting the identification" of a particular person under surveillance.[51] The new law orients the permissibility of the search on the person instead of the device (like a cell phone) that is being used. By eliminating the need (and time) to get a new court order whenever a suspect flees a particular jurisdiction, Section 206, in theory, reduces the chance that the proverbial moving target will evade detection by switching phones across geographical space. At the same time, however, observing a person rather than a electronic instrument is akin to authorizing a "blank warrant," which in turn increases the possibility that nonforeign intelligence information will be recovered since there is no advance judicial finding that a specific device is a credible source of illicit or dangerous data. In other words, Section 206 is controversial since the parties reacting to the surveillance order do not have to be identified, and, as a result, it compels acquiescence to the validity of the warrant on its face.[52]

The new law also strengthens the government's power to conduct extended surveillance and physical searches (Section 207),[53] and it facilitates the interception of Internet and telephone communications through pen trap orders, if the FISA order is not aimed exclusively at protected First Amendment activities of American persons (Section 214).[54] Business records and other tangible evidence can be seized through a FISA order in Section 215, but only if the attorney general can certify that taking the items is in furtherance of an international terrorist or covert intelligence investigation and, as in Section 214, the order is not directed solely at protected First Amendment activities of a "United States person."[55] Section 215 differs from 214 in one important respect, however: It prohibits business owners from revealing to anyone that the FBI has conducted a search or seizure pursuant Section 215. This latter requirement, some say, is tantamount to an unconstitutional "gag order."[56]

While these alterations to FISA are undoubtedly important, the most profound and far-reaching change to existing law is found in Section 218. Prior to September 11, in order to maintain a separation from domestic internal security, FISA informed applicants desiring secret FISC approval that "the purpose" of the investigation is to get foreign intelligence. In response to 9/11, the Bush administration advocated altering the "the purpose" to read "*a* purpose," a difference giving the attorney general virtually unlimited authority to pursue FISA warrants for any reason connected to gathering foreign intelligence data. In light of federal case law that predominately held that FISA evidence was admissible so long as the "primary purpose" of the FISA warrant was to get foreign intelligence, enough political opposition surfaced in the Senate to defeat the original proposal. The modified, and final version of Section 218 thus states that there must be "a significant purpose" behind the FISA warrant.[57] While the compromise [the Bush administration accepting the "a significant purpose" language] does not go as far as the initial Bush proposal, it still grants the executive branch a vast amount of discretion to obtain FISA warrants based on nonforeign, or law enforcement rationales. As one commentator put it, "[f]ederal law enforcement can now obtain FISA warrants with the intent of using them in criminal matters, so long as intelligence gathering is also a significant purpose of the request."[58] While opponents fear Section 218 is a license to invade privacy and civil rights, the government can counter that it is pliable enough to capture incriminating evidence while preserving the ideal underlying the 1970s reform since FISA warrants, in theory, ought not to be granted for domestic law enforcement purposes.[59]

New Immigration Restrictions

The 1996 Anti-terrorism and Effective Death Penalty Act (AEDPA) enhanced the government's ability to detain or deport non-U.S. citizens to the point where Congress was contemplating, prior to September 11, new laws to ameliorate AEDPA's harsh impact.[60] In addition, the Supreme Court decided two opinions shortly before the tragedy that purported to go in the direction that Congress was contemplating. On April 24, 2001, in *Immigration and Naturalization Service v. St. Cyr* (2001) a divided Court (5:4) affirmed the right of a resident alien charged with committing a crime of moral turpitude to utilize habeas corpus to test the limits of executive detention and also ask the attorney general to waive deportation (if the resident alien was threatened with it) under AEDPA and the Illegal Immigration Reform and Immigrant Responsibility Act of 1996.[61] On June 28, 2001, in *Zadvydas v. Davis* (2001) the Court (5:4) limited the attorney general's power to detain indefinitely an alien when it was unlikely that deportation could be accomplished in the reasonably foreseeable future.[62] At first blush, both *St. Cyr* and *Davis* appeared to give aliens a Fourteenth Amendment due process liberty interest, and therefore some constitutional protection, to be free from potentially arbitrary detentions from the executive branch.

September 11 quickly reversed any prolonged recognition of such rights.[63] Besides strengthening the government's border to the north with a variety of measures,[64] Subtitle B of Title IV ("Enhanced Immigration Provisions") gives the attorney general ample discretion and expanded authority to stop terrorist aliens from entering the country, as well as to detain and deport them. Two provisions, Sections 411 and 412, are illustrative. The former defines the circumstances under which aliens are deportable. Under prior law they were deportable if they were inadmissible at the time they came into the United States or, more significantly, if they participated in terrorist activity once they entered. Section 411 redefines and expands the number of grounds by which an alien is barred from entry into the country or, alternatively, deportable. Hence, the provision applies if the alien is engaging in terrorist activity or represents a terrorist organization. Likewise, it pertains to those who: 1) espouse terrorist activity; 2) are the spouse or child of an inadmissible alien; and 3) associate with a terrorist organization with the intent to threaten the United States. In general, Section 411 attempts to keep out of the country persons who engage, advocate, or support terrorist activities that may endanger America. They include, of course, entities designated as "terrorist organizations" or those that give material support for planned or actual acts of terror.[65]

Perhaps the most ominous provision is Section 412, which grants the attorney general legal authority to detain suspected alien terrorists for up to seven days upon certification (by the attorney general and not a court) that the alien is inadmissible or deportable on terrorism-related grounds (e.g., terrorism, espionage, sabotage, sedition); or there are "reasonable grounds to believe that the alien is engaged in any other activity that endangers the national security of the United States."[66] If a certification is made, within the seven days the attorney general must initiate removal proceedings or charge the alien with a criminal offense or, if neither is done, release the alien.[67] An alien who is detained but is likely not to be removed in "the reasonably foreseeable future" can be held for additional periods of six months upon recertification that indicates that their release will threaten national security or imperil community (or individual) safety.[68] While there is no limitation on the number of six-month periods an alien can be incarcerated in the event of nonremoval, Section 412 explicitly affords the detainee a right to file a writ of habeas corpus in federal court.[69] Moreover, the attorney general must file a report about the actions he has taken in invoking Section 412 to Congress on a periodic basis (every six months).[70]

Section 412 is especially problematic considering that the Bush administration initially urged (but did not get) the adoption of a detention law that freed the attorney general from having *any* responsibility to file *any* charges supporting the confinement. Notably, this provision is different and more open-ended than Sections 422 and 423 of ADEPA since they only give the executive power to hold, and then remove, aliens who are convicted of a crime.[71] The PATRIOT Act, therefore, gives the attorney general virtually unlimited discretion to take away the liberty of a person *who the attorney general reasonably believes* is a terrorist. Even though Congress was mindful of the Supreme Court's *Davis* ruling in crafting Section 412's language, it remains an open constitutional question whether in times of national emergency the attorney general has the kind of broad discretion that the law vests in him to detain suspected terrorist aliens where removal to another country is impracticable or impossible.[72]

Anti-Terrorist Money Laundering Provisions

As with the 1996 Antiterrorism and Effective Death Penalty Act, Congress realized that the government must assert better control over the adverse influence money was having in spreading terrorist activity. Money laundering was widely viewed as being especially insidious because it is a set of actions calculated to hide the origin of large sums of money that provide the material support, or means, to accomplish destructive acts of terror. Through the process of placement, layering, and integration, the paper trail of illicit money is obscured and replaced by the perception that the financial transaction in question is legitimate. Its effects are compounded in the Internet age where "e-money" is funneled to cyber accounts that are extremely hard to trace or identify. The scope of the problem is indeed astonishing. The International Monetary Fund estimates that up to $500 billion annually is laundered in the United States alone. Worldwide, the number is believed to be between $590 billion and $1.5 trillion.[73]

Yet, before September 11 the American political environment was not conducive to expanding what began in the AEDPA antiterrorist funding provisions. While tougher restrictions were contemplated, legislative proposals seeking to increase the financial community's duty to superintend suspicious financial transactions more carefully stalled. Banks, which were interested in the best bottom line, were not eager to embrace more costly regulatory measures. It also did not help that Senator Phil Gramm (R-TX), who chaired the Senate Banking Committee, did not endorse mandatory disclosure rules that would expose the details of financial minutia. Civil libertarians, who saw visions of "Big Brother," also protested because the new laws would reveal sensitive financial information to law enforcement personnel. Indeed, new regulations that were proposed in December 1998 were rescinded in March 1999 because a large portion of the nearly 300,000 public comments received objected to them on grounds that privacy interests would be violated.[74]

The political climate began to change with George W. Bush's ascension to the White House since part of his criminal justice policy agenda included a desire to adopt money laundering restrictions. Vermont Senator Jim Jeffords's June 2001 defection from Republican to independent status made a difference as well since Senator Gramm lost control of the Banking Committee when the Democrats took control of the Senate. The World Trade Center and Pentagon assaults that autumn provided the final impetus for impeding the flow of money that contributed to September 11's terrorism. First, on September 24, 2001, the president issued Executive Order 13244, freezing assets of at least twenty-seven individuals and banking institutions. Four days later the United Nations adopted several resolutions aimed at directing nation states to effectuate various antiterrorism financial initiatives.[75] The following month witnessed legislative action by Congress, even though the House of Representatives signaled that it wanted to include the regulations in a separate bill that could be more thoughtfully considered. Yet the Senate pushed for including them in one package, and what emerged was the PATRIOT Act's Title III: "International Money Laundering Abatement and Anti-Terrorist Financing Act of 2001."[76]

Whereas AEDPA was directed at compelling (either through regulation or the imposition of criminal penalties) U.S. banks to stop the flow of money from identified foreign terrorist organizations,[77] Title III goes further by expanding government control over monies distributed in domestic and international commerce. Title III's gist can be described under two general headings: 1) more stringent record keeping, disclosure, and information sharing requirements; and, 2) the imposition of new crimes and penalties, including forfeiture and confiscation. The key provisions are outlined next.

Record Keeping, Disclosure, and Information Sharing

Under prior law, financial institutions were required to file with the Department of the Treasury and the Internal Revenue Service a variety of reports (e.g., Cash Transaction Reports [CRTs] and Suspicious Activities Reports [SARs]) detailing the particulars behind transactions exceeding certain amounts.[78] In addition to mandating that all financial institutions establish anti–money laundering programs (with appropriate procedures and an employee training program), the PATRIOT Act expands the coverage of reporting and disclosure; and, whenever possible, it takes advantage of seizing information that was given to one agency but not another in cases where such an exchange was prohibited by law.[79] As Section 358 well illustrates, data that previously would be limited to the Treasury Department or the IRS can be shared among the relevant actors in charge of internal security and foreign intelligence.[80] In addition, the United States government is authorized to adopt select regulations that are designed to encourage, direct, and compel domestic banks to take certain steps to combat money laundering.[81]

Thus, with consultation and notice to certain agencies, Section 311 empowers the Secretary of the Treasury to promulgate "special measures" upon finding "reasonable grounds" to conclude that a financial institution or jurisdiction (or related account or transaction) that is operating out of the United States is a "primary money laundering concern." The special regulations may include a number of strategies to abate laundering, such as requiring domestic banks to record or report certain transactions or, alternatively, undertaking reasonable methods to ascertain the beneficial ownership of correspondent (i.e., foreign bank) accounts.[82] Section 312 similarly obliges U.S. financial institutions that maintain (private bank or correspondent) financial ledgers for non-U.S. persons to adopt "due diligence" policies and procedures that are aimed at detecting money laundering activities running through those accounts. Foreign banks that are doing business under off-shore licenses are subject to additional rules as well.[83] Under Section 313, certain United States financial entities are statutorily barred from having a correspondent account in the U.S. for a foreign bank that lacks a physical presence in the country (shell banks). Section 313 also mandates that U.S. banks take reasonable precautions in seeing that correspondent accounts are not servicing shell banks indirectly. Such a step, for example, might include getting written certifications from the correspondent account holders that they are not doing business with any shell banks.[84]

Other parts of the PATRIOT Act direct that a wider range of financial and nonfinancial businesses file CRTs and SARs in situations involving the exchange of large sums of money. Many of the new requirements relate to the Treasury Department's Financial Crimes Enforcement Network (FinCEN) unit, which is specifically charged under the PATRIOT Act (Section 361) to enforce the act's proscriptions in a secure bureaucratic network that connects financial institutions to the government.[85] With due notice and consultation with relevant agencies, the treasury secretary is directed pursuant to Section 356 to establish rules that make registered brokers and dealers (including futures commodity merchants, commodity trading advisors, and commodity pool operators) file SARs (with FinCEN) for suspicious transactions exceeding $5,000. Nonfinancial trades or businesses, which were previously only obligated to account to the IRS, must now file transaction reports to disclose pertinent information involving the receipt of more than $10,000 in coins or currency under Section 365.[86] Moreover, Sections 351 and 355 combine to provide immunity (from civil liability) to those financial institutions or its officers that file SARs under certain circumstances (including making employment references to other banks). And government officials, and not just the officers and employees of financial institutions (as under prior law), are prohibited from disclosing what they suspect in filing the SARs to those who are involved in the suspicious activity.[87]

New Crimes and Penalties

The PATRIOT Act deters and punishes a variety of offenses that relate to money laundering, smuggling, or economic terrorism. One significant change is departing from the usual constitutional rule that money-laundering prosecutions can only be brought in the geographical district where the money transfer took place. Under Section 1004, the crime itself is treated as a continuing offense, a distinction that permits prosecution in the place where the crime that created the funds transpired.[88] Enhanced civil and criminal penalties, moreover, are outlined in Section 363 for violations of the PATRIOT Act's special measures or due diligence provisions (in Sections 311 and 312).[89] In order to prevent the use of laundered funds originating from foreign crimes, Section 315 lists several new "foreign corruption offenses" and makes them money laundering crimes in the United States, including crimes of violence, bribery of a public official, misappropriation, theft, embezzlement of public funds (by or for the benefit of a public official), smuggling, and offenses relating to bilateral extradition treaties to which the United States is a party.[90] Public corruption in administering the framework of money laundering laws is made a federal crime in Section 329, as is knowingly, and therefore illegally, engaging in money transmitting businesses (Section 373).[91] Participation in counterfeiting schemes is severely punished, moreover, as a brand of economic terrorism in Sections 374 and 375. Not only are domestic and foreign counterfeiting activities covered, but the sections also bar possession of electronic counterfeiting paraphernalia (i.e., having an electronic image of a U.S. security document, or an analog or digital copy).[92]

Apart from the new crimes and increased penalties, the PATRIOT Act skirts preexisting jurisprudence concerning the law of forfeiture and confiscation to accomplish its antiterrorist objectives. Past law barred false reporting of transporting cash sums of $10,000 or more into the United States, with a confiscation as a penalty in lieu of a criminal fine. But, grossly disproportionate confiscations (e.g., $350,000) originating from the act of not declaring the sums at custom borders were held unconstitutional in

United States v. Bajakian (1998), a case Congress was well aware of in drafting the PATRIOT Act's new bulk cash prohibition. Hence, under Section 371, the same act (i.e., falsely reporting or not declaring large sums of money at the border) is made into a smuggling offense, notably to avoid the problem of having the courts nullify the law (and its confiscation component) as a disproportionate, and therefore an unconstitutional, "excessive fine" under the Eighth Amendment.[93] Civil and criminal forfeitures are made into penalties for violating other nonreportings of asset crimes as well.[94]

Perhaps the most troublesome and potentially unconstitutional sections dealing with forfeiture as a penalty are 806 and 106. Both break from the American legal tradition of statutory forfeiture and institute, in lieu thereof, principles normally associated with the common law forfeiture of estate. Statutory forfeiture is reflected in two kinds of statutes, for example: taking property associated with the commission of certain crimes or, alternatively, authorizing government seizure of enemy assets during wartime. With forfeiture of estate, the property's relationship to the crime is irrelevant and all property is lost on the basis of ownership. Also, the principle of attainder is a characteristic as well, which means that all property is lost forever and does not have any possibility of being recovered by the felon's heirs.[95]

Accordingly, Section 106 permits the president or his delegate to confiscate property within the United States belonging to a foreign entity that has attacked (or helped in attacking) the United States. The provision is analogous to section 5(b) of the Trading with the Enemy Act (TWEA) and, after 1977, a more limited version of TWEA in the International Economic Emergency Powers Act (IEEPA). Until the enactment of the IEEPA, the president, under section 5(b), had the legal power to confiscate, and vest, enemy property in the United States during either war or national emergency.[96] The Justice Department perceived Section 106 as a new weapon that returned to the president broad constitutional authority to take the property of enemies in times of unconventional conflict (i.e., where no formal declaration of war has been made). Although confiscation can be legally challenged, in exercising judicial review the court has the option to give the government a chance to offer classified evidence in secret *(ex parte* and *in camera)* to relieve the United States of having to choose between electing to confiscate or declining to in fear of disclosing sensitive information implicating national security.[97]

Section 806 is inapplicable to foreign entities, but it authorizes confiscation of any and all property of any individual, entity, or organization that fosters domestic or international terrorism against the property of the United States or its citizens, regardless of where it is found.[98] While the confiscation is subject to the same judicial controls as Section 106, the scope of 806 is nonetheless breathtaking given the expansive definitions of terrorism that trigger its applicability.[99] Furthermore, in addition to making ownership (instead of the property's relationship to the crime's occurrence) the touchstone for confiscation, both sections are unusual because the terrorist does not have to be convicted of any crime before they apply; and both are silent about giving an exemption to the terrorist's heirs. As such, both have the potential to be voided on constitutional grounds, especially since they tend to operate in a punitive, instead of remedial, fashion.[100]

Protecting (or Destroying) Freedom through Law

Executive Action

The PATRIOT Act is only part of the story in America's war against terror. While it has extensive ramifications, it represents Congress's initial answer to the threat. For his part, President George W. Bush acted swiftly as well by exercising his own constitutional powers as the nation's chief executive and commander in chief. Any qualms about his ability to exercise constitutional powers were eliminated shortly after 9/11 with the passage of a joint resolution by Congress on September 18 that helped to unify the country in its pursuit of terrorists. While the resolution is not a formal declaration of war, it symbolized the principle that the president had the power to act militarily against the sponsors of international terrorism.[101] That standard ratified the president's decision to use the U.S. army to topple the Taliban in Afghanistan and, later, upset Saddam Hussein's regime in Iraq in pursuing and destroying weapons of mass destruction that conceivably could fall into terrorist hands. Also, before the military campaigns, President Bush invoked his Article II powers to issue several executive orders in the aftermath of 9/11. On September 24, 2001, the president issued Executive Order 13244, which froze the assets of suspected terrorists and the banking institutions they utilized. On October 8, 2001, through Executive Order 13228, a new White House entity was created, the Office of Homeland Security, forerunner to the massive reorganization of the executive branch that culminated in the creation of the Department of Homeland Security (2002). And, on November 13, 2001 Bush announced a military order authorizing the trial of suspected terrorists by military tribunals instead of criminal courts.[102]

These actions were part of a larger strategy to centralize executive authority in the Department of Justice, the agency under the direct control of the nation's chief law enforcement officer, Attorney General John Ashcroft. With Ashcroft at the helm, the fight against terrorism has become preemptive and unrelenting. In his words, an aggressive approach is necessary because "[t]here are no second chances in the campaign to prevent another September 11 . . . [and] if we fail in our responsibility to secure justice, we invite the risk of additional criminality[,] . . . the security of our nation and the survival of freedom."[103] With the help of Viet Dinh, the assistant attorney general, the so-called Ashcroft Doctrine assumes that: 1) prevention stops terrorist-induced catastrophes from happening; 2) a strong government is essential to secure, enduring liberty; 3) terrorist behavior is not simply a criminal act but rather an act of war; and, 4) civil liberties must yield in applying rules of war to terrorist conflicts.[104] Indeed, these ideals are responsible for creating a "parallel legal system" where "terrorism suspects—

U.S. citizens and non-citizens alike—may be investigated, jailed, interrogated, tried and punished without legal protections guaranteed by the ordinary system." The weapons of choice are many: indefinitely detaining executive-designated "enemy combatants"; employing "material witness" warrants; covertly using wiretaps and counterintelligence techniques for law enforcement purposes; and trying noncitizen terrorists through military commissions or, conversely, removing them from the country through closed, or secret, deportation hearings. There is evidence, too, that the PATRIOT Act's material support provision is working efficiently, snaring at least thirty persons (ranging from the American Taliban to New York lawyers and Florida college professors) since 9/11.[105]

On June 5, 2003, the U.S. House of Representatives vicariously explored the significance of the Ashcroft Doctrine by holding hearings about the PATRIOT Act and its impact. During his testimony before the Judiciary Committee, the attorney general touted the administration's efforts and credited the legislation as the principal bulwark of America's defense against terror. It has been instrumental, he explained, in cracking terrorist cells operating in Buffalo, Portland, Seattle, and Detroit since 9/11 because it enabled investigators to gather key evidence against those who trained in Al Qaeda camps but also lived stateside. The PATRIOT Act's severe penalties have also permitted prosecutors to leverage suspects into disclosing critical information about planned terrorist activities after agreeing to plead guilty to avoid long prison sentences. The combination of prevention and preemption, in other words, has reaped detailed intelligence reports secured through more than 18,000 subpoenas and search warrants; and, under FISA, more than 1,000 international terrorist suspects have been targeted, and at least 170 were the subject of emergency FISA warrants. The increase in emergency warrants, Ashcroft observed, is more than three times the total number secured in the last twenty-three years before 9/11. Moreover, Ashcroft testified that more than $125 million dollars and assets in "terror's money trail" have been seized, a success reaped from isolating 600 bank accounts pursuant to 70 investigations.[106]

As the attorney general's comments imply, the government's response to 9/11 has been pervasive and, on occasion, has reaped substantial rewards, as in the high-profile arrest of Iyman Faris, an American citizen and truck driver from Columbus Ohio. He was captured in April 2003 after the government learned he supported the Jihad against his own country by scouting ways in which rail systems and landmarks like the Brooklyn Bridge could be destroyed in a new wave of post-9/11 attacks.[107] Yet the visible accomplishments in the war against terror must be measured against what the attorney general failed to mention in his House testimony. He omitted reference, for example, to the existence and operation of non–PATRIOT Act surveillance and data-mining programs, like the FBI's Carnivore Diagnostic Tool (renamed DCS-1000)and the Defense Department's research project, the Terrorist (formally known as the "Total") Information Awareness System (TIA). Whereas DCS-1000 enables the FBI to sniff packets of information contained in Internet transmissions (typically e-mail) to see if one is sent by a suspect, TIA is a data integration system that lets the military compile databases of digital information pertaining to suspected terrorists and nonterrorist citizens alike for defensive purposes. While these systems are at the front edge of the technological assault against terrorism, and in spite of safeguards that allow each to operate with some oversight, DCS-1000 and TIA have great potential for reducing individual privacy to an unprecedented degree, especially if they are used for purposes that have little to do with terrorism. As conservative pundit William Safire portends,

> [E]very purchase you make with a credit card, every magazine subscription you buy and medical prescription you fill, every Web site you visit and e-mail you send and receive, every academic grade you receive, every bank deposit you make, every trip you book and every event you attend—all these transactions and communications will go into [the TIA database].[108]

Notably, although TIA is a recent innovation, the government reportedly has supplemented its ability to superintend Internet traffic with at least two other surveillance technologies that predate 9/11, the"Eschelon" (that monitors messages around the world for the National Security Agency) and "key logger" (that records keystrokes from a target computer) systems.[109]

The apprehension that "Big Brother" is upon us is accompanied by a related fear that government can sacrifice liberty with heavy-handed, if not arbitrary, applications of law in calamitous times. Perhaps that is why Ashcroft said little about the DOJ Office of the Inspector General's (IG) report that was critical of the treatment of aliens received as detainees who were held by the government on immigration charges in relation to the FBI's Pentagon/Twin Towers Bombings (PENTTBOM) investigation that was launched in the aftermath of 9/11. The lack of emphasis is curious, though, because the report was performed in accordance with a requirement imposed by the PATRIOT Act and publicly released before his House testimony. Nonetheless, it should have been a focal point of analysis, if for no other reason than it demonstrated how easy it is for government to abuse those who it believes represent a national security threat under the extraordinary exigency of an event like September 11. Although it acknowledged the difficulty in meeting the challenge of respecting rights and maintaining order under such circumstances, the report concluded that there were "significant problems in the way the September 11 detainees were treated."[110]

Inspector General Glenn A. Fine observed that most of the 762 detainees were held in two facilities, the Bureau of Prison's Metropolitan Detention Center (MDC) in Brooklyn, New York, and the Passaic County Jail in Paterson, New Jersey. Hence the IG directed his attention on those facilities and, specifically, a sample of 119 of the 475 detainees that were held at those locations. After conducting extensive interviews (of the detainees, their attorneys, agency personnel, and special interest group representatives) and examining various documentation (INS Alien Files, facility records, field office records, agency policies/procedures, and agency databases including litigation and detention histories), the IG found that some of the detainees suffered "certain conditions of confinement" that were "unduly harsh, such as illuminating the detainees' cells for 24 hours a day." Also, the IG said "the evidence indicates a pattern of physical and verbal abuse by some correctional officers at the MDC against some September 11 detainees." Moreover, the IG discovered that "the MDC's restrictive and inconsistent policies on telephone access for detainees prevented them from obtaining legal counsel in a timely manner." Beyond these specific findings, the IG criticized the FBI and the INS for instituting an unwritten "hold until cleared" policy that not only confused those who were detained, but also, in conjunction with a "no bond" policy, led to a slow clearance process and lengthy detention periods. The average clearance process took eighty days "primarily because [the INS] was understaffed and not given sufficient priority by the FBI." This kind of injustice, the report suggested, was especially acute for those aliens who were swept up in the "chaotic aftermath of September 11" and held even though they were only a coincidental part of the PENTTBOM investigation and, therefore, had no connection to terrorism.[111]

Although Ashcroft expressed "some sympathy" during his House testimony for the mistreatment of some detainees, the IG's findings are relatively predictable, since the policy of the attorney general is to make few apologies because he is justified on the grounds of national security. Several provocative executive actions underscore the wide swath of this rationale. In addition to the PENTTBOM investigation, approximately six weeks after 9/11, Ashcroft approved a Bureau of Prisons' regulation that vested exclusive discretion in the attorney general to order that ordinarily privileged communications between an inmate and legal counsel be monitored, if there was "reasonable suspicion to believe" that they could "further or facilitate acts of terrorism." Also, acting in accordance with the PATRIOT Act's direction to strengthen American borders, the attorney general used his regulatory authority in November 2002 to establish special registration procedures that required gender-specific (males only) aliens from select countries (mostly Muslim) to track their presence within the United States as part of the "National Security Entry-Exit Registration System." All aliens who were subject to the targeted group had to comply with the edict (by, among other things, being fingerprinted, photographed, and interrogated by an immigration official and re-registering annually) or face deportation.[112] In fortifying the barriers to entry, Ashcroft took the controversial step of reversing a Board of Immigration Appeals order by declaring in a legal opinion, *In Re D-J* (2002), that illegal immigrants seeking asylum in the United States did not have a right to be released on bond for national security reasons, regardless of whether the immigrant in custody actually presented a flight risk or a danger to the community.[113]

Judicial Deference

The government's acquisition of new powers to investigate, detect, and preempt acts of terrorism have been matched by a corresponding increase in governmental secrecy and, significantly, judicial deference. This is best illustrated by an appeals court ruling issued from the D.C. Circuit in June,

2003. In *Center for National Security Studies v. U.S. Department of Justice,* the court, in a 2:1 decision, rejected a Freedom of Information Act request by public interest groups to reveal, among other things, the identity of detainees who were being held by the government as potential terrorist threats as part of the September 11 investigation. The judicial conflict expressed in the majority and dissenting opinions show that two disparate rationales were counterpoised against the other: a compelling interest in keeping critical information secret on the grounds of national security and, conversely, an equally compelling interest in giving citizens critical information about what the government is doing in achieving national security.[114]

In opting for nondisclosure, Judge Sentelle's majority opinion reasoned that deference to the executive's judgment is warranted because "America faces an enemy just as real as its former Cold War foes, with capabilities beyond the capacity of the judiciary to explore."[115] To do otherwise, he continued,

> would enable al Qaeda or other terrorist groups to map the course of the investigations and thus develop the means to impede it. . . . A complete list of names informing terrorists of every suspect detained by the government at any point during the September 11 investigation would give terrorist organizations a composite picture of the government investigation, and since these organizations would generally know the activities and locations of is members on or about September 11, disclosure would inform terrorists of both the substantive and geographic focus of the investigation. This information could allow terrorists to better evade the ongoing investigation and more easily formulate or revise counter-efforts.[116]

The government's interest in maintaining secrecy, Sentelle concluded, was firmly established on statutory (Freedom of Information Act exemption) grounds and not outweighed by countervailing First Amendment or common law (right to access to public records) rationales.[117]

For dissenting Judge Tatel, though, the outcome not only undercut the Freedom of Information Act's purpose, but it also set a dangerous precedent of judicial acquiescence. In Tatel's view, the court must play a "meaningful role in reviewing FOIA exemption requests," lest it capitulate to what the executive wants on the untenable basis of agreeing with the government's claim that the court, and the citizenry, must "simply trust its judgment." Under this logic, the court only fulfills its obligation to "do the job Congress assigned to it" by insisting that government "provides a rational explanation for claiming exemption from FOIA's disclosure requirements" (with the help, for example, of an *in camera* inspection affidavit).[118]

Center for National Security Studies is important because it reflects an almost irrefutable presumption that what the executive does in the name of national security is constitutional. As such, the case illustrates that the deference principle is rapidly becoming part of the post-9/11 legal landscape. Indeed, Judge Sentelle observed as much by listing several cases in the majority opinion that, in the court's view, "wisely respected the executive judgment in prosecuting the national response to terrorism."[119] Yet, as one critic complains, any successes attributable to a paradigm that protects freedom through law have been reaped, perhaps, at a substantial cost to civil liberties with the onset of a "New McCarthyism."[120] This charge, it seems, is apt in light of Judge Sentelle's endorsement of the executive prerogative by analogizing the modern terrorist to a cold war–like enemy. As the next section explains, it is likely that dissent to the PATRIOT Act and what it represents will not be silenced any time soon. Rather, lament will continue to be recorded in the pages of legal opinions for as long as the lessons of history concerning governmental abuse are forgotten while the historical struggle against terrorism lasts.

The Fourth Amendment and Enhanced Surveillance

The PATRIOT Act's place in history will be forged, in large part, by how well the courts defend executive power against claims that its exercise violates the Fourth Amendment prohibition against unreasonable search and seizure and its corresponding respect for personal privacy. Broadly, the Fourth Amendment stands as a barrier to general searches of persons or property without a warrant. For a warrant to issue, a neutral magistrate must make a finding that the application is factually specific and supported by probable cause of some wrongdoing. While the Supreme Court has crafted exceptions to the warrant requirement, its preference for a warrant has been overshadowed by its tendency since the Warren Court (1953–69) to evaluate Fourth Amendment claims through *Katz*'s "reasonable expectation of privacy" standard and, in general, assessing if the police action in a particular case is "reasonable."[121] Although the existence of satellites, thermal imaging, biometric identification devises, DNA "fingerprinting," wiretaps, and the Internet are ripe fodder for developing constitutional law, with the exception of cases like *Kyllo v. U.S.* (2001) and, more indirectly, *Barnicki v. Vopper* (2002) and *U.S. v. American Library Association, Inc.* (2003), the Supreme Court has been slow in considering how these technologies affect constitutional law outcomes.[122]

Nor has the Court yet wrestled with the enhanced surveillance provisions of the PATRIOT Act, but it has made rulings in analogous cases. In *Smith v. Maryland* (1979), the Court upheld the government's use of pen registers, a practice that is expanded by PATRIOT Act Section 216. Specifically, the ruling held there is no legitimate expectation of privacy, and hence no Fourth Amendment concern, because there is no "search" in protecting against wiretap interception of the numbers a person dials to, and from, a telephone.[123] Even though Section 216 amends several laws to allow pen register and trap devises to capture Internet and e-mail transmissions (and not just telephone calls) on a nationwide basis (with little opportunity to challenge, in a specific regional court, their validity), it might withstand constitutional challenge because it erects a statutory bar on appropriating the "content" of the messages that are monitored. Still, as some in the legal academy and criminal defense bar observe, the PATRIOT Act does not define what "content" is (e.g., if a subject line on an e-mail is addressing or routing information, or content), and that kind of uncertainty is prone to abuse since surveillance targets can only hope to rely on the government's reassurance that the computer is configured correctly to capture only that information that is part of the initial warrant. Besides having faith in the operator's competence, one must also believe in the operator's integrity because, in Carnivore searches for example, a record of the search is never kept, even though the operator can easily switch (using a radio button) between "full" (revealing entire messages) and "pen" (showing only addressing data) during surveillance.[124] As one attorney put it, "since Section 216 empowers the government to use its Carnivore . . . system of tracking and collecting electronic information, the notion of the government acting within reasonable limits without defense and court pressure is fanciful."[125]

Section 213, the sneak-and-peek provision, is likewise problematic because it sanctions the surveillance practice of entering a person's property secretly for the purpose of seizing evidence, with only delayed notice. While notice may be afforded (to the subject of the warrant if a court generally finds it reasonable to do so), it is done so only *after* the intrusion. Hence judicial oversight is minimal and the surveillance target has no chance to test the warrant's legal sufficiency in court before it is executed. As a result, it seems contrary to Rule 41 of the Federal Rules of Criminal Procedure (which required that officers leave a copy of the warrant and inventory of what they seized after the warrant is executed, along with disclosing their action to a judge afterward) and, concomitantly, repudiates the common law "knock-and-announce" principle embedded in judicial interpretations of the Fourth Amendment. For instance, the Supreme Court in *Wilson v. Arkansas* (1995) held that the Fourth Amendment incorporates the common law requirement that police knock and announce their identity (and purpose) when entering a dwelling. Sneak and peak, therefore, undercuts *Wilson*'s rationale and, perhaps more pejoratively, condones what civil libertarians have referred to as "black bag" searches—a law enforcement technique they derisively trace back to the period when the FBI or CIA abused citizens' rights in overzealous prosecutions in the days before the implementation of the 1970s reforms. Allowing the executive branch this kind of discretion also tends to obliterate any distinctions that are left between the domestic and foreign intelligence communities, since delayed notification is not just confined to uncovering suspected terrorist activity. Instead, as some critics complain, it applies to any suspected criminal behavior and is judged on a standard that is below typical Title III or Rule 41 probable cause requirement (and that affords advance notice and an opportunity to contest). Worse still, since the government never has to tell you it conducted a search, sneak and peak "treat[s] the Fourth Amendment protections as if they were written in pencil, easily erased and malleable, tied to the crisis-of-the-day level of paranoia."[126]

A similar difficulty exists with the PATRIOT Act's endorsement of roving wiretaps, a "bug" that follows the individual under surveillance from one geographical region to another instead of centering on a device (i.e., a telephone). Although prior law permitted roving wiretaps in criminal investigations (if the government could prove that the target was using the line being watched), they were barred in FISA surveillance. But, with Section 206, roving bugs are permitted for FISA-oriented "intelligence" wiretaps. If a suspect under surveillance is prone to switching phones, or moving from computer to computer, in order to avoid detection then the government will be able to place all of the phones or computers that are under suspicion and in use under a roving wiretap, an authorization that compromises the particularity requirement of a Fourth Amendment warrant. In other words, the warrant can never specify what is being searched because any and all of the devices that the suspect is using are incapable of being identified with any certainty in a fluid investigation where the target is constantly moving. Moreover, roving wiretaps inherently sweep too broadly since the target's communications are captured along with all of the conversations and transmissions from innocent third parties who are using the same device and who, in the end, are left with no Fourth Amendment remedy.[127]

A related issue is the breadth of the PATRIOT Act in expanding FISA wiretap authority, an important subject because a FISA warrant is not only sanctioned behind closed doors in a secret courtroom but also through a probable cause standard that is less rigorous than the one imposed in a Title III search. In theory FISA warrants are issued if there is probable cause that the person under surveillance is connected to a foreign power. Yet the PATRIOT Act's Section 218, and its replacement of the pre-9/11 "purpose" standard with the new "significant purpose" test, increases the likelihood that FISA warrants (which are supposed to be aimed at gathering foreign intelligence) could also reap evidence of unrelated or nonterrorist criminal acts that the government only discovered through the FISA wiretap. Under the new PATRIOT Act language, if there is a significant purpose in gathering foreign intelligence, then the government has the power to discover, and use, evidence of criminal acts that are unrelated to the original purpose of the warrant. Hence there are few controls in place to limit the scope of the government's surveillance of a target (criminal, terrorist, foreign, or other- wise). Cloaking the warrant procedure under a cover of searching for foreign intelligence, therefore, allows the special FISA Court to degrade the Fourth Amendment's probable cause requirement (that requires that facts exist showing evidence that a crime has occurred) since surveillance is sanctioned by a court without specific proof that the suspect has engaged in any criminal behavior. Thus some critics describe Section 218 as an "end- run around" the Fourth Amendment.[128] Notwithstanding this claim, in its first-ever ruling, dated November 18, 2002, the Foreign Intelligence Surveil- lance Court of Review (Review Court) squarely confronted, and upheld, the PATRIOT Act's extension of FISA to investigations whose primary purpose is law enforcement.[129]

In doing so, the three-judge appeals panel in *In Re Sealed Case* overturned a May 17, 2002 en banc decision by the Foreign Intelligence Surveillance Court (FISC). The FISC erred, the Review Court held, in maintaining that the FISA statute required that a proverbial "wall" of separation exist between law enforcement and counterintelligence agencies of the federal

government. Such a wall, the Review Court opined, was artificially constructed by a precedent set by the Fourth Circuit in *U.S. v. Truong Dinh
Hung* (1980), a case that did not even rely upon FISA's legislative history to
reach its ill-founded conclusion that there was a "primary purpose" FISA
requirement (that excludes evidence from a warrantless electronic search
from the point after which the foreign investigation purpose becomes
primarily concerned with law enforcement goals). Ironically, the Review
Court observed, several other circuits followed the Fourth Circuit precedent, a trend that was mirrored in 1995, when the FBI promulgated
"minimization" procedures in their guidelines governing FISA searches.
Those standards, the Review Court observed, perpetuated the erroneous
Truong Dinh Hung standard and actually led to the issue the Court was
deciding since the 2002 Department of Justice regulations (new "Intelligence
Sharing Procedures" that jettisoned the primary purpose rule) were promulgated to replace the 1995 guidelines. In finding that FISA's legislative history
did not support the common law supporting the primary purpose test, the
Review Court cast it aside and toppled the illusionary wall that wrongfully
created a distinction between foreign intelligence and criminal law enforcement that, according to positive law, simply did not exist. Consequently, as a
matter of statutory construction, the Review Court endorsed the attorney
general's 2002 guidelines that, pursuant to the PATRIOT Act and its FISA
amendments that adopted "the significant purpose" language, facilitated
interagency cooperation in the war against terror. The PATRIOT Act, in
other words, authorizes a FISA warrant for gathering foreign intelligence
even if other evidence of criminality is discovered.[130]

While the Review Court's construction of the PATRIOT Act and FISA
settled the question on appeal, the Court also considered whether a FISA
warrant was constitutionally reasonable as a Fourth Amendment "warrant." Although it conceded that a FISA order might not be a warrant for
Fourth Amendment purposes, it avoided answering the issue directly and
instead explored the underlying question of whether FISA surveillances were
reasonable. In stating that there is "no definitive jurisprudential answer" in
determining if Congress's rejection of *Truong*'s primary purpose test is
constitutional, the Review Court still held that the FISA procedures "certainly come close" to "meet[ing] the minimum Fourth Amendment warrant
standards," if for no other reason than understanding that the threat the
nation faces in confronting terrorism is genuine. Hence, the Review Court
concluded, the FISA warrant process is a reasonable exercise of governmental power as the executive's way to confront the danger in the interest of
preserving national security.[131]

In re Sealed Case has been appealed, but as of June 2003 it is uncertain if
the Supreme Court will opt to hear the case. A review of the writ of certiorari
(dated February 18, 2003) and the underlying cases leading up to it shows
how unusual the request is, mostly because the litigation itself is unprecedented.[132] The writ, notably, addresses the initial question of whether any
nongovernmental entity can actually maintain an appeal if they lose the case.
That issue exposes the reality that the litigation itself (and whether the writ is

proper) is in uncharted legal terrain, simply because the FISC and the Review Court are secret courts that have never made any of their decisions public. The uncertainty surrounding the legitimacy of the appeal is also exacerbated in light of the fact that the government is the sole party involved in FISA application requests and, significantly, hardly ever loses since the wiretap authority, in some form, has always been granted. Thus, when the government never loses, there is no need for an appeal (to any court). Yet, with much fanfare the lower court, FISC, deliberately disseminated its May 17, 2002 opinion by releasing it to the chairman of the Senate Judiciary Committee.[133] One can only speculate as to why (since that has never happened before), but it is clear from the tenor of the opinion—and the conclusion it reached—that the court was trying to open up, in a provocative fashion, the FISA process for public viewing by airing a judicial result that has profound consequences in post-9/11 American political society.

As it turns out, it was important to get a glimpse of the May 17 FISC rationale. One learns, for example, from the May 17 opinion that the attorney general had guidelines in effect in 1995 that adhered to the primary purpose requirement and, therefore, supported the practice that a "wall" should be in place as a routine part of interagency intelligence operations. The wall's function was to provide a barrier (essentially a system of internal oversight and review of key documents) that prevented agents conducting foreign intelligence investigations from conveying what they learned about ancillary criminal acts to law enforcement personnel. In this way the wall protects American citizens and legal aliens from having unauthorized communications disclosed. The opinion also recounts how disturbing it was for FISC judges to learn (from government officials, at their initiative) of at least seventy-five incidents proving that FISC judges were mislead by the government during the warrant application procedure. As the FISC chief judge, Royce Lamberth, wrote, these included: 1) "an erroneous statement in the FBI Director's FISA certification that the target of the FISA was not under criminal investigation"; 2) "erroneous statements in the FISA affidavits of FBI agents concealing the separation of the overlapping intelligence and criminal investigations, and the unauthorized sharing of FISA information with FBI criminal investigators and assistant U.S. attorneys"; and 3) "omissions of material facts from FBI FISA affidavits relating to a prior relationship between the FBI and a FISA target, and the interview of a FISA target by an assistant U.S. attorney."[134] Thereafter, and in conjunction with an in-house inquiry being conducted to explore possible ethics violations, the court convened specially to hear from the FBI to "consider the troubling number of inaccurate FBI affidavits in so many FISA applications." After doing so it took "supervisory action" to insure, among other things, that FBI agents understood the primary purpose procedure, presumably to avoid abuse—"like information sharing and unauthorized disseminations to criminal investigators and prosecutors"—from occurring in the future.[135]

The upshot of the May 17 opinion is that it reveals, first hand, that the special (and secret) court in charge of administering FISA warrants requests saw, and chose to communicate publicly, how prone the executive branch was to making serious and unethical mistakes that violate the civil rights of innocents. The errors in presenting the affidavits to the FISC are even more troubling if one considers that Judge Lamberth said in a rare 1997 public speech that the court "always ha[s] the personal approval of the attorney general as the last stop before the application is presented to us [i.e., the court] for approval." As Lamberth described it, "the political accountability that the attorney general must personally assume for each surveillance is an important safeguard, and we [i.e., the court] consistently find the applications well-scrubbed by the attorney general and her [i.e., Janet Reno's] staff before they are presented to us."[136] Accordingly, if one assumes the process has not changed much in the transition from the Reno to Ashcroft regimes, the May opinion demonstrates, quite persuasively, that there are sound reasons for having a wall in the first place, especially if one recalls that FISA itself was in essence a legislative act of reform designed to curb the kind of executive abuse that led up to the statute's passage. In short, the opinion underscores that FISA was a law bred in reform, and the primary purpose standard naturally evolved to become a routine part of agency intelligence and law enforcement operations and greatly impacted the way in which foreign intelligence was gathered. Indeed, insiders familiar with the FISA process reveal how entrenched the standard has been in preparing FISA warrants for court review.[137] But, as 9/11 and the response to it shows, the logic that built FISA—and its underlying rationale that helped institutional-ize the wall and the primary purpose test—was quickly dispatched to the dustbin of constitutional law in the sweeping, and deferential, reasoning found in the Review Court's *In Re Sealed Case* ruling. One could justify the action for the reasons being cited by those favoring the result: that the separation between agencies led to an information block that contributed to the 9/11 tragedy. On the other hand, one could also point out that the government—including the judicial branch—ought to be obligated to weigh very carefully whether it is best to jettison a reform rationale that is already in place (and serves salutary purposes) whole cloth and without exploring alternative means that are consistent with national security goals and the aim of preserving civil liberty.

"One of the Many Sad Legacies of September 11"

One of the PATRIOT Act's requirements is that several of the aforemen-tioned provisions will expire, or sunset, on December 31, 2005.[138] Yet the PATRIOT Act and its cousin, the Ashcroft Doctrine, will continue to be "one of the many sad legacies of September 11" as civil libertarians will be compelled to continue their own war in the nation's courtrooms to try to withstand the government's terrifying assault on personal freedom by allegedly protecting it through law.[139] While this essay has concentrated its attention on the law's impact on the Fourth Amendment, the PATRIOT Act and what it represents in the war against terror has many other civil liberty ramifications that are taken up elsewhere in this book and in the literature.

One, for example, is the executive's mandatory detention and removal strategy, a principle of immigration control that raises not only questions of substantive and procedural due process but also racial profiling and, in the end, fundamental justice. The strategy, it has been reported, profoundly affects *all* those connected to a suspected terrorist, as illustrated by the (unexplained) arrest and detention of an Ohio man (Ashraf Al-Jailani) who was arrested at work in October 2003 for allegedly having ties to extremist Muslims. Since his arrest and detention by the FBI, the man's family has been destroyed: While he has languished in a Pennsylvania prison, the INS has told his wife that he is going to be deported and, shortly thereafter, took custody of her children (and is seeking their permanent removal) because she is incapable of paying her bills while suffering from depression. As of June 2003, Al-Jailani remains incarcerated even though, in March, an immigration judge ruled that he ought to be released on bond on the grounds that there was not enough evidence to hold him. That decision, though, was blocked by federal officials who maintain that he is associated with terrorism.[140] While the Supreme Court has yet to confront the issue directly, in *Demore v. Kim* (2003), where the mandatory detention of a criminal alien who is deportable on the basis of committing a minor theft crime was upheld, the Court gave a hint that it will be very difficult to prevent the attorney general from aggressively enforcing his immigration policy in detaining aliens, and perhaps later even U.S. citizens, for an indefinite period, so long as the confinement is required in the interest of national security.[141]

The litigation testing the boundaries of executive action will proceed apace in the near future and there is a distinct possibility that the PATRIOT Act's sunset provisions will be supplanted by new legislation that recaptures what will expire. While praising the legislation at the House Judiciary Committee hearing in June 2003, Attorney General Ashcroft ironically made a plea for Congress to give the executive branch more power to fight terrorism by citing the PATRIOT Act's shortcomings. Indeed, Ashcroft's request was foreshadowed by the Justice Department's intention to lobby for expanded law enforcement powers, as expressed in a legislative proposal it drafted in January 2003. Notably, the new idea, styled "The Domestic Security Enhancement Act of 2003," or "PATRIOT Act II," was drafted in secret (allegedly as an "early discussion draft" and not a final commitment, and distributed to the Speaker of the House, Dennis Hastert [R-IL], and Vice President Richard Cheney on January 10) and obtained, and then distributed, by the Center for Public Integrity.[142] The draft generally proposes to increase the government's power to increase surveillance, control immigration, expand the range of criminal penalties for terrorist activity, and, significantly, strip American citizenship from those who engage in terrorism. Many of the new powers will vest unparalleled discretion in the Office of Attorney General, with fewer judicial controls than are already in place because of the first PATRIOT Act. Thus civil libertarians, predictably, are very concerned about the prospect of another PATRIOT Act that compounds, in their view, the mistakes of the original legislation.[143]

While it is premature to know if PATRIOT Act II will be enacted, the likelihood that it will become law may depend on two things. If the United States is the subject of another devastating terrorist attack on a magnitude that meets or exceeds 9/11, there is perhaps nothing that would stand in the way of its approval by the American people. The events of Oklahoma City and the World Trade Center/Pentagon attacks demonstrate quite clearly that Americans want quick answers to their fear of terror, and PATRIOT Act II surely will become the third of a triad of antiterrorist legislation initiatives that are born in large part from the politics of apprehension and response. Whether PATRIOT Act II becomes law, moreover, will also depend, in part, on whether the nation's courts will act as the balance wheel of justice or, alternatively, a rubber stamp of acquiescence to the executive. Acting in either capacity will likely define what the PATRIOT Act and its progeny will mean to republican liberty. In the end, however, transversing the path of balance is the nation's best hope for sustained liberty whereas the other alternative only guarantees that government will have more of a free hand in taking liberty away. The saddest legacy of 9/11 might be the failure of courts to live up to their responsibility to preserve individual rights instead of abdicating it by saying they are not in a position to second guess the executive. Indeed, a good case can be made that questioning the exercise of arbitrary authority under the pretext of maintaining a secure nation is precisely what courts are supposed to be doing, if for no other reason than it is extremely difficult to regain liberty once it is lost.

Chapter 2

1. Woodrow Wilson, *Congressional Government: A Study in American Politics* (Baltimore: The John Hopkins University Press, 1981), 43. Alexander Hamilton explained the value of having "energy in the executive" in *Federalist Nos. 70–77*, see Clinton Rossiter, ed., *The Federalist Papers* (New York: Mentor, 1999). On the issue (and reluctance) of inserting a bill of rights into the proposed constitutional framework, see Jack N. Rakove, *Original Meanings: Politics and Ideas in the Making of the Constitution* (New York: Vintage Books, 1996), 288–338.
2. U.S. House, Constitution Subcommittee, "Anti-Terrorism Investigations and the Fourth Amendment after September 11: Where and When Can the Government Go to Prevent Terrorist Attacks?" 108th Cong. 2d sess., May 20, 2003, p. 3 of 28, available at http://www.lexis.com in *FDCH Political Transcripts file* (viewed June 3, 2003). See also "Uniting and Strengthening America by Providing Appropriate Tools Required to Intercept and Obstruct Terrorism (USA PATRIOT Act)," P.L. 107–56, 115 Stat. 272 (2001).
3. U.S. House, Constitution Subcommittee. "Anti-Terrorism Investigations and the Fourth Amendment after September 11," p. 4 of 28. Academics, pundits, and civil rights activists have uniformly criticized the breakneck speed with which the PATRIOT Act was enacted, a process (in their view) lacking serious and thoughtful deliberation. See, e.g., Jennifer C. Evans, "Hijacking Civil Liberties: The USA PATRIOT Act of 2001," *Loyola University Chicago Law Journal* 33 (2002): 933, 967–68 (noting that the Senate debated it for only one day); Michael T. McCarthy, "USA PATRIOT Act," *Harvard Journal on*

Legislation 39 (2002): 435, 439 (acknowledging the act has select sunset provisions, but still suggesting the "paucity of committee and floor debate, along with decisions to short-circuit the typical amendment process" makes it appear that "Congress had indeed acted as a rubber stamp" of what the executive has to do in times of great crisis); editorial, "A Panicky Bill," *Washington Post*, 26 October 2001, p. A34 (calling it "panicky legislation that, in seeking to reduce one set of dangers, unnecessarily creates another"); Ronald Weich, *Insatiable Appetite: The Government's Demand for New and Unnecessary Powers after September 11* (October 15, 2002), available at http://www.aclu.org: 3–4 (viewed June 13, 2003) (noting that the House and Senate did not have a conference committee to reconcile differences, ordinarily done with all legislation).

4. McCarthy, "USA PATRIOT Act," 439.
5. Rensselaer Lee and Raphael Perl, "Terrorism, the Future, and U.S. Foreign Policy," *CRS-14. Issue Brief for Congress. Congressional Research Service. The Library of Congress* (updated October 18, 2002), pp. 438–9.
6. McCarthy, "USA PATRIOT Act," 441; Frederick P. Hitz, "Unleashing the Rogue Elephant: September 11 and Letting the CIA be the CIA," *Harvard Journal of Legislation and Public Policy* 25 (2002): 765, 772.
7. See William Zolla II, "The War At Home: Rising Tensions between Our Civil Liberties and Our National Security," *Chicago Bar Association Record* 17 (2003): 32, 33 (observing that the sad legacy will be the "perpetual friction between individual liberties and national security"). The idea of protecting freedom through law is inspired by a debate that occurred between Viet D. Dinh (assistant attorney general, Office of Legal Counsel) and Nadine Strossen (president of the American Civil Liberties Union) on August 31, 2002, at the Sheraton Boston hotel during the annual meeting of the American Political Science Association. During the debate Mr. Dinh defended the PATRIOT Act as "protecting freedom through law"; whereas, for Strossen, the legislation was described as law that only destroyed personal freedom. Mr. Dinh's comments are echoed in Paul Rosenzwieg's testimony in House subcommittee debates on the PATRIOT Act's impact on the Fourth Amendment, suggesting that the "difficult challenge" of reconciling the competing interests of order and liberty is framed by whether we should give the executive too much power and risk violation of civil liberties; or, conversely, give the government too little power and risk public safety. See U.S. House, Constitution Subcommittee, "Anti-Terrorism Investigations and the Fourth Amendment after September 11."
8. Lee and Perl, "Terrorism, the Future, and U.S. Foreign Policy"; Charles Doyle, "Terrorism: Section-by-Section Analysis of the USA PATRIOT Act" *CRS Report for Congress* (updated December 10, 2001): CRS-1 to CRS-59.
9. USA PATRIOT Act, Sections 201–225.
10. Slacker raids were conducted by volunteer members of the American Protective League (APL), a group that informally assisted the fledging Federal Bureau of Investigation in trying to uncover acts of disloyalty. The APL volunteers arrested, searched, and tapped the telephones of suspects, as well as performed slacker raids to eliminate draft dodging. The Palmer raids were named after President Woodrow Wilson's attorney general, A. Mitchell Palmer, who, with presidential approval, aggressively used governmental authority to arrest thousands of individuals who were suspected of being communists, but often without probable cause. William C. Banks and M. E. Bowman, "Executive Authority for National Security Surveillance," *American University Law Review*

- 50 (2000): 1, 23–26. The raids were prompted by a politically inspired bombing of Palmer's home in Washington, D.C. Six thousand immigrants in thirty-three cities were detained, many in overpopulated "bull pens," and had confessions beaten out of them. In the end, 556 were deported for their political associations, but not for any role they played in the bombing. David Cole and James X. Dempsey, *Terrorism and the Constitution: Sacrificing Civil Liberties in the Name of National Security* (New York: The New Press, 2002), 150.
11. Evans, "Hijacking Civil Liberties," 933, 950.
12. Hitz, "Unleashing the Rogue Elephant," 769.
13. Remarks of Senator Patrick Leahy (D-VT) in U.S. Senate, "U.S.A. PATRIOT Act," *Congressional Record* vol. 147, S 10990, 107th Cong. 1st sess., October 25, 2001, pp. 6–7 of 89, available at http://www.lexis.com (viewed June 3, 2003). Open-ended investigations began in the New Deal period where, for example, the Justice Department began the practice of using wiretaps for federal law enforcement purposes. Yet much of the abuse occurred during the tenure of FBI Director J. Edgar Hoover. In 1936, President Franklin D. Roosevelt charged Hoover with the duty of investigating domestic subversion and the agency responded by amassing scores of files on the lives of private citizens. Hoover, in the 1950s period of McCarthyism, implemented as an official policy the practice of wiretapping private property without prior authorization from the attorney general in situations where the FBI deemed that the national interest required it. Advances in surveillance technology in the military facilitated the creation of an electronic watch lists of persons, or targets, related to intelligence or nonintelligence activities in the 1960s. Banks and Bowman, "Executive Authority for National Security Surveillance," 26–31; Americo R. Cinquegrana, "The Walls (and Wires) Have Ears: The Background and First Ten Years of the Foreign Intelligence Surveillance Act of 1978," *University of Pennsylvania Law Review* 137 (1989): 793, 797. Moreover, through operations titled "CHAOS," the CIA was involved with putting moles in American student groups that were opposed to the Vietnam War for the purpose of discovering if there were any subversive, foreign connections. Hitz, "Unleashing the Rogue Elephant," 770. The FBI's COINTELPRO domestic surveillance operation (from roughly 1956 to 1971), concerning antiwar protesters and other suspected dissidents, also led to illegal wiretapping, illegal break-ins, and widespread abuses of civil rights and liberties. Cole and Dempsey, *Terrorism and the Constitution,* 73–76; Gerald H. Robinson, "We're Listening! Electronic Eavesdropping, FISA, and the Secret Court," *Willamette Law Review* 36 (2000): 51, 53.
14. Both were initiatives by President Gerald Ford in 1975. The (Nelson) Rockefeller Commission's purpose was to study if any CIA operations exceeded the agency's legal authority and make appropriate recommendations. The (Frank) Church Committee systematically investigated all aspects of the intelligence community, including the impact of government secrecy and whether there was sufficient oversight of intelligence activities. Banks and Bowman, "Executive Authority for National Security Surveillance," 32–34.
15. Ibid.
16. Ibid., 33; McCarthy, "USA PATRIOT Act," 441–42; Hitz, "Unleashing the Rogue Elephant," 770.
17. Banks and Bowman, "Executive Authority for National Security Surveillance," 33; McCarthy, "USA PATRIOT Act," 441–42.
18. *Katz v. U.S.,* 389 U.S. 347 (1967) overturned *Olmstead v. United States,* 277 U.S. 438 (1928), which held that there could not be a "search" (and a warrant

was not needed) for Fourth Amendment purposes unless the police conducted a physical search, or intrusion, of property. The "reasonable expectation of privacy" standard actually was derived from Justice John Marshall Harlan II's concurrence and that standard became the touchstone for prospective Supreme Court Fourth Amendment privacy cases. *Katz,* 360 (Harlan, J. concurring). Also, Justice Stewart's opinion for the Court avoided the question of whether there ought to be a national security exception to the warrant requirement. *Katz,* 358, n. 23. Yet while Justice Byron White favored a national security exception, his position brought a sharp rebuke from his colleagues on the bench. See *Katz,* 362 (White, J. concurring); 359 (Douglas, J. concurring).

19. *Berger v. New York,* 388 U.S. 41 (1967): 54–59.
20. 18 U.S.C. Sects. 2510–2520 (1968). The predicate offenses are listed in 18 U.S.C. Sect. 2516. Doyle, "The USA PATRIOT Act: A Legal Analysis," *CRS Report for Congress* (April 15, 2002), CRS-2 to CRS-3, CRS-3, n. 9. See also Robert A. Pikowsky, "An Overview of the Law of Electronic Surveillance Post September 11, 2001," *Law Library Journal* 94 (2002): 601, 603–604.
21. 18 U.S.C. 2511(3)(1968). See also Sharon H. Rackow, "How the USA PATRIOT Act Will Permit Governmental Infringement upon the Privacy of Americans in the Name of 'Intelligence' Investigations," *University of Pennsylvania Law Review* 150 (2002): 1651, 1659; Cinquegrana, "The Walls (and Wires) Have Ears," 801.
22. *United States v. United States District Court,* 407 U.S. 297 (Powell, J. Opinion for the Court): 315 and 318.
23. Ibid., 320 and 321–322.
24. Ibid., 323.
25. Whereas in 1973 Attorney General Levi instituted guidelines to cabin executive discretion in conducting electronic services (e.g., limiting surveillance to foreign targets), at least four courts of appeals strongly suggested that the president has the authority to conduct warrantless searches on national security grounds if the primary purpose of the investigation was to target, and obtain, foreign intelligence. Cinquegrana, "The Walls (and Wires) Have Ears," 803–806 (citing cases).
26. Foreign Intelligence Surveillance Act of 1978, Pub. L. No. 95–511, 92 Stat. 1783, 50 U.S.C. Sections 1801 et seq. (2003). See also Remarks of Senator Leahy in U.S. Senate. "U.S.A. PATRIOT Act," 7 of 89.
27. Ibid., Section 1803. The FISC Court "conducts all of its hearings in a secret windowless courtroom, sealed from the public by cipher-locked doors on the top floor of the Department of Justice." See Patrick S. Poole, "Inside America's Secret Court: The Foreign Intelligence Surveillance Court," available at http://fly.hiwaay.net/~pspoole/fiscshort.html (viewed November 20, 2002).
28. Cinquegrana, "The Walls (and Wires) Have Ears," 812–813.
29. Doyle, "The USA PATRIOT Act: A Legal Analysis," CRS-8. See 50 U.S.C. Section 1804(a)(7)(B). See, e.g., *United States v. Truong Dinh Hung,* 629 F.2d 908 (4th Cir. 1980), which was a pre-FISA case establishing the origin of the "primary purpose" test. In developing this limitation on FISA searches, *Truong* reasoned that courts would be in a position to grant a non-FISA warrant at the point that the government's efforts in monitoring a target primarily became a criminal investigation. Doyle, "The USA PATRIOT Act: A Legal Analysis," CRS-9, n. 19 (discussing *Truong*). Generally court approval is not required to collect foreign intelligence if the attorney general certifies under oath that the electronic surveillance is directed solely at communications between foreign

powers and that all minimization procedures have been followed. 50 U.S.C. Section 1802 (2003); Robinson, "We're Listening!," 60; Louis A. Chiarella and Michael A. Newton, "So Judge, How Do I Get That FISA Warrant? The Policy and Procedure for Conducting Electronic Surveillance," *Army Lawyer* 1997 (1997): 25, 30.

30. "Intelligence" consists of "foreign intelligence" (offensive in nature, occurring beyond the United States) and "counterintelligence" (protection against intelligence activities directed against the United States). Counterintelligence relates to protecting national security and hence is different from "domestic law enforcement" (which punishes criminal behavior) and "domestic security" (which safeguards the government from internal threats that are unrelated to foreign powers). Chiarella and Newton, "So Judge, How Do I Get That FISA Warrant?" 26–30. Hence, FISA does not regulate domestic security investigations (ibid., 30). Also, while FISA pertains to electronic surveillance and physical searches (intruding into premises or property to gather information surreptitiously), it does not apply to surveillance employed outside of the United States (ibid., 30).

31. 50 U.S.C. Sections 1804 ("Applications for court orders"), 1805 ("Issuance of order"), and 1806 ("Use of information") generally outline the application procedure for FISA searches. See Alison A. Bradley, "Extremism in the Defense of Liberty? The Foreign Intelligence Surveillance Act and the Significance of the USA PATRIOT Act," *Tulane Law Review* 77 (2002): 465, 474–8 (describing the mechanics of the FISA application process).

32. This difference is illustrated by the warrant procedures (for criminal investigations) set out in the *Federal Rules of Criminal Procedure* (Rule 41). Also, under Rule 41 the target of the search is entitled to get a copy of the warrant and an itemization of what was seized. A FISA search remains secret and the target does not get any notification that a search happened. Daniel J. Malooly, "Physical Searches Under FISA: A Constitutional Analysis," *American Criminal Law Review* 35 (1998): 411, 416–417.

33. As Doyle puts it, "Defendants often questioned whether authorities had used a FISA surveillance order against them in order to avoid the predicate crime threshold for a Title III order." Doyle, "The USA PATRIOT Act: A Legal Analysis," CRS-8 to CRS-9.

34. Approval authority for electronic surveillance rests with various personnel in the executive branch bureaucracy and who precisely has it is contingent upon "the type of person, the location, and the type of situation involved." Chiarella and Newton, "So Judge, How Do I Get That FISA Warrant?" 32. Arguably, then, there is enough vagueness in FISA's statutory definitions to muddle the determination of who falls within the law's coverage, or when. Thus, in practice, American citizens or permanent residents may be particularly at risk to FISA warrants because executive discretion determines when they are knowingly engaging in spying for foreign powers or, alternatively, about to commit a crime involving U.S. laws. Robinson, "We're Listening!," 58.

35. Gregory E. Birkenstock, "The Foreign Intelligence Surveillance Act and Standards of Probable Cause: An Alternative Analysis," *Georgetown Law Journal* 80 (1992): 843, 852. See 50 U.S.C. Section 1801(b)(2)(A)-(B).

36. Joginder S. Dhillon and Robert I. Smith, "Defensive Information Operations and Domestic Law: Limitations on Government Investigative Techniques," *Air Force Law Review* 50 (2001): 135, 165–166. See 18 U.S.C. Section 1801(h) and 1804 (a).

37. John W. Whitehead, "Forfeiting 'Enduring Freedom' for 'Homeland Security': A Constitutional Analysis of the USA PATRIOT Act and the Justice Department's Anti-Terrorism Initiatives," *American University Law Review* 51 (2002): 1081, 1088–1090.
38. Doyle, "The USA PATRIOT Act: A Legal Analysis," CRS-2.
39. Doyle, "The USA PATRIOT Act: A Legal Analysis," CRS-2 to CRS-5.
40. Sections 201, amending 18 U.S.C. Section 2516(1), and 202, amending 18 U.S. Section 2516(1)(c); Doyle, "The USA PATRIOT Act: A Legal Analysis," CRS-8. These sections also added terrorism and chemical weapons to the list of prohibited criminal conduct. See Joshua L. Dratel, "Fourth Amendment Implications of the USA PATRIOT Act," *Champion* 26 (2002): 51. Authority to intercept messages from a protected computer system is given through Section 217. Section 217, amending the Federal Wirtetap Act, 18 U.S.C. Section 2511. Doyle, "The USA PATRIOT Act: A Legal Analysis," CRS-8; Pikowsky, "An Overview of the Law of Electronic Surveillance Post September 11, 2001," 610.
41. Section 203(b), amending disclosure provisions of Rule 6(e)(3)(C) of the *Federal Rules of Criminal Procedure*. See *Federal Rules of Criminal Procedure* (amended to December 1, 2002), Rule 6(e)(3)(D), outlining "exceptions" to general rule of grand jury secrecy and nondisclosure, and referring to statutory definitions of "foreign intelligence," "counterintelligence," or "foreign intelligence information," available at http://www.law.ukans.edu/research/frcrilII. htm (viewed February 13, 2003).
42. Rule 6(e)(3)(D)(ii), available at http://www.law.ukans.edu/research/frcrilII.htm (viewed February 13, 2003); Doyle, "The USA PATRIOT Act: A Legal Analysis," CRS-20 to CRS-23.
43. Section 209, amending the Federal Wiretap Act, 18 U.S.C. Section 2510(1), and the Stored Communications Act, 18 U.S.C. Section 2703. This section thus equates voice mail to e-mail, and makes it subject to a court order. Doyle, "The USA PATRIOT Act: A Legal Analysis," CRS-7.
44. Prior law allowed more limited access to records such as subscriber names, addresses, telephone numbers, and telephone billing records. Section 210, amending the Stored Communications Act, 18 U.S.C. Section 2703(c)(2). Pikowsky, "An Overview of the Law of Electronic Surveillance Post September 11, 2001," 609. Getting payment information without a court order is critical in quickly thwarting the attempt by ISP users to avoid detection by employing false names. Doyle, "The USA PATRIOT Act: A Legal Analysis," CRS-6, n. 13.
45. Section 211, amending the Cable Communications Policy Act, 47 U.S.C. Section 551; Pikowsky, "An Overview of the Law of Electronic Surveillance Post September 11, 2001," 609; Doyle, "The USA PATRIOT Act: A Legal Analysis," CRS-7, n. 15. Also, Section 212 allows Internet service providers to reveal the content of subscriber data on a volunteer basis if the ISP believes it has information that risks immediate harm, death, or physical injury. Section 212, amending the Stored Communications Act, 18 U.S.C. Sections 2702–03. Pikowsky, "An Overview of the Law of Electronic Surveillance Post September 11, 2001," 610.
46. Section 216, amending 18 U.S.C. Section 3121(c), 3123(a), 3123 (b)(1), 3123 (d)(2), 3124(b), 3124(d), 3127(1)-(4); Pikowsky, "An Overview of the Law of Electronic Surveillance Post September 11, 2001," 610; Doyle, "The USA PATRIOT Act: A Legal Analysis," CRS-5 to CRS-6, CRS-5, n. 11, CRS-6, n.12; Whitehead, "Forfeiting 'Enduring Freedom' for 'Homeland Security,'" 1106 (explaining the difference between trap/trace and pen registers).

47. Section 219 amends Rule 41 of the *Federal Rules of Criminal Procedure* and gives judges the authority to issue search and seizure warrants for any district if it pertains to domestic or international terrorism activities. Section 219, amending Rule 41(a) and 18 U.S.C. Section 2703. See *Federal Rules of Criminal Procedure* (amended to December 1, 2002), Rule 41, available at http://www.law.ukans.edu/research/frcrVIII.htm (viewed February 14, 2003). Doyle, "The USA PATRIOT Act: A Legal Analysis," CRS-66 and CRS-67. Section 220 also gives nationwide effect to securing access to e-mail that is stored by third parties, allowing courts in one district to issue an access order for any other district in the country. Section 220, amending the Stored Communications Act, 18 U.S.C. Section 2703. Doyle, "The USA PATRIOT Act: A Legal Analysis," CRS-6 and CRS-7.

48. Section 213, amending 18 U.S.C. Section 3103a. See also Whitehead, "Forfeiting 'Enduring Freedom' for 'Homeland Security,'" 1110–1111; Steven A. Osher, "Privacy, Computers, and the PATRIOT Act: The Fourth Amendment Isn't Dead, But No One Will Insure It," *Florida Law Review* 54 (2002): 521, 533–534.

49. Whitehead, "Forfeiting 'Enduring Freedom' for 'Homeland Security,'" 1110–1111; Doyle, "The USA PATRIOT Act: A Legal Analysis," CRS-62 to CRS-66.

50. Section 208, amending 50 U.S.C. Section 1803(a); Doyle, "The USA PATRIOT Act: A Legal Analysis," CRS-15.

51. Section 206, amending 50 U.S.C. 1805(c)(2)(B).

52. Dratel, "Fourth Amendment Implications of the USA PATRIOT Act," 54; Whitehead, "Forfeiting 'Enduring Freedom' for 'Homeland Security,'" 1105.

53. Section 207, amending 18 U.S.C. Sections 1805(e)(1) and 1824(d) (extending physical searches from forty-five to ninety days; and extending surveillance and physical searches involving orders pertaining to agents of foreign power to 120 days, with further extensions for up to one year). Doyle, "The USA PATRIOT Act: A Legal Analysis," CRS-15.

54. Section 214, amending 50 U.S.C. Section 1842. Doyle, "The USA PATRIOT Act: A Legal Analysis," CRS-17.

55. Section 215, amending 50 U.S.C. Section 1861. Doyle, "The USA PATRIOT Act: A Legal Analysis," CRS- 17 to CRS-18.

56. Whitehead, "Forfeiting 'Enduring Freedom' for 'Homeland Security,'" 1099–1100. But Section 215 also immunizes the person producing the tangible items in good faith from civil liability. Doyle, "The USA PATRIOT Act: A Legal Analysis," CRS- 17 to CRS-18.

57. Section 218, amending 50 U.S.C. Section 1804(a)(7)(B); Doyle, "Terrorism: Section by Section Analysis of the USA PATRIOT Act," CRS-14 to CRS-15.

58. McCarthy, "USA PATRIOT Act," 443–444.

59. McCarthy, "USA PATRIOT Act," 444–445.

60. McCarthy, "USA PATRIOT Act," 448–449.

61. *Immigration and Naturalization Service v. St. Cyr*, 533 U.S. 289 (2001) (Stevens, J.).

62. *Zadvydas v. Davis*, 533 U.S. 678 (2001)(Breyer, J.).

63. McCarthy, "USA PATRIOT Act," 448–449.

64. Title IV ("Protecting the Border") and Subtitle A ("Protecting the Northern Border") contains Sections 401 to Section 405. They generally: 1) provide appropriations for increasing the personnel and equipment of the Border Patrol,

Customs Service, and INS (Sections 401, 402); 2) provide funding to allow the State Department and the INS to assimilate criminal records' information relative to visa and admission applications into the U.S. (Section 403); 3) remove the overtime ceiling amount for INS overtime pay (Section 404); and 4) provide appropriations for studying the feasibility of improving the FBI's Integrated Automated Fingerprint Identification System relative to reliably screening visa applications (Section 405). Other provisions in Title IV's Subtitle B (and elsewhere) command the attorney general, for example, to analyze the feasibility of implementing biometric identification systems to bar terrorists from entering the country (Sections 1007 and 1008) or tightening restrictions governing foreign student visa programs (Section 416) and facilitate sharing of the State Department's visa lookout data with other countries for the purpose of preventing terrorism or related crimes (Section 413). Doyle, "The USA PATRIOT Act: A Legal Analysis," CRS- 49 to CRS-50.

65. Ibid., CRS-50 to CRS-51.
66. Section 412(3); Doyle, "The USA PATRIOT Act: A Legal Analysis," CRS-51.
67. Section 412(5); Doyle, "The USA PATRIOT Act: A Legal Analysis," CRS-51.
68. Section 412(6) and 412(7).
69. Section 412(b); Doyle, "The USA PATRIOT Act: A Legal Analysis," CRS-51. Denials of habeas corpus writs, however, are only appealable to the U.S. Court of Appeals for the District of Columbia circuit (ibid).
70. Section 412(c); Doyle, "The USA PATRIOT Act: A Legal Analysis," CRS-51.
71. Sections 422 and 423, *Antiterrorism and Effective Death Penalty Act of 1996*, Pub. L. 104–132, 110 Stat. 1214–1319 (1996); McCarthy, "USA PATRIOT Act," 449.
72. The due process rights of aliens under the Fifth Amendment are implicated, as are the association rights of noncitizens under the First Amendment. McCarthy, "USA PATRIOT Act," 449–451. The question still remains an open one even in light of the Supreme Court's ruling in *Demore v. Kim*, 538 U.S. 956 (2003) (upholding constitutionality of mandatory detention of lawful permanent resident alien who is convicted of a crime and deportable). See Shirin Sinnar, "Patriotic or Unconstitutional? The Mandatory Detention of Aliens Under the USA PATRIOT Act," *Stanford Law Review* 55 (2003): 1419, 1446–1452.
73. Jonathan P. Straub, "The Prevention of E-Money Laundering: Tracking the Elusive Audit Trail," *Suffolk Transnational Law Review* 515 (2002): 517–520. The money laundering process begins with depositing unlawful monies into financial institutions (placement). The funds are then are moved around through a variety of complex transactions that hide the funds' origin (layering). Thereafter, the illegitimate funds are put into the mainstream of legitimate commerce (integration) (ibid., 517); U.S. Department of State and Bureau for International Narcotics and Law Enforcement Affairs, "International Narcotics Control Strategy Report" (2001), 2 of 153, available at http://www.state.gov/g/inl/rls/nrcrpt/2001/rpt/8487.htm (viewed February 18, 2003). "E-Money" facilitates money laundering by creating a cyber "paper" trail that is virtually unregulated and hence difficult to discover because "person to person" transactions are replaced by direct communications between computer users. Straub, "The Prevention of E-Money Laundering," 515, 519–520.
74. McCarthy, "USA PATRIOT Act," 447; Andrew Ayers, "The Financial Action Task Force: The War on Terrorism Will Not Be Fought on the Battlefield," *New York Law School Journal of Human Rights* 18 (2002): 449, 458.

75. Ayers, "The Financial Action Task Force," 458, nn. 64 and 66; U.S. Department of State and Bureau for International Narcotics and Law Enforcement Affairs, "International Narcotics Control Strategy Report (2001)," 2 of 153.

76. In addition to general sections (Sections 301 to 303), Title III has three subtitles: "International Counter Money Laundering and Related Matters" (Subtitle A); "Bank Secrecy Act Amendments and Related Improvements" (Subtitle B); and "Currency Crimes and Protection" (Subtitle C). Sections 311 to 377, PATRIOT Act. See also McCarthy, "USA PATRIOT Act," 447–448. The Senate's view to add the laundering restrictions in a comprehensive antiterrorist bill won the day and the concerns raised by critics on privacy grounds were never fully addressed (ibid., 448).

77. Sec. 302(a) (permitting the Secretary of Treasury to force U.S. banks to freeze its assets); Sec. 303(a) (imposing criminal sanctions for knowingly attempting, conspiring, or providing foreign terrorist organizations with "material support or resources").

78. Banks, credit unions, and other certain institutions to the Treasury Department must report cash transactions over $10,000. Banks must file suspicious activity reports as well if a transaction involving more than $5,000 looks suspicious. Doyle, "The USA PATRIOT Act: A Legal Analysis," CRS-25.

79. Section 352, amending 31 U.S.C. Section 5318(h); U.S. Department of State and Bureau for International Narcotics and Law Enforcement Affairs, "International Narcotics Control Strategy Report (2001)," 16 of 153.

80. Section 358, amending 31 U.S.C. Section 5311. Regarding suspected terrorist activities, Section 358 generally permits the sharing of the Bank Secrecy Act information with the intelligence community and better governmental access to consumer financial information and credit reports held by banks by amending the Right to Financial Privacy Act and the Fair Credit Reporting Act. U.S. Department of State and Bureau for International Narcotics and Law Enforcement Affairs, "International Narcotics Control Strategy Report (2001)," 16 of 153.

81. McCarthy, "USA PATRIOT Act," 448.

82. Section 311, amending 31 U.S.C. Section 5318; U.S. Department of State and Bureau for International Narcotics and Law Enforcement Affairs, "International Narcotics Control Strategy Report (2001)," 15 of 153.

83. Section 312, amending 31 U.S.C. Section 5318. U.S. Department of State and Bureau for International Narcotics and Law Enforcement Affairs, "International Narcotics Control Strategy Report (2001)," 16 of 153.

84. Section 313, amending 31 U.S.C. Section 5318; U.S. Department of State and Bureau for International Narcotics and Law Enforcement Affairs, "International Narcotics Control Strategy Report (2001)," 7 and 16 of 153.

85. Section 361, amending Subchapter I of chapter 3 of Title 31 of the U.S. Code. FinCEN previously was empowered to act under federal regulation but not a statutory mandate. Doyle, "The USA PATRIOT Act: A Legal Analysis," CRS-27.

86. Section 365, amending Subchapter II of chapter 53 of Title 31 of the U.S. Code.

87. Section 351, amending 31 U.S.C. Section 5318(g)(3); Section 355, amending 12 U.S.C. Section 1828; Doyle, "The USA PATRIOT Act: A Legal Analysis," CRS-26 to CRS-27.

88. Section 1004, amending 18 U.S.C. 1956(i). The change is predicated on the Supreme Court's analysis, in dicta, that suggested the accused could be tried in more than one place if the launderer got the funds in one district but moved them to another in furtherance of the crime. Doyle, "The USA PATRIOT Act: A

Legal Analysis," CRS-26 to CRS-40. See also *United States v. Cabrales,* 524 U.S. 1 (1998). The act has another extraterritorial jurisdiction provision in Section 377 (making 18 U.S.C. Section 1029, prohibiting credit card, PIN number, and other access devices, applicable overseas if the card or device is controlled by an American entity and the instrument or fruits of the crime pass through the United States). Section 377, amending 18 U.S.C. Section 1029; Doyle, "The USA PATRIOT Act: A Legal Analysis," CRS-39.

89. Section 363, amending 31 U.S.C. Section 5321(a); Doyle, "The USA PATRIOT Act: A Legal Analysis," CRS-36.

90. Section 315, amending sundry existing statutes and regulations; Doyle, "The USA PATRIOT Act: A Legal Analysis," CRS-35.

91. Sections 329 and 373, respectively; Doyle, "The USA PATRIOT Act: A Legal Analysis," CRS-36 and CRS-37.

92. Sections 374 and 375; Doyle, "The USA PATRIOT Act: A Legal Analysis," CRS-37.

93. Section 371, amending 31 U.S.C. Section 5316; Doyle, "The USA PATRIOT Act: A Legal Analysis," CRS-38 to CRS-39. See also *United States v. Bajakian,* 524 U.S. 321 (1998).

94. Section 372, amending 31 U.S.C. Section 5317 (relating to reporting of domestic coins or currency transactions involving $10,000 or more; and amending 31 U.S.C. Section 5324 (relating to "smurfing," or structuring transactions to avoid reporting requirements); Doyle, "The USA PATRIOT Act: A Legal Analysis," CRS-39.

95. Doyle, "The USA PATRIOT Act: A Legal Analysis," CRS-40 to CRS-45.

96. The IEEPA limited section 5(b) by not expressly having a provision allowing the vesting of property in the United States, and section 5(b) was changed to governing property seizure "during time of war." Doyle, "The USA PATRIOT Act: A Legal Analysis," CRS-40.

97. Doyle, "The USA PATRIOT Act: A Legal Analysis," CRS-41.

98. Section 806, amending 18 U.S.C. Section 981(a)(1)(G); Doyle, "The USA PATRIOT Act: A Legal Analysis," CRS-42 to CRS-43.

99. For instance, "international terrorism," inter alia, means activities that involve violent acts or acts dangerous to human life that are a violation of United States (or state) criminal law if committed within the United States (or state). "Domestic terrorism" generally encompasses the same acts. 18 U.S.C. Section 2331; Doyle, "The USA PATRIOT Act: A Legal Analysis," CRS-42 n. 86.

100. In other words, they are not directed at capturing property that is part of a crime or part of the fruits of a crime. Doyle, "The USA PATRIOT Act: A Legal Analysis," CRS-44 to CRS-45. The sections might be challenged as "excessive fines" violations of the Eighth Amendment. Also, since the Justice Department has advocated Section 806 on the basis it is akin to the Racketeer Influenced and Corrupt Organizations (RICO) law's criminal forfeiture provisions, Doyle observes that either section is suspect as a violation of the Fifth Amendment's double jeopardy clause, or the ex post facto clause (ibid., CRS-45).

101. See William Zolla II, "The War At Home: Rising Tensions between Our Civil Liberties and Our National Security," *Chicago Bar Association Record* 17 (2003): 32, 33.

102. "Detention, Treatment, and Trial of Certain Non-Citizens in the War Against Terrorism," 66 Federal Register 57833 (November 13, 2001); David Cole, "Enemy Aliens," *Stanford Law Review* 54 (2002): 953, 977. See also Ayers, "The Financial Action Task Force," 458, nn. 64 and 66; U.S. Department of

State and Bureau for International Narcotics and Law Enforcement Affairs, "International Narcotics Control Strategy Report (2001)," 2 of 153. "Detention, Treatment, and Trial of Certain Non-Citizens in the War Against Terrorism," 66 Federal Register 57833 (November 13, 2001).

103. "Remarks of Attorney General John Ashcroft," U.S. Attorneys Conference New York City, October 1, 2002, Available at http://www.usdoj.gov/ag/speeches/2002/100102agremarkstousattorneysconference.htm.

104. Aschroft's aggressive style of law enforcement in the terrorist war is described in Siobhan Gorman, "The Ashcroft Doctrine," *National Journal,* 21 December 2002, pp. 3712–9. See ibid., p. 3713. The attorney general said there were no second chances in a speech delivered to the U.S. Attorney's Conference in New York City on October 1, 2002 (ibid., 3716–17). The assistant attorney general's perspective is found in Viet D. Dinh, "Freedom and Security After September 11," *Harvard Society for Law and Public Policy* 25 (2002): 399–406.

105. Siobhan Roth, "Material Support Law: Weapon in War on Terror," *Legal Times,* 5 May 2003, p. 11. See also Charles Lane, "In Terror War, 2nd Track For Suspects: Those Designated 'Combatants' Lose Legal Protections," *Washington Post,* 1 December 2002, p. A1.

106. Ashcroft's comments are reprinted in "Testimony of Attorney General John Ashcroft, U.S. House of Representatives, Committee on the Judiciary, June 5, 2003," available at http://www.usdoj.gov (viewed June 12, 2003). See generally Susan Schmidt, "Tougher Terror Laws Proposed," *Akron Beacon Journal,* 6 June 2003, p. A3.

107. Shannon McCaffrey, "Ohio Man Aided Bin Laden," *Akron Beacon Journal,* 20 June 2003, p. A1.

108. Safire published his commentary in a *New York Times* article and is quoted in Will Thomas DeVries, "Protecting Privacy in the Digital Age," *Berkeley Technology Law Journal* 18 (2003): 283; 305, n. 173. Carnivore's purpose, application, and limitations are explained in Donald M. Kerr's congressional statement before the U.S. Senate's Committee on the Judiciary on September 6, 2000. "Statement for the Record of Donald M. Kerr, Assistant Director, Laboratory Division, Federal Bureau of Investigation on Carnivore Diagnostic Tool," available at http://www.fbi.gov/congress/congress00/kerr090600.htm (viewed June 20, 2003). The Terrorism Information Awareness program's purpose, use, and limitations are explained in the Defense Advanced Research Project Agency's "Terrorism Information Awareness (TIA) System" website, http://www.darpa.mil/iao/TIASystems.htm (viewed June 20, 2003; this site was removed subsequent to this viewing). See generally Aaron Y. Strauss, "A Constitutional Crisis in the Digital Age: Why the FBI's 'Carnivore' Does Not Defy the Fourth Amendment," *Cardozo Arts and Entertainment Law Journal* 20 (2002): 231–58.

109. Mark G. Young. "What Big Eyes and Ears You Have!: A New Regime for Covert Governmental Surveillance," *Fordham Law Review* 70 (2001): 1017, 1029–30.

110. U.S. Department of Justice, Office of the Inspector General, "The September 11 Detainees: A Review of the Treatment of Aliens Held on Immigration Charges in Connection with the Investigation of the September 11 Attacks" (April 2003), available from the American Civil Liberties Union website, at http://www.aclu.org, p. 195 (viewed on June 2, 2003). See also Schmidt, "Tougher Terror Laws Proposed," A3.

111. U.S. Department of Justice, Office of the Inspector General, "The September 11 Detainees," pp. 195–198. See also Schmidt, "Tougher Terror Laws Proposed," A3.

112. "National Security: Prevention of Acts of Violence and Terrorism," 66 *Federal Register* 55062 (October 31, 2001); "Registration of Certain Nonimmigrant Aliens from Designated Countries," 67 *Federal Register* 67765 (November 6, 2002). See also, *Hamdi v. Rumsfeld,* 296 F.3d 278 (4th Cir. 2002)(reversing lower court order allowing alleged enemy combatant unmonitored access to counsel).

113. *In Re D-J,* 23 I. & N. Dec. 572 (A.G. 2003).

114. *Center for National Security Studies v. U.S. Department of Justice,* 2003 U.S. App. LEXIS 11910 (D.C. Cir. 2003).

115. Ibid., *26.

116. Ibid., *27–8.

117. Ibid., *44–56.

118. Ibid., *61, *81.

119. Ibid., *40. Judge Sentelle observed that only the Sixth Circuit, in *Detroit Free Press v. Ashcroft,* 303 F.3d 681 (6th Cir. 2002) held that the First Amendment prohibited a blanket closure of special interest deportation hearings. A majority of courts, he countered, have ruled otherwise: *Hamdi v. Rumsfeld,* 316 F.3d 450 (4th Cir. 2003) (rejecting the habeas petition of a U.S. citizen challenging his military detention and designation as an enemy combatant); *Global Relief Foundation v. O'Neill,* 315 F.3d 748 (7th Cir. 2002) (validating that the PATRIOT Act can employ *ex parte,* classified evidence in proceedings to freeze terrorist organizations' assets); and *Hamdi v. Rumsfeld,* 296 F.3d 278 (4th Cir. 2002) (reversing lower court order allowing alleged enemy combatant unmonitored access to counsel).

120. David Cole, "The New McCarthyism: Repeating History in the War on Terrorism," *Harvard Civil Rights–Civil Liberties Law Review* 38 (2003): 1–30.

121. See Akhil Reed Amar, "Fourth Amendment First Principles," *Harvard Law Review* 107 (1994): 757, 762; *Katz,* 389 U.S. 347 (1967).

122. *Kyllo v. U.S.,* 533 U.S. 27 (2001) (requiring a warrant when police use thermal imaging to discover heat patterns inside a home); *Barnicki v. Vopper,* 532 U.S. 514 (2001) (First Amendment protects disclosure of contents of illegally intercepted cell phone conversations relating to public issues; *U.S. v. American Library Association, Inc.,* 2003 U.S. LEXIS 4799 (2003) (libraries can be compelled under federal law to install filters blocking pornographic images from Internet pursuant to Spending Power). See generally Young, "What Big Eyes and Ears You Have!"

123. *Smith v. Maryland,* 442 U.S. 735 (1979).

124. Young, "What Big Eyes and Ears You Have!" 1071–72.

125. Dratel, "Fourth Amendment Implications of the USA PATRIOT Act," 51. See also McCarthy, "USA PATRIOT Act," 445–46.

126. Osher, "Privacy, Computers, and the PATRIOT Act," 533, 534, n. 106. See also Evans, "Hijacking Civil Liberties," 980–981; *Wilson v. Arkansas,* 514 U.S. 927 (1995). Rule 41(d) states: "Execution and Return With Inventory. The officer taking property under the warrant shall give to the person from whom or from whose premises the property was taken a copy of the warrant and a receipt for the property taken or shall leave the copy and receipt at the place from which the property was taken. The return shall be made promptly and shall be accompanied by a written inventory of any property taken. The inventory shall

be made in the presence of the applicant for the warrant and the person from whose possession or premises the property was taken, if they are present, or in the presence of at least one credible person other than the applicant for the warrant or the person from whose possession or premises the property was taken, and shall be verified by the officer. The federal magistrate judge shall upon request deliver a copy of the inventory to the person from whom or from whose premises the property was taken and to the applicant for the warrant." Rule 41(d). *Federal Rules of Criminal Procedure,* at Cornell's Legal Information Institute website, available at http://www.law.cornell.edu/topics/criminal_procedure.html (viewed June 25, 2003). See also Doyle, "The USA PATRIOT Act," CRS-62 to 66.

127. Osher, "Privacy, Computers, and the PATRIOT Act," 530; Dratel, "Fourth Amendment Implications of the USA PATRIOT Act," 54.

128. American Civil Liberties Union, "FISA: End-Run Around the Fourth Amendment," available at http:///www.aclu.org (viewed June 13, 2003).

129. *In Re Sealed Case,* 310 F.3d 717 (Foreign Int. Surv. Ct. Rev. 2002).

130. Ibid. See also *United States v. Truong Dinh Hung,* 629 F.2d 908 (4th Cir. 1980): 915.

131. The Review Court relied heavily on the Supreme Court's *Keith* decision to reach its conclusion as to Fourth Amendment reasonableness (ibid.).

132. The writ of certiorari can be downloaded at the ACLU website. See "In the Courts," at http://www.aclu.org (viewed June 24, 2003); ACLU, "In Legal First, Groups Urge High Court to Review Secret Court Ruling on Government Spying," available at http:///www.aclu.org (viewed June 24, 2003).

133. Reportedly the May 2002 opinion was the first instance where the Department of Justice lost a FISA application request. The chief justice of the FISC apparently agreed with the chairman of the Senate Judiciary Committee's decision to release it. See "The 'Secret Court,'" available from the *Courts.Net* website, at http://www.courts.net/secret.htm, p. 3 of 4 (viewed June 24, 2003).

134. *In Re All Matters Submitted to the Foreign Intelligence Surveillance Court* (Foreign Int. Sur. Ct., May 17, 2002), available online from the Federation of American Scientists website, at http://www.fas.org/irp/agency/doj/fisa/fisc051702.html. All seven judges joined this opinion without dissent.

135. Ibid.

136. Judge Lamberth's speech, and the question and answer session that followed, occurred at a breakfast meeting sponsored by the American Bar Association's Standing Committee on Law and National Security. The judge also said that the validity of the application is certified by an "applicable agency official and an affidavit of the investigating agent" before it reaches the attorney general for approval. "Intelligence on the FISA Court," *Legal Times,* 14 April 1997, 18.

137. See generally Chiarella and Newton, "So Judge, How Do I Get That FISA Warrant?"

138. Via PATRIOT Act Section 224, these include Sections 203 (sharing grand jury information), 208 (seizure of stored voicemail), 211 (access to cable company communication service records), 213 (sneak and peak) and 216 (pen and trace devise amendments). Doyle, "The USA PATRIOT Act: A Legal Analysis," CRS-10 n. 22.

139. William Zolla II, "The War At Home: Rising Tensions between Our Civil Liberties and Our National Security," *Chicago Bar Association Record* 17 (2003): 32, 33.

140. Carl Chancellor, "Nightmare Without End," *Akron-Beacon Journal,* 20 June 2003, A10.
141. *Demore v Kim,* 538 U.S. 956 (2003). See also Daniel Kanstoom, "From the Reign of Terror to Reigning in the Terrorists: The Still-Undefined Rights of Non-Citizens in the 'Nation of Immigrants,'" *New England International and Comparative Law Annual* 9 (2003): 47–107; Cole, "Enemy Aliens," 966–974.
142. Charles Lewis and Adam Mayle, "Justice Dept. Drafts Sweeping Expansion of Anti-Terrorism Law," available at http://www.publicintegrity.org (viewed June 25, 2003).
143. See, e.g., Timothy H. Edgar, "Section-by-Section Analysis of Justice Department draft 'Domestic Security Enhancement Act of 2003,' also known as 'PATRIOT Act,'" available at http://www.aclu.org (viewed June 22, 2003). A copy of the draft legislation can be found at the Center for Public Integrity's website, at http://www.publicintegrity.org/dtaweb/home.asp (viewed June 25, 2003).

Chapter 3

Presidential Power, Judicial Deference, and the Status of Detainees in an Age of Terrorism

Otis H. Stephens, Jr.

Introduction

The murderous attacks of September 11, 2001 marked a turning point in America's escalating war on terrorism. Prior to that date, suspected terrorists had typically been prosecuted in accordance with a law enforcement model based on the well-defined procedures of the American criminal justice system. For example, in accordance with the *law enforcement model,* Ramzi Yousef, the mastermind behind the 1993 bombing of the World Trade Center, was tried and convicted in 1998 in United States District Court.[1] After 9/11, however, the emphasis changed abruptly, and the procedural rules associated with criminal trials began to yield to claims of military exigency in the war on terrorism. The expanded use of presidential power in the immediate aftermath of 9/11 reflects this basic shift to a *military justice model.*

Responding to widespread fear and anger, as well as demands for retaliation and protection from future attacks, on September 14, 2001, President George W. Bush proclaimed a "Declaration of National Emergency by Reason of Certain Terrorist Attacks."[2] Congress promptly adopted a joint resolution authorizing the president to use "all necessary and appropriate force" against the 9/11 terrorists and those who harbored them.[3] Then in October 2001, the president initiated military operations in Afghanistan (Operation Enduring Freedom) resulting a few months later in the overthrow of the Taliban regime and the destruction of many of the Al Qaeda cells and training camps operating in that country. Meanwhile, on November 13, 2001, citing the previously noted joint resolution and his constitutional and statutory authority as commander in chief, President Bush issued a sweeping military order authorizing the detention of non-U.S. citizens suspected of committing or otherwise being involved in acts of international terrorism against "the United States, its citizens, national security, foreign policy, or economy. . . . "[4] The order also provided for the trial of such detainees before military tribunal "for violations of the laws of war and other applicable laws. . . . " Pursuant to this order as implemented by the secretary of defense, at least 640 noncitizen detainees have reportedly been imprisoned at Guantanamo Bay, Cuba, where they remain awaiting formal charges.

Three additional classes of detainees have figured prominently in the post–September 11 War on Terror: 1) *INS detainees*: aliens taken into custody by the Immigration and Naturalization Service; 2) *criminal detainees*: typically American citizens charged with involvement in terrorist activities; and 3) *material witness detainees*: persons detained following the issuance of a material witness warrant to secure their testimony before a grand jury. These classes of individuals were the focus of a lawsuit brought by a number of public interest groups against the Department of Justice seeking information regarding persons detained in connection with the investigation of the terrorist attacks. On August 2, 2002, the District Court for the District of Columbia ruled in the case of *Center for National Security Studies v. Department of Justice* that the Department of Justice was required under the Freedom of Information Act (FOIA) to disclose names of detainees and their attorneys but was not required to disclose information regarding their arrest, detention, and release.[5]

Reviewing this decision on June 17, 2003, the District of Columbia Court of Appeals reversed the decision of the lower court and held that the Justice Department was not required to provide the requested information in light of the law enforcement exemptions in FOIA.[6] In addition, the court ruled that the First Amendment did not require release of the requested information. In his opinion for the majority, Judge Sentelle expressed unwillingness to "convert the First Amendment right of access to criminal judicial proceedings into a requirement that the government disclose information compiled during the exercise of a quintessential executive power—the investigation and prevention of terrorism."[7] Judge Sentelle distinguished this decision from the ruling in *Detroit Free Press v. Ashcroft,* which recognized a First Amendment right of access to deportation proceedings.[8] He viewed the *Detroit Free Press* decision as applying to "adjudicative" information rather than the "investigatory" information sought by the public interest groups.[9]

In a powerful dissent, Judge Tatel noted that the limited exemptions in the Freedom of Information Act "do not obscure the basic policy that disclosure, not secrecy, is the dominant objective of the Act." His view is summed up in the following statement:

> Rather than hold the government to clearly established standards governing FOIA exemptions, the court sustains the government's vague, ill-explained decision to withhold information, invoking principles of deference and engaging in its speculation to fill in the gaps in the government's showing. In my view, the court's approach drastically diminishes if not eliminates the judiciary's role in FOIA cases that implicate national-security interests.[10]

Judge Tatel's criticism serves to underscore the extent to which the majority in this case and most judges in other cases discussed in the following pages have deferred to executive authority.

This chapter analyzes the legal status of noncitizen and citizen detainees in the aftermath of the September 11 attacks. It examines the sources and scope of President Bush's power to detain noncitizens and to try them before military commissions. In addition, it compares this power with the president's authority to designate citizens as enemy combatants and to detain them indefinitely without affording them the constitutional rights ordinarily granted to federal criminal defendants. Finally, this chapter considers the implications of viewing the post–September 11 expansion of presidential power as an endorsement of the military model as distinguished from the law enforcement model of criminal justice.

Historical Background of Military Commissions

The framers of the U.S. Constitution, distrustful of the concentration of governmental authority, divided several important powers, including the war power, between Congress and the president. Congress, for example, was granted the power to raise and support an army and navy, to declare war, "to define and punish piracies and felonies committed on the high seas, and offenses against the law of nations," and to "make rules for the government and regulation of the land and naval forces."[11] The president, however, was designated as "commander in chief" and given the broad power to "take care that the laws be faithfully executed. . . . "[12] The writ of habeas corpus is recognized with the negative statement that "the privilege of the writ of habeas corpus shall not be suspended, unless when in cases of rebellion or invasion the public safety may require it."[13] Although Congress is authorized to suspend the writ, the Constitution does not formally bar the president from doing so if public safety requires such action. President Abraham Lincoln unilaterally suspended the writ of habeas corpus at the beginning of the Civil War, and Congress later approved this action. Military commissions were frequently used to try both military personnel and civilians during the Civil War. For the most part, the authority of these commissions was upheld. However, in *Ex parte Milligan,* decided a year after the end of hostilities, the Supreme Court held that the military trial of a civilian on charges of disloyalty outside the theater of military operations, while the civil courts remained open, violated the defendant's Fifth and Sixth Amendment rights.[14]

It is generally recognized that under its Article I, Section 8 powers, Congress has the authority to provide for the creation of military commissions or to authorize the president to create such commissions. The Supreme Court recognized the latter alternative in upholding the president's power to establish military commissions in the World War II cases of *Ex parte Quirin*[15] and *In Re Yamashita.*[16]

A more difficult question is whether the president can exercise this power independently. In the 1952 case of *Madsen v. Kinsella,* the Supreme Court answered this question in the affirmative.[17] This case came to the Court via a petition for habeas corpus filed by Yvette Madsen, a United States citizen, to review her murder conviction by a military commission. She had been convicted of murdering her husband, a lieutenant in the United States Air Force, in their military quarters in Frankfort, Germany. Madsen claimed, among other things, that the commission itself was unconstitutional. Rejecting this contention, the Supreme Court recognized the inherent power of the president to establish military commissions: "in the absence of attempts by Congress to limit the President's power, it appears that, as Commander in Chief of the Army and Navy of the United States, he may in time of war establish and prescribe the jurisdiction and procedure of military commissions."[18] Congress, the Court emphasized, had made no attempt to limit the president's power with respect to military commissions. It seems clear that the power of the president to establish military tribunals, either with or without congressional authorization, was well-established long before November 13, 2001.

President Bush's order establishing military tribunals closely paralleled President Franklin D. Roosevelt's proclamations pertaining to the Nazi saboteur incident in the summer of 1942.[19] In mid-June of that year, eight German soldiers, after receiving extensive training in the techniques of sabotage, were transported by submarine to the east coast of the United States, four coming ashore on Long Island and four in Florida. They landed secretly at night and buried their uniforms along with explosives presumably intended for use in the destruction of various war facilities and other property. Dressed in civilian clothing, they attempted to conceal their identity as they mingled with the population and traveled to New York City, Chicago, and other urban centers. Before any acts of destruction were undertaken, two of the saboteurs had second thoughts and provided the Federal Bureau of Investigation with information about the ill-conceived plot. Before the end of June, all of the saboteurs were incarcerated.

In an attempt to reassure a civilian population still reeling from the devastating attack on Pearl Harbor, Roosevelt issued two military orders on July 2, 1942. The first of these provided that enemies entering this country for purposes including sabotage were subject to the laws of war and the jurisdiction of military tribunals. The order further provided that "such persons shall not be privileged to seek any remedy or maintain any proceeding directly or indirectly, or have any such remedy or proceeding sought in their behalf, in the courts of the United States, or of its States, territories, and possessions. . . . "

In the second order, Roosevelt set up a military tribunal for trial of the Nazi saboteurs, relying on his authority as "President and as Commander in Chief of the Army and Navy, under the Constitution and statutes of the United States, and more particularly the Thirty-Eighth Article of War. . . . " Convictions by this seven-member tribunal required a two-thirds vote. The order sought to preclude judicial review by providing that "The record of the trials, including any judgment or sentence, shall be transmitted directly to [the President] for [his] action thereon."

This hastily created military commission, operating in strict secrecy, proceeded immediately to the trial of the saboteurs. The procedure followed by the commission did not include many of the constitutional protections guaranteed in civil trials. Nevertheless, the saboteurs were provided with able defense counsel consisting of legally trained military officers. The defense argued that the president had exceeded his constitutional powers by barring the defendants from the civil courts and by ordering their trials before a military commission. They also argued that the commission had not been established in accordance with the existing provisions of the Articles of War. Defense counsel was also concerned that the president retained the sole power to review the commission's decision. They feared that the trial would be rushed to conclusion and sentences carried out without notice or time to permit a constitutional challenge in the Supreme Court.

The District Court for the District of Columbia denied petitioners applications for habeas corpus.[20] By complicated steps involving issuance of writs of habeas corpus and certiorari, the Supreme Court justices, who were scattered throughout the country during their summer recess, were individually contacted and rushed back to Washington. In a special term convened for this case only, they heard oral arguments on July 29 and 30 and rendered a brief per curiam decision on July 31 in *Ex Parte Quirin* denying defendants' applications for leave to file petitions for habeas corpus. The Court concluded that the "alleged offenses . . . could be tried by a military commission, that the commission was lawfully constituted, and that the petitioners were lawfully held for trial."[21] Undeterred by these events, the military trial proceeded, the defendants were speedily convicted, and in early August 1942, six of the eight defendants were executed in Washington, D.C.

Because of the importance of the issues raised in *Ex parte Quirin,* the Supreme Court on October 29, 1942, issued an opinion elaborating on its July 31 per curiam decision. Writing for eight members of the Court (Justice Frank Murphy not participating), Chief Justice Harlan Fiske Stone distinguished this decision from the Court's famous Civil War era ruling in *Ex parte Milligan.* In *Milligan,* as previously noted, the Court held that martial law could not "be applied to citizens in states which have upheld the authority of the government, and where the courts are open and their process unobstructed." In *Quirin,* the Court acknowledged that the civilian courts were open at the time of the saboteurs' trials and that one of the defendants was technically an American citizen. However, it did not regard these factors as critical. Rather, it limited its analysis to the question of whether the actions of these petitioners, regardless of their status as soldiers and not civilians, were violations of the law of war. Stone concluded that by entering the United States, "armed with explosives intended for the destruction of war industries and supplies . . . without uniform or other emblem signifying their belligerent status, or by discarding that means of identification after entry, such enemies become unlawful belligerents subject to trial and punishment"[22] Having found that the petitioners were properly charged with the offense of unlawful belligerency, the Court asserted that Roosevelt was authorized to order their trials by a military commission. In short, the Court concluded that the president had lawfully constituted and convened the military commission, that the petitioners were held in lawful custody, and that they failed to "show cause for their discharge."[23]

Despite the opaque language of Stone's opinion, it was clear that the Supreme Court was unwilling to limit the president's power to establish military commissions for the trial of enemy belligerents. Given the strong public approval of Roosevelt's handling of the Nazi saboteur incident, anything other than judicial deference would have been surprising. Nevertheless, it is important to recognize that in the very process of affirming the constitutionality of President Roosevelt's action, the Supreme Court was asserting, in opposition to his order, the power of judicial review—that is, the power "to say what the law is."[24]

Military Tribunals Since 9/11

Relying heavily on the precedent established in *Ex parte Quirin,* President Bush's military order of November 13, 2001 authorized military tribunals to depart from "the principles of law and the rules of evidence generally recognized in the trial of criminal cases in the United States District Courts."[25] As justification for this departure from the law enforcement model, President Bush emphasized his determination "that an extraordinary emergency exists for national defense purposes, that this emergency constitutes an urgent and compelling government interest, and that issuance of this order is necessary to meet this emergency."[26] The order granted the secretary of defense broad authority to establish and implement regulations. Under this authority, a number of regulations were adopted in early 2002 restoring certain procedural guarantees. These include the right to privately retained counsel and a provision requiring a unanimous vote of the commission for imposition of the death penalty. For other convictions and sentences, a two-thirds vote of the commission, as provided in the original order, remains intact. Like Roosevelt's 1942 proclamations, Bush's military order sought to preclude judicial review of convictions and sentences. The order provided for "review and final decision" by the president or the secretary of defense as his designee. The November 13 military order has been the subject of heated debate among legal scholars, civil liberties groups, and other interested parties.[27]

As previously noted, several hundred non-U.S. citizens have been detained and imprisoned at Guantanamo Bay, Cuba, under the president's November 13 order. A number of unsuccessful efforts have been made by, and on behalf of, these persons to challenge the constitutionality of their detention. For example, in *Coalition of Clergy v. Bush,* the Ninth U. S. Circuit Court of Appeals affirmed an order dismissing a habeas corpus petition on the ground that the clergy, lawyers, and law professors bringing the action were not proper "next friends" of the detainees.[28]

Al Odah v. U.S. involved three separate actions brought by nationals from Kuwait, Australia, and Great Britain, in the D.C. District Court, challenging the legality and conditions of their confinement. From adverse judgments, these individuals sought review in the Court of Appeals for the District of Columbia. On March 11, 2003, Judge Randolph, writing for a three-judge panel, delivered an opinion holding that the "privilege of litigation" does not extend to aliens in military custody outside the territory of the United States.[29] The court relied heavily on the Supreme Court's 1950 decision in *Johnson v. Eisentrager.*[30] That case arose from the convictions of twenty-one German nationals by an American military tribunal in China for having engaged in military activity against the United States after the surrender of Germany on May 8, 1945, but before the surrender of Japan the following August. After their convictions, these individuals were repatriated to Germany and confined in the U. S. army prison at Landsberg. They petitioned the United States District Court for the District of Columbia for writs of habeas corpus to review the legality of their detention. Their case ultimately reached the Supreme Court. Speaking through Justice Jackson, the Court ruled that the "privilege of litigation" had not been extended to these prisoners. It is important to note that the petitioners in *Al Odah,* like the German prisoners in *Eisentrager,* had at no relevant time been within the territorial jurisdiction of the United States.

Al Odah and his fellow petitioners argued that under the existing lease agreement between the United States and Cuba, Guantanamo Bay is in essence a territory of the United States and that the government exercises sovereignty over this territory. Judge Randolph noted that for a variety of reasons, including the fact that Guantanamo Bay is neither a state nor an insular possession, the United States does not exercise sovereignty over this military base. In short, the court held that the detainees were in the same position as the prisoners in *Eisentrager.* Since the courts were not open to them, they could not "seek release based on violations of the Constitution or treaties or federal law. . . . " By denying jurisdiction, the court thus avoided dealing with the question of the president's constitutional authority to issue the November 13 order. On a separate issue, the District of Columbia Circuit disagreed with the Ninth Circuit by ruling that relatives who were assisting the petitioners in this litigation qualified as "next friends" available to file the lawsuit. The court reasoned that these relatives, unlike the clergy, lawyers, and law professors in the Ninth Circuit case, had a "significant relationship" with the detainees.

Reacting strongly to the court's denial of jurisdiction, attorneys for the petitioners vowed to seek either en banc review in the Court of Appeals or a petition for certiorari in the Supreme Court. Critics maintain that the court's opinion sets a dangerous precedent since its reasoning is not limited to times of war. They argue that the decision allows U.S. officials to detain any noncitizen abroad in times of peace as well as war without judicial review. By contrast, Justice Department officials welcomed the decision as "an important victory in the war on terrorism. . . . In times of war, the President must be able to protect our nation from enemies who seek to harm innocent Americans."[31]

The *Al Odah* decision illustrates the lengths to which American courts will go to avoid constitutional questions that relate to the president's exercise of war powers. As in other cases discussed below, this posture of judicial deference indicates that most judges are inclined to take a realistic view of the limits of judicial policymaking in this area. Judicial deference, however, is not synonymous with abdication. The Supreme Court may yet have occasion to address the constitutionality of the president's November 13th order. Whether it should address this substantive issue or treat it as a "political question" remains a perplexing problem.

Detention of United States Citizens since 9/11

In the post–September 11 era, courts have not reached agreement in deciding cases involving U.S. citizens designated as enemy combatants. In *Hamdi v. Rumsfeld,* the Fourth Circuit Court of Appeals has in effect adhered to the military justice model.[32] On the other hand, the United States District for the Southern District of New York in *Padilla v. Rumsfeld* has opted, at least to some extent, for the criminal justice model. These distinct approaches are examined in the following paragraphs.[33]

Yaser Esam Hamdi was captured by American forces while fighting for the Taliban in Afghanistan in the fall of 2001.[34] Initially detained at Guantanamo Bay, Hamdi was removed to the Naval Brig in Norfolk, Virginia, in April 2002, when authorities learned that he was a United States citizen. There he remains awaiting the filing of criminal charges by the government. A federal public defender and a private citizen filed "next friend" habeas petitions on Hamdi's behalf in May 2002. In June, Hamdi's father, Esam Fouad Hamdi, as "next friend," also filed for habeas corpus. After resolving the question of who had standing to bring a habeas petition on Hamdi's behalf, the court appointed the public defender to represent him, required the government to allow Hamdi unmonitored access to counsel, and ordered the government to answer the habeas petition. Thus began a complicated series of proceedings in the U.S. District Court for the Eastern District of Virginia and the Fourth Circuit Court of Appeals. On remand from the Fourth Circuit Court of Appeals, the District Court, on August 16, 2002, held that Hamdi was entitled to due process of law and certified for appeal the question of whether a declaration by Under Secretary of Defense Michael Mobbs was sufficient "to establish that continuing military detention did not violate [the] detainee's due process rights."[35]

Ultimately, on January 8, 2003, the Fourth Circuit remanded the case with directions to dismiss Hamdi's habeas corpus petition. Chief Judge J. Harvey Wilkinson, writing for a three-judge panel, held that the Mobbs declaration was a "sufficient basis upon which to conclude that the Commander in Chief [had] constitutionally detained Hamdi pursuant to the war powers entrusted to him by the United States Constitution."[36] In addition, the court held that Hamdi's detention was authorized by Congress; that he did not have a right under the Geneva Convention to a formal hearing to determine his status as enemy belligerent; and that the district court's order impermissibly conflicted with the constitutional war-making powers of the president and Congress.

As in the *Al Odah* case, involving noncitizen detainees, the court in *Hamdi* emphasized the necessity of extreme judicial deference in relation to military authority. The following excerpt from Judge Wilkinson's opinion clearly conveys this view:

> The constitutional allocation of war powers affords the President extraordinarily broad authority as Commander in Chief and compels courts to assume a deferential posture in reviewing exercises of this authority. And, while the Constitution assigns courts the duty generally to review executive detentions that are alleged to be illegal, the Constitution does not specifically contemplate any role for courts in the conduct of war, or in foreign policy generally. Indeed, Article III courts are ill-positioned to police the military's distinction between those in the arena of combat who should be detained and those who should not.[37]

Wilkinson maintained that the court was in no position to determine the facts concerning Hamdi's conduct "while amongst the nation's enemies. . . . " Relying heavily on *Ex parte Quirin,* the court cautioned against the risk of "obstructing war efforts authorized by Congress and undertaken by the executive branch."

Finally, Judge Wilkinson made it clear that judicial deference, although extreme in this situation, was not to be confused with abdication of judicial responsibility. Thus, he wrote:

> Cases such as Hamdi's raise serious questions which the courts will continue to treat as such. The nation has fought since its founding for liberty without which security rings hollow and for security without which liberty cannot thrive. The judiciary was meant to respect the delicacy of the balance and we have endeavored to do so. The events of September 11 have left their indelible mark. It is not wrong even in the dry annals of judicial opinion to mourn those who lost their lives that terrible day. Yet we speak in the end not from sorrow or anger but from the conviction that separation of powers takes on special significance when the nation itself comes under attack. Hamdi's status as a citizen, as important as that is, can not displace our constitutional order or the place of the courts within the Framers' scheme.[38]

Throughout his opinion, Judge Wilkinson adheres to the military justice model. Although he recognizes that judicial review "does not disappear during wartime," he leaves no doubt that, in his view, the judiciary is in no position to second-guess military judgments.

By contrast, in considering Jose Padilla's challenge to detention as an "enemy combatant," Federal District Judge Michael Mukasey accorded greater weight to procedural requirements. An American citizen by birth,

Padilla was arrested in Chicago on May 8, 2002, by Department of Justice officers on a material witness warrant issued by the United State District Court for the Southern District of New York to secure his testimony before a grand jury. Padilla was promptly removed from Chicago to New York, where he was detained by the Justice Department at the Metropolitan Detention Center. He appeared before the District Court on May 15 and attorney Donna R. Newman was appointed to represent him. On May 22, Padilla, represented by Newman, moved to vacate the warrant. On June 9, the government notified the court that it was withdrawing the subpoena and the court vacated the warrant. The government at that time disclosed that President Bush had designated Padilla an "enemy combatant" and had directed Secretary of Defense Donald Rumsfeld to detain him. The Defense Department immediately took custody of Padilla and transferred him to the Consolidated Naval Brig in Charleston, South Carolina.[39] It was alleged that Padilla had conspired with senior Al Qaeda members in Afghanistan for the purpose of building and detonating a radioactive "dirty bomb." He remains imprisoned at Charleston, and criminal charges have yet to be filed against him.

On June 11, Newman filed a petition for habeas corpus, challenging the lawfulness of Padilla's detention and seeking an order permitting him to consult counsel. At this point, Padilla had no direct access to the court. Thus, Newman acted for him as "next friend." On December 4, 2002, Judge Mukasey ruled that Newman, as Padilla's attorney, had standing as "next friend"; that the secretary of defense, rather than the president, was the proper respondent; that the District Court in New York retained jurisdiction to hear the case; that President Bush had authority to order Padilla's detention despite his United States citizenship; that Padilla could consult with counsel while pursuing his petition; and that the "some evidence" standard applied in determining whether Padilla was lawfully detained. Mukasey acknowledged that the government could invoke enemy combatant law and classify citizens as enemy combatants even in the absence of a declaration of war. This authority is derived from the president's constitutional power as commander in chief: "Even assuming that a court can pronounce when a 'war' exists, in the sense that word is used in the Constitution . . . a formal declaration of war is not necessary in order for the executive to exercise its constitutional authority to prosecute an armed conflict—particularly when, as on September 11, the United States is attacked."[40] In reaching this conclusion, the court relied heavily both on *Ex parte Quirin* (1942) and *The Prize Cases* (1863).[41] In the latter, the Supreme Court rejected a challenge to the president's power to impose a blockade, an act of war, on the secessionist states. It made no difference to a majority of the Justices that the Union had not formally declared war on the Confederacy. While acknowledging that the president has no power to initiate or declare a war, the Court recognized that "war may exist without a declaration on either side. . . . " When another country imposes war on the United States, the president "does not initiate that war, but is bound to accept the challenge without waiting for any special legislative authority. . . . "[42] Judge Mukasey added that even if Congressional authority were "deemed necessary," such authority was provided by the joint resolution of Congress passed in the immediate aftermath of 9/11. Although Mukasey discussed the nebulous concepts of "lawful combatant," "unlawful combatant," and "enemy combatant," he again deferred to the president's judgment in placing Padilla in the latter category. In short, Mukasey regarded the exercise of presidential power to detain enemy aliens as a political question and refused to speculate on whether and when such power might be limited.[43]

Apart from the question of presidential power, Judge Mukasey did recognize Padilla's right to challenge his detention by means of a habeas corpus petition. To facilitate the exercise of this right, Mukasey concluded that Padilla would be permitted to consult with counsel. Since no criminal charges had been brought against Padilla, his right to counsel did not derive from the Constitution's Sixth Amendment. Nor was the court willing to invoke the self-incrimination clause or the due process clause of the Fifth Amendment in support of Padilla's contentions. Rather, Padilla's right to counsel was grounded in the habeas corpus statutes. Although recognizing that these statutes "do not explicitly provide a right to counsel for a petitioner in Padilla's circumstances," Judge Mukasey concluded that certain provisions permitted the appointment of counsel if the court determines that "the interests of justice so require."[44] Mukasey asserted that: "It would frustrate the purpose of the procedure Congress established in habeas corpus cases, and of the remedy itself, to leave Padilla with no practical means whatever for following that procedure."[45] Mukasey distinguished Padilla's situation from that of Hamdi (who was not accorded the right to counsel), pointing out that Padilla initially had access to counsel after his capture but before his designation as an enemy combatant. In conclusion, the court directed Secretary of Defense Rumsfeld "to permit Padilla to consult with counsel solely for the purpose of submitting to the court facts bearing upon his petition. . . . " Mukasey allowed access to counsel on the condition that "Padilla [would not] use his attorneys for the purpose of conveying information to others."[46]

On March 11, 2003, after hearing the government's motion to reconsider various aspects of the order implementing the December 4, 2002, decision, Judge Mukasey reaffirmed Padilla's right to consult counsel.[47] The judge issued rulings on further procedural motions by Padilla and the government on April 9, 2003.[48] At this writing, no further judicial decisions have been rendered in the *Padilla* case. It should be recalled that the District Court in the *Hamdi* case was also inclined to give some weight to the petitioner's contentions. The Fourth Circuit, however, totally rejected these contentions and dismissed Hamdi's petition. It will be interesting to see whether, if appealed, Judge Mukasey's recognition of Padilla's statutory right to counsel will be similarly rejected. In any event, the initial District Court decision in *Padilla,* while recognizing the president's broad power to wage war on terrorism, provides at least a limited endorsement of the criminal justice model.

Conclusion

Over the years, American courts have, with few exceptions, been unwilling to limit the president's war-making power. The Supreme Court has recognized broad "inherent" executive power in the field of foreign policy—sometimes maintaining that this power transcends the Constitution itself.[49] In spite of a strong inclination toward judicial deference, however, the Supreme Court and lower courts as well have nurtured the principle of judicial review. Even in the aftermath of 9/11, courts seem unwilling to relinquish this ultimate authority.

Since the World War II era, the constitutional rights of criminal defendants, as well as First Amendment freedoms of expression, have undergone major expansion. Even though some trimming back has occurred during the Rehnquist era, individuals enjoy far greater constitutional protections in these areas than during any previous period in American history. Americans have become accustomed to exercising their greatly expanded rights and liberties. This fact may help to explain the growing public debate over governmental limitations on such freedoms since 9/11. No significant debate of this kind occurred during World War II, as exemplified by the wide public approval of Franklin Roosevelt's handling of the Nazi saboteur case.[50] Even the forcible "relocation" of approximately 120,000 Americans of Japanese ancestry aroused only mild protests at the time. Moreover, in the Supreme Court's widely publicized decision on this issue, a majority of the Justices gave their stamp of constitutional approval to the government's action.[51]

Many critics of the Bush administration's war on terrorism are deeply concerned about the extent to which the procedural requirements of the criminal justice system have been brushed aside. These persons are not convinced that the traditional law enforcement model is inadequate to deal with the threat of international terrorism. As they see it, the criminal justice system has become just another casualty in the war on terrorism. On the other hand, defenders of the president's antiterrorism policies accept his assertion that we are at war with Al Qaeda. They believe that the military model is far more appropriate than the law enforcement model in dealing with detainees suspected of having ties with Al Qaeda. They reject the view that the American justice system is threatened by limiting the terrorists' access to criminal courts.

Tension between the criminal justice and military justice models is vividly illustrated by the government's ongoing effort to prosecute Zacarias Moussaoui. Approximately one month before the September 11, 2001 attacks, Moussaoui, a French citizen and admitted Al Qaeda member, was arrested because criminal investigators were suspicious of his activities at a

Minnesota flight school. In December 2001, Moussaoui was indicted on several counts of conspiracy linking him with other Al Qaeda members in hijacking the planes that destroyed the World Trade Center and damaged the Pentagon, killing thousands of people.[52]

According to one news source, Moussaoui is the only person "charged in the United States in connection with the September 11 attacks." Attorney General John Ashcroft announced the indictment with "great fanfare. . . . as an example of how the United States could prosecute terrorists in the criminal justice system."[53] Facing a possible death penalty if convicted, Moussaoui has pursued a vigorous defense. Originally provided with court-appointed counsel, Moussaoui nevertheless insisted on representing himself. While granting his request, the trial court appointed his attorneys to serve as standby counsel.

In September 2002, Moussaoui filed a motion seeking access to a critically important witness held by military authorities at Guantanamo Bay, Cuba. This individual, also an Al Qaeda member, is alleged to have played a central role in planning the September 11 attacks. The government opposed this request contending that access to this "enemy combatant" would be gravely harmful to national security and foreign relations interests. Moussaoui, however, contended that in the context of a criminal prosecution, denial of access to the potentially favorable witness was fundamentally unfair.

On March 10, 2003, the District Court granted Moussaoui limited access to his presumed Al Qaeda associate. In granting this limited access, the court sought to strike a balance between the legitimate security concerns of the government and the "equally compelling right of a defendant in a capital prosecution to receive the fair trial to which he is entitled under the Constitution and laws of the United States." The court concluded that: "When the Government elected to bring Moussaoui to trial in this civilian tribunal, it assumed the responsibility of abiding by well-established princi- ples of due process. . . . To the extent that the United States seeks a categorical, 'wartime' exception to the Sixth Amendment, it should recon- sider whether the civilian courts are the appropriate fora in which to *prosecute* alleged terrorists captured in the context of an ongoing war."[54]

The government appealed this District Court decision, continuing to press its national security argument. On June 26, 2003, the Court of Appeals for the Fourth Circuit dismissed the government's appeal on technical, jurisdictional grounds. Chief Judge Wilkins, writing for a three-judge panel, noted that the question before the court was "one of extraordinary impor- tance, presenting a direct conflict between a criminal defendant's right 'to have compulsory process for obtaining witnesses in his favor' (U. S. Const. 6th Amendment) and the government's essential duty to preserve the security of this nation and its citizens."[55]

Asserting that the court was fully prepared "to rule on the substantive questions at issue," Wilkins noted that the court, nevertheless, was "com- pelled to conclude" that it lacked authority to do so.[56] Because the order of the District Court was not a final one, there was no basis for an appeal at the time. Officials have indicated that if they lose the appeal on substantive grounds, they will move the case to a military tribunal rather than comply with the district court order.[57] If this is the outcome, the government's choice would clearly reflect its preference for the military justice model and its reluctance to adhere to a criminal justice model in addressing the threat of international terrorism.[58]

Although the Bush administration has moved far toward endorsing a military justice model, it has not uniformly followed this approach. Thus, John Walker Lindh, the "American Taliban," was permitted to plead guilty to criminal charges in a United States District Court in Alexandria, Virginia.[59] The factual parallels between Lindh's case and that of Yaser Esam Hamdi are striking. Yet Hamdi remains in detention, held without criminal charges at the Naval Brig in Norfolk, Virginia. The exceptions exemplified by the Lindh case and by the recent criminal conviction of the "Al-Qaeda shoe-bomber" Richard Reid do not necessarily indicate that the administration has departed from its apparent preference for the military justice model.[60]

Throughout American history, threats to national security have been accompanied by demands for expanded governmental power and the curtailment of civil liberties. The justification has always been that such restrictions are necessary to enable the government to protect the safety of the people. These restrictions have traditionally been temporary and civil liberties have been restored once the perceived crisis has ended. With the ongoing war on terrorism, are we entering a new era? Will existing restrictions on civil liberties turn out to be permanent rather than temporary? Today, distrust of government is widespread among Americans. If we experience another serious terrorist attack, many will question the efficacy of the government's approach to the war on terrorism. Some will call for the restoration of procedural protections while others will call for even greater restrictions on civil liberties.

No doubt the United States Supreme Court will have ample opportunity to review various constitutional questions pertaining to the war on terrorism. It may re-examine the *Ex parte Quirin* precedent, which many legal scholars believe should not apply to the Guantanamo Bay detainees. In any event, in light of the historical record, it would be surprising if the Justices seriously challenged the president's endorsement of a military justice model in dealing with the threat of international terrorism.

Chapter 3

1. For background, see Stephen Dycus, et al., *National Security Law* (New York: Aspen Publishers, 2002), pp. 826–827.
2. Proclamation 7463, "Declaration of National Emergency by Reason of Certain Terrorist Attacks" (September 14, 2001). Available at http://www.whitehouse. gov/news/releases/2001/09/20010914–4.html.
3. "Sense Of Congress Regarding Terrorist Attacks," Pub. L. No. 107–40, 115 Stat. 224 (2001).

4. "Military Order of November 13, 2001—Detention, Treatment, and Trial of Certain Non-Citizens in the War against Terrorism," (November 13, 2001), 66 Federal Register No. 222, pp. 57833–6.
5. *Center for National Security Studies v. Department of Justice,* 215 F. Supp. 2d 94 (2002).
6. 2003 WL 21382899.
7. Ibid., p. 18
8. 2002 WL 1972919.
9. *Detroit Free Press v. Ashcroft,* 303 F.3d 681 (2002).
10. 2003 WL 21382899.
11. U.S. Constitution, Art. I, Sec. 8.
12. U.S. Constitution, Art. II, Sec. 2 and Sec. 3.
13. U.S. Constitution, Art. I, Sec. 9.
14. *Ex parte Milligan,* 71 U.S. 2 (1866). For further historical background see William H. Rehnquist, *All the Laws but One: Civil Liberties in Wartime* (New York: Alfred A. Knopf, 1998).
15. *Ex parte Quirin,* 317 U.S. 1 (1942).
16. *In Re Yamashita,* 327 U.S. 1 (1946).
17. *Madsen v. Kinsella,* 343 U.S. 341 (1952).
18. Ibid., p. 348. For background, see Timothy C. MacDonnell, "Military Commissions and Courts-Martial: A Brief Discussion of the Constitutional and Jurisdictional Distinctions between the Two Courts," *Army Lawyer* (March 2002): 19–40.
19. For general background on the Nazi saboteur episode, see Alex Abella and Scott Gordon, *Shadow Enemies: Hitler's Secret Terrorist Plot against the United States* (Guilford, CT: Globe Pequot Press, 2003), and Carl Brent Swisher, *The Supreme Court in Modern Role,* rev. ed. (New York: New York University Press, 1965), 118–22.
20. Noted in *Ex parte Quirin* 317 U.S. 1 (1942): 18.
21. Swisher, *The Supreme Court in Modern Role,* p. 120.
22. *Ex parte Quirin,* p. 37.
23. *Ex parte Quirin,* p. 48.
24. *Marbury v. Madison 5* U. S. 137 (1803).
25. "Military Order of November 13, 2001," Section 1(f).
26. Ibid., Section 1(g).
27. Many legal scholars and civil liberties groups have been highly critical of the November 13 military order. For example, see Neal K. Katyal and Laurence H. Tribe, "Waging War, Deciding Guilt: Trying the Military Tribunals," *Yale Law Journal* 111 (2002) and Jordan Paust, "Antiterrorism Military Commissions: Courting Illegality," *Michigan Journal of International Law* 23 (fall 2001). On the other hand, a number of scholars have defended the constitutionality of Bush's order. See, for example, Ruth Wedgwood, "Al Qaeda, Terrorism, and Military Commissions," *American Journal of International Law* 96 (2002) and Ronald J. Seivert, "War on Terrorism or Global Law Enforcement Operation?" *Notre Dame Law Review* 78 (2003). For a balanced appraisal concluding that the president's order is constitutional under *Ex parte Quirin,* but that it is inconsistent with international law, of which the laws of war are a subcategory, see Christopher M. Evans, "Terrorism on Trial: The President's Authority to Order the Prosecution of Suspected Terrorists by Military Commission," *Duke Law Journal* 51 (2002).
28. *Coalition of Clergy v. Bush,* 310 F.3d. 1153 (2002).

29. *Al Odah v. United States,* 321 F.3d 1134 (2003).
30. *Johnson v. Eisentrager,* 339 U.S. 763 (1950).
31. *American Bar Association E-Report,* e-mail report to ABA members, sent March 14, 2003.
32. *Hamdi v. Rumsfeld* 316 F.3d 450 (2003).
33. *Padilla v. Bush* 233 F.Supp.2d 564 (2002).
34. For a detailed account of the *Hamdi* litigation, see Nickolas A. Kacprowski, "Stacking the Deck against Suspected Terrorists: The Dwindling Procedural Limits on the Government's Power to Indefinitely Detain United States Citizens as Enemy Combatants," *Seattle Law Review* 26 (2003): 651
35. See case history in *Hamdi v. Rumsfeld* 316 F.3d 450 (2003), pp. 460–3.
36. *Hamdi,* p. 459.
37. Ibid., p. 474.
38. Ibid., p. 477.
39. See *Padilla v. Bush* 233 F.Supp. 2d 564.
40. Ibid., p. 589.
41. *The Prize Cases* 67 U.S. 635 (1863).
42. Ibid., p. 668.
43. U.S. District Court Judge Mukasey discusses the distinctions in combatant status: "The laws of war draw a fundamental distinction between lawful and unlawful combatants. Lawful combatants may be held as prisoners of war, but are immune from criminal prosecution by their captors for belligerent acts that do not constitute war crimes. . . . Four criteria generally determine the conditions an armed force and its members must meet in order to be considered lawful combatants: 1) To be commanded by a person responsible for his subordinates; 2) To have a fixed distinctive emblem recognizable at a distance; 3) To carry arms openly; and 4) To conduct their operations in accordance with the laws and customs of War. . . . Those who do not meet those criteria, including saboteurs and guerrillas, may not claim prisoner of war status. . . . Although in the past unlawful combatants were often summarily executed, such Draconian measures have not prevailed in modern times in what some still refer to without embarrassment as the civilized world. . . . Rather, as recognized in *Quirin,* unlawful combatants generally have been tried by military commissions. . . . Although unlawful combatants, unlike prisoners of war, may be tried and punished by military tribunals, there is no basis to impose a requirement that they be punished. Rather, their detention for the duration of hostilities is supportable—again, logically and legally—on the same ground that the detention of prisoners of war is supportable: to prevent them from rejoining the enemy. . . . The President designated Padilla an 'enemy combatant' based on his alleged association with al Qaeda and on an alleged plan undertaken as part of that association. The point of the protracted discussion immediately above is simply to support what should be an obvious conclusion: when the President designated Padilla an 'enemy combatant,' he necessarily meant that Padilla was an unlawful combatant, acting as an associate of a terrorist organization whose operations do not meet the four criteria necessary to confer lawful combatant status on its members and adherents." *Padilla v. Bush,* pp. 592–593
44. Ibid., p. 600. See also 18 U.S.C. Sect. 3006A(2)(B) (2000).
45. Ibid., p. 602.
46. Ibid., p. 605.
47. *Padilla v. Rumsfeld* 243 F. Supp. 2d 42 (2003).
48. 2003 WL 18581570.

49. E.g., see *U.S. v Curtiss-Wright Export Corporation*, 299 U.S. 304 (1936).

50. For a perceptive comparison of popular attitudes then and now, see Jack Goldsmith and Cass R. Sunstein, "Military Tribunals and Legal Culture: What A Difference Sixty Years Make," *Constitutional Commentary* 19 (2002): 261.

51. See *Korematsu v. United States*, 323 U.S. 214 (1944). But see also *cf Ex parte Endo* 323 U.S. 283 (1944) ordering the release of a relocation center detainee whose "loyalty" to the United States had been confirmed. See also Patrick O. Gudridge, "Remember Endo?" *Harvard Law Review* 116 (2003): 1933.

52. Jerry Markon, "U.S. Tries to Block Access to Witness for Terror Trial," *Washington Post*, 2 April 2003 and the case history in *U.S. v. Moussaoui*, U.S. App. LEXIS 12894 (2003).

53. Markon, "U.S. Tries to Block Access to Witness for Terror Trial."

54. 2003 WL 21263699.

55. *U.S. v. Moussaoui*, p. 2.

56. *U.S. v. Moussaoui*, p. 3.

57. Jerry Markon, "Appeals Court Rebuffs U.S. in Moussaoui Case," *Washington Post*, 27 June 2003.

58. E.g., see Eric Lichtblau, "Wide Impact from Combatant Decision Is Seen," *New York Times*, 25 June 2003, p. A14. Writes Lichtblau: "President Bush's decision to declare a Qatari student an enemy combatant signals a more aggressive approach against terrorism suspects in the face of new threats from Al Qaeda, and it increases the chances that Zacarias Moussaoui will wind up in a military brig as well, officials and legal observers said today. Administration officials said the decision to imprison the student, Ali Saleh Kahlah al-Marri, in a brig in South Carolina on Monday, less than a month before he was scheduled to go on trial in a federal court in Illinois, was intended in part to try to cull more information from him about possible links to Al Qaeda. That avenue would probably have been foreclosed if Mr. Marri's case had gone to trial next month. . . . The decision to make Mr. Marri an enemy combatant represented the first time that the administration has dropped criminal charges against a suspect and moved him into military custody. The person most affected by the precedent, officials said, could be Mr. Moussaoui, who is facing terrorism and conspiracy charges in Alexandria, Va., in connection with the attacks of Sept. 11, 2001."

59. *U. S. v. Lindh*, 227 F. Supp. 2d 565 (E.D.Va.2002).

60. *U. S. v. Reid*, 2001 WL 1688908.

Chapter 4

Activist Judges, Responsive Legislators, Frustrating Presidents:

International Human Rights, National Security, and Civil Litigation against Terrorist States

John C. Blakeman

One year after the September 11, 2001 terrorist attacks on the World Trade Center and Pentagon, with the subsequent loss of over 3,000 lives, a new front in the ongoing war on terrorism opened in the Federal District Court for the District of Columbia. Far removed from the plains and mountains of Afghanistan, over 900 named and unnamed plaintiffs, all victims or surviving relatives of the terrorist attacks, sued Osama Bin Laden, members of Al Qaeda, members of the royal family of Saudi Arabia, the Republic of Sudan, and various international banks and Muslim charities operating in the United States.[1] The civil lawsuit charges the defendants with sponsoring, financing, or otherwise materially supporting acts of terrorism in violation of U.S. and international law. Specifically the complaint alleges that material support provided by the defendants facilitated acts of torture, aircraft sabotage, and extrajudicial killing.[2] The plaintiffs request $100 trillion in damages.

Civil litigation against individuals and foreign states that sponsor and engage in acts of terrorism uses the federal courts to punish wrongdoers for civil wrongs and torts defined by federal and international law. Unlike federal criminal prosecutions against captured terrorists, where the end result is the imprisonment or execution of convicted criminals, civil litigation relies on noncriminal international and federal law to hold states that sponsor terrorism financially accountable for their actions. Private plaintiffs and trial lawyers, not government officials, initiate lawsuits, and indeed government agencies may have little control over how civil litigation in the war against terrorism develops since the plaintiffs amass evidence, structure legal arguments, and try to convince a civil jury that the defendants committed various violations of the law. For one scholar, it is fair to ask whether civil litigation is "an appropriate normative tool for combating state-sponsored terrorists," and whether "unleashing lawyers, lawsuits, procedural rules, delay, and other characteristics of American-style tort litigation on foreign state defendants" may unduly interfere with the ability of the United States to wage an aggressive, and successful, global campaign against terrorism.[3]

Fighting terrorism through civil litigation is a risky process, no doubt. Plaintiffs may find it difficult to establish appropriate proof of the defendants' complicity, and even if the plaintiffs are successful they will find it extremely difficult to collect damage awards from evasive individuals and noncompliant states in the global community. Yet, as the Seventh Circuit notes in *Boim v. Quranic Literacy Institute*, a recent civil lawsuit against organizations that fund terrorist activities in Israel, "if we failed to impose liability on aiders and abettors who knowingly and intentionally funded acts of terrorism, we would be thwarting Congress' clearly expressed intent to cut off the flow of money to terrorists at every point along the causal chain of violence."[4] Additionally, "there would not be a trigger to pull or a bomb to blow up without the resources to acquire such tools of terrorism and to bankroll the persons who actually commit the violence." Thus, not only should individual terrorists be punished, but also "the organizations, businesses and nations that support and encourage terrorist acts" must be accountable in civil litigation and "are likely to have reachable assets" that can be used to satisfy lawsuit awards. The Seventh Circuit concluded that "the only way to imperil the flow of money and discourage the financing of terrorist acts is to impose liability on those who knowingly and intentionally supply the funds to the persons who commit the violent acts."

In referring to Congressional intent in extending civil liability in federal law to cover terrorist acts, the Seventh Circuit points out that lawsuits in the war on terrorism are sanctioned and supported by the federal government. Although the government has little control over how specific civil trials develop, it has created a basic framework that facilitates litigation. Federal courts are receptive to hearing claims against individual terrorists and the states that sponsor them. Courts are also more than willing to incorporate and expand existing international legal norms prohibiting terrorist activities such as torture, extrajudicial killing, kidnapping, and hijacking, in order to hold terrorists accountable. As well, Congress positively validates federal court decisions in civil lawsuits against rogue states and has amended federal law several times since the early 1980s to make suing terrorists easier. As courts and litigants encounter legal barriers to suing terrorist states, Congress quickly responds to remove them. Although Congress and the courts agree on civil lawsuits as one tool for holding terrorists accountable, the executive branch has yet to fully support this development. Indeed, several plaintiffs have won large damage awards arising out of terrorism sponsored by Iran, Iraq, and Cuba, and have sought to collect hundreds of millions of dollars in damages through the seizure of foreign state–owned property in the United States. The general reaction by the executive, though, is to rely on national security and diplomatic concerns and block the efforts of federal courts to force states to pay. Private plaintiffs seeking to vindicate their specific rights initiate civil lawsuits, but in litigation against terrorist states a much larger political process is at work that ultimately affects how civil lawsuits are conducted, and whether or not they are successful. Federal courts and Congress extend international human rights standards and facilitate such litigation, but the executive branch injects national security concerns to block the payment of judgments against defendant states. Plaintiffs often win large damage awards against terrorist states, but the awards regularly go uncollected.

The Starting Point: *Filartiga v. Pena-Irala*

A civil lawsuit against a Paragyuan police officer initiated the dialogue between federal courts, Congress, and the presidency about how state-sponsored terrorist activities should be punished. The case and subsequent action by Congress links international human rights norms prohibiting terrorist conduct to the development of federal law on terrorism. In 1979, Dr. Joel Filartiga and his daughter, both Paraguayan nationals, filed a civil lawsuit in the federal district court in the Eastern District of New York against Americo Pena-Irala, a former Paraguayan police chief residing illegally in the United States. Filartiga accused Pena of torturing and killing his son in 1976, in Paraguay, in order to punish the father for his outspokenness against the Paraguayan government. Pena-Irala's conduct, according to Filartiga, violated international law prohibitions against torture and extrajudicial killing. To gain access to a federal district court, Filartiga used a little-know federal statute, the Alien Tort Claims Act (ATCA) passed in 1793 by the first Congress. The ATCA allows district courts to try all cases "where an alien sues for a tort only [committed] in violation of the law of nations." The origins of the ATCA are murky, to say the least, and it has rarely been used in over 200 years of federal practice.[5] However, the terms of the statute are clear: Aliens can sue in American federal courts to punish violations of international tort law. The district court dismissed the case due to lack of federal jurisdiction, indicating that even if international law prohibited torture, there was no way federal courts could adjudicate such claims. On appeal, the Second Circuit reversed, and importantly set the stage for future civil litigation against individuals and states the perpetrate acts of terrorism. For the circuit court, modern international law roundly condemns torture:

> Among the rights universally proclaimed by all nations . . . is the right to be free of physical torture. Indeed, for purposes of civil liability, the torturer has become like the pirate and slave trader before him hostis humani generis, an enemy of all mankind. Our holding today, giving effect to a jurisdictional provision enacted by our First Congress, is a small but important step in the fulfillment of the ageless dream to free all people from brutal violence.[6]

By so finding, the 2nd Circuit validated Filartiga's allegations and facilitated the use of the ATCA for lawsuits against individuals who use torture as a means of state repression. On remand, the district court found in favor of Filartiga and awarded over $10 million in damages against Pena-Irala (the judgment has yet to be collected).

Significantly, *Filartiga* prompted an important debate about how and when federal courts should be open to international human rights litigation. For the Second Circuit, the ATCA allows aliens to sue for violations of international torts, so it only remains for courts to discern what kind of conduct is prohibited by international law. However, only individuals could be sued under the ATCA, not foreign states, as under international law sovereign states are generally immune from the jurisdiction of another state's courts. Thus, Filartiga could sue Pena-Irala but not sue the Paraguayan regime that most likely encouraged and officially sanctioned Pena-Irala's conduct. Immunity issues were not the only problems noticed in *Filartiga* either. Other circuit courts began to question whether a substantive basis for federal jurisdiction even existed for civil cases concerning violations of international law prohibitions on torture and terrorism.

In a subsequent case, *Tel-Oren v. Libyan Arab Republic,* several American, Israeli, and Dutch citizens injured by a Palestine Liberation Organization (PLO) bus highjacking in Israel sued the PLO in the United States for committing acts of terrorism against them.[7] Libya was also named in the lawsuit since it allegedly sponsored the terrorists involved. The Circuit Court for the D.C. Circuit dismissed the case, although the judges on the three judge panel did not agree on the reasons. For Judge Robb, federal courts are inherently unable to adjudicate disputes concerning acts of terrorism due to foreign policy issues, thus the case presented a political question better resolved by another branch of government. Judge Edwards ruled that international law only applies to sovereign states, as opposed to nonstate actors such as the PLO. Thus courts did not have subject matter jurisdiction. Finally, Judge Bork argued that the ATCA grants only limited subject matter jurisdiction to federal courts. If plaintiffs want to use the statute to sue for violations of torture and terrorism prohibited by modern, twentieth-century international law, Congress must specifically define a cause of action by amending the statute itself.

In response to lingering problems concerning whether federal courts could rely on international law to punish state-sanctioned torture and summary execution, Congress passed the Torture Victim Protection Act (TVPA) in 1992 and codified current international law into U.S. federal law. The statute grants a cause of action—a substantive basis for a lawsuit—for torture and extrajudicial killing committed outside the United States.[8] The House Judiciary Committee's report on the bill points out "official torture and summary execution violate standards accepted by virtually every nation."[9] In addition, "torture" and "extrajudicial killing" are defined in "accordance with international standards," thus the House makes clear that international law informs the development of American federal law. Likewise, the Senate report indicates "the purpose of this legislation is to provide a Federal cause of action against any individual who, under actual or apparent authority or under color of law of any foreign nation, subjects any individual to torture or extrajudicial killing."[10] The TVPA carries out the intent of various international treaties, ratified by the Senate, that prohibit torture. Importantly, both the House and Senate reports make clear that only individuals can be sued under the TVPA.

With the TVPA Congress essentially codified the *Filartiga* reasoning into federal law, and thus gave civil lawsuits against individuals who violate international law a solid statutory footing. Importantly, the statute's reach is only limited to individuals who torture and kill with the sanction and support of a sovereign state government; it does not cover the conduct of sovereign states themselves that sponsor and fund terrorist activities. Individuals who commit terrorist acts can be accountable, but not the states that fund, support, and sponsor those acts. Although the TVPA framework was incomplete, nonetheless Congress and federal courts used international law as a normative framework to guide the development of federal laws against terrorism. With *Filartiga* and the subsequent TVPA, international law served to link international human rights norms against terrorist activities with the developing federal laws that allow victims of terrorism to seek compensation from terrorists themselves.

Defining Immunity Down

Suing individual terrorists does help punish those who specifically perpetrate violence against others, but as the Filartigas found out, large damage awards against individuals who cannot pay means that justice is fleeting, at best. Thus, as the 7th Circuit stated in *Boim,* it makes more sense to sue states that sponsor and fund terrorist activities in order to "imperil the flow of money and discourage the financing of terrorist acts." Since many foreign governments have property and other assets in the United States, it is theoretically easy for courts to seize those assets to satisfy civil judgments arising out of litigation. However, international and federal law often place foreign states and their assets beyond the reach of federal courts because of the doctrine of sovereign immunity, which stipulates that no state or its courts shall exercise jurisdiction over another sovereign states. Two post-*Filartiga* cases demonstrate how immunity interferes with litigation against states, and how Congress responded yet again to facilitate litigation against terrorist states.

The first, *Saudi Arabia v. Nelson,* concerns an American citizen who moved to Saudi Arabia after being hired by a Saudi hospital. The Saudi police ultimately detained Nelson after he reported safety problems in the hospital to his superiors. He was shackled and allegedly tortured by the police, and only released after the intervention of a U.S. Senator. Nelson subsequently sued Saudi Arabia in 1988 in a federal district court, accusing the Saudi government of violating various international human rights laws against battery, torture, unlawful imprisonment, and mental anguish. The district court dismissed the case on the grounds that Saudi Arabia, as a sovereign state, was immune from litigation under the federal Foreign Sovereign Immunities Act passed in 1976. A circuit court reversed, and on appeal from the Saudi government the U.S. Supreme Court ruled 6–3 that Saudi Arabia was indeed immune. Under the 1976 Foreign Sovereign Immunities Act, foreign states cannot be sued except for a narrow band of conduct such as tortious and negligent behavior committed within the United States, or for commercial activities either in the United States or abroad that cause harm to a plaintiff. As Justice Souter noted for the Court, Nelson's case concerns the "abuse of the power of its police by the Saudi Government, and however monstrous such abuse undoubtedly may be, a foreign state's exercise of the power of its police has long been understood . . . as peculiarly sovereign in nature."[11] Heinous though its alleged conduct is, Saudi Arabia did not fall under any of the FSIA's immunity exceptions, and the litigation was subsequently terminated.

The second case, *Smith v. Socialist People's Libyan Arab Jamahiriya,* arises out of the 1988 bombing of Pan Am Flight 103 over Lockerbie, Scotland, that killed 259 passengers and crew and 11 people on the ground.[12] Agents from the Libyan secret service were implicated in the bombing after a long investigation, and subsequently several families of the victims filed suit against Libya in 1994 for wrongful death, battery, and violations of international law. Like Scott Nelson's case, however, this lawsuit was dismissed. Under the Foreign Sovereign Immunities Act, Libya as a sovereign state is immune from civil litigation except for its commercial activities. With both *Nelson* and *Smith* preventing civil lawsuits against states that either use torture or terrorism as official state policy, Congress again modified the law.

A brief overview of the international law on sovereign immunity is important to set the context for Congressional policymaking. Historically, international law recognized that sovereign states are absolutely immune from another state's courts and that absolute nature of immunity stems from the unqualified legal equality of states in the international system. Although states differ in terms of economic and social resources, they are nonetheless juridically equal and independent of one another in terms of legal status. In U.S. foreign relations law, absolute immunity conferred to sovereign states is based on early Supreme Court decisions, especially the *Schooner Exchange v. M'Faddon* from 1812 in which the Court declared that "this perfect equality and absolute independence of sovereigns, and this common interest impelling them to mutual intercourse" means that one sovereign state will not exercise jurisdiction over another.[13] The *Schooner Exchange* rule recognizes absolute immunity, meaning that no state can be sued in another state's courts.

By the mid 1950s, however, the United States defined a more restrictive form of immunity in response to states that engaged in commercial transactions and then sought to shield themselves from litigation under rules of absolute immunity. As the State Department indicated, states that engage in commercial behavior such as the buying and selling of basic goods or property act like private business entities in the marketplace and should generally not be allowed to claim immunity if sued over their commercial conduct. In practice, federal judges often sought the State Department's advice in specific cases and would accordingly grant or deny immunity to a foreign state if the State Department so requested. Political and diplomatic reasons often affected the waivers of immunity, and to make the process less dependent on State Department politics, and more predictable for American litigants, Congress passed the Foreign Sovereign Immunities Act in 1976. The FSIA codified the existing State Department practice of denying immunity to states engaged in commercial behavior. By so doing, Congress placed immunity decisions squarely in the hand of federal courts and provided concise statutory guidelines governing such cases.

The primary exception to sovereign immunity concerned the commercial activities of foreign states. As the *Nelson* and *Smith* cases point out, Saudi Arabia and Libya were not engaged in commercial activities when Scott Nelson was allegedly detained and tortured, nor when Libyan agents bombed Flight 103. Thus, neither state could be sued for its conduct in violation of international law. In addition, the Supreme Court construes the FSIA as the only way a federal court can take jurisdiction over a foreign state. In *Argentine Republic v. Amerada Hess Shipping Corp,* Amerada Hess tried to use the ATCA to sue Argentina for the destruction of one of its oil tankers in the South Atlantic during the Falklands Conflict. The Court determined that Argentina was immune from litigation since its destruction of the ship was not commercial activity falling under the FSIA. As well, the "text and structure of the FSIA demonstrate Congress' intention that the FSIA be the sole basis for obtaining jurisdiction over a foreign state in our courts."[14]

The FSIA did make immunity decisions more predictable, but it also prevented victims of terrorism from suing those states that sponsored illegal terrorist activities. Thus, the FSIA had to be amended if civil litigation against foreign states was to be encouraged. With the 1996 Antiterrorism and Effective Death Penalty Act (AEDPA) Congress did exactly that, and removed immunity for terrorist states that commit certain kinds of terrorist activities in violation of federal and international law. The FSIA now reads:

§ 1605. General exceptions to the jurisdictional immunity of a foreign state

(a) A foreign state shall not be immune from the jurisdiction of courts of the United States or of the States in any case—

(7) in which money damages are sought against a foreign state for personal injury or death that was caused by an act of torture, extrajudicial killing, aircraft sabotage, hostage taking, or the provision of material support or resources . . . for such an act if such act or provision of material support is engaged in by an official, employee, or agent of such foreign state while acting within the scope of his or her office, employment, or agency.

The AEDPA amendment only applied to victims who are U.S. nationals. As well, it only waives immunity for certain foreign states defined as "terrorist states" by the State Department, and therefore does not bring all foreign states within its reach.[15] Additionally, the AEDPA amendment simply grants a forum to civil claims. That is, it empowers federal courts to remove state immunity and thereby allow a lawsuit to proceed. It does not, however, provide a cause of action or substantive basis of law for those claims. To eradicate doubt about its intent in holding terrorist states accountable, Congress created a cause of action for litigants. The Civil Liability For Acts of State-Sponsored Terrorism Law[16] was also passed in 1996 to ensure that federal courts would have subject matter jurisdiction over state-sponsored terrorism. As a result, the AEDPA and Civil Liability for Acts of State Sponsored Terrorism Law now give federal courts the ability to waive foreign state immunity for litigation concerning terrorism and the subject matter jurisdiction to adjudicate such claims. Significantly, both statutes rely on the TVPA's definitions of torture, extrajudicial killing, and other terrorist activities, definitions that are ultimately grounded in international human rights law.

Suing, Winning, but Not Collecting

Several plaintiffs successfully relied upon the 1996 law changes to sue terrorist states. One of the first cases under the new legal regime is *Alejandre v. Republic of Cuba.* Three private American pilots conducting air searches for Cuban refugees in international waters, for the humanitarian group Brothers to the Rescue, were shot down and killed by the Cuban air force in international airspace. The families of the pilots sued Cuba in the District Court for the Southern District of Florida. Judge James King found Cuba liable for the "unprovoked firing of deadly rockets at defenseless, unarmed civilian aircraft," which falls under the AEDPA's prohibition of extrajudicial killing. The AEDPA in turn relies on the TVPA's definition of extrajudicial killing: "deliberated killing not authorized by a previous judgment pronounced by a regularly constituted court affording all the judicial guarantees which are recognized as indispensable by civilized people."[17] As Judge King further notes, Cuba's conduct violated "clearly established principles of international law . . . the fact that the killings were premeditated and intentional, outside of Cuba's territory, wholly disproportionate, and executed without warning or process makes this act unique in its brazen flouting of the law."[18] So brazen, in fact, that a large punitive damage award is warranted, as Judge King points out, to show "condemnation of human right abuses" and "to deter other international actors from engaging in similar practices." The Alejandre plaintiffs were awarded a total of $187,627,911 in total damages, of which the punitive portion is $137,700,000.

Other plaintiffs have had similar success. Steven Flatow, a U.S. citizen, sued Iran for sponsoring a Hamas terrorist bombing in Israel that killed his daughter, Alisa Flatow, also a U.S. citizen. Judge Royce Lamberth of the District Court for the District of Columbia found Iran liable for sponsoring

acts of international terrorism, and awarded $247,000,000 in compensa-
tory and punitive damages to the Flatow family.[19] As Judge Lamberth
argued, "terrorism has achieved the status of almost universal condemnation, as have slavery genocide, and piracy, and the terrorist is the modern
era's *hosti humani generis*—an enemy of all mankind."[20]

The *Alejandre* and *Flatow* cases are by no means the only successful
lawsuits against terrorist states. Joseph Cicippio, David Jacobsen, and Frank
Reed successfully obtained a judgment against Iran of $65,000,000 in
compensation for their kidnapping and detention by the Hezbollah, a
Lebanese Islamic group that receives material support from Iran.[21] Terry
Anderson, also kidnapped and tortured for six years by the Hezbollah, sued
Iran and received a $340,000,000 judgment.[22] The families of two U.S.
nationals killed in a Hamas bombing in Israel received a $327,000,000
judgment against Iran, similar to the *Flatow* judgment.[23] Finally, several
American citizens who were unlawfully kidnapped, detained, and tortured
by Iraq for over 200 days while removing land mines as civilian contractors
on the Iraq-Kuwait border successfully sued the Republic of Iraq.[24] The
District Court for the District of Columbia awarded almost $13,000,000
collectively in damages.

The damage awards listed above show that civil litigation against terrorist states works, at least in terms of finding states liable and then awarding
compensatory damages to cover plaintiffs' suffering and extensive punitive
awards to punish and deter terrorist states in the future. As the *Alejandre*
court puts it, punitive damages are explicitly linked to the international
community's consensus that terrorist acts will not be tolerated, and thus
serve "to redress conduct so heinous that it has been condemned by the
world community." Likewise, "punitive damages help reinforce the consensus of the community of humankind that horrific abuses against the person
will not be tolerated."[25] One significant question remains however, which
is: How are terrorist states actually forced to satisfy these huge damage awards?

The *Flatow* litigation here is instructive. The Islamic Republic of Iran
owns property in the United States, such as its former embassy and other
diplomatic properties in Washington D.C., and consular properties throughout
the United States. Even though Iran and the United States have no diplomatic
relations, the property nonetheless remains the sovereign territory of Iran,
and in fact some of it is managed and leased by the federal government, with
proceeds going into commercial bank accounts maintained by the federal
government. To satisfy the $247 million damage award against Iran, Steven
Flatow asked the D.C. district court to attach (seize and force the sale of) the
Iranian embassy and chancery, the Iranian ambassador's residence, the
Iranian military attaché's residence, and the Minister of Cultural Affairs's
residence, all in Washington, D.C. In addition, Flatow sought the funds in
the bank accounts set up for the revenue generated by leasing the Iranian
properties to third parties. The Clinton administration intervened in the case
and asked the district court to quash the writs of attachment. In the

administration's terms, federal law and international treaties to which the United States is a party do not allow seizure of a sovereign state's diplomatic property. The FSIA, for example, allows courts to attach property owned by foreign states only if used for commercial activities. Since the Iranian embassy and other properties were used for diplomatic purposes, they were immune from seizure. The Clinton administration also argued that the federal Foreign Missions Act and the Vienna Convention on Diplomatic Relations prohibit attachment. The district court granted the administration's motion and exclusively relied on the FSIA. The court noted that attaching Iran's embassy and other diplomatic properties "would expand the class of cases arising under the Act beyond those limited, enumerated exceptions to immunity prescribed by Congress, and thus would expose foreign states to far greater liability than was originally contemplated" by Congress.[26] The court also found that the bank accounts in question belonged to the United States, and were thus immune from attachment due to the doctrine of sovereign immunity.

In addition to relying on the FSIA and other statutes and treaties to block seizure of Iran's diplomatic properties, the Clinton administration had one other power at its disposal. Section 117 of the Omnibus Consolidated and Emergency Supplemental Appropriations Act of 1999 allowed the president to exercise control over the assets of terrorist states in the United States on grounds of national security. Under §117, the U.S. Treasury could block access to those assets, and President Clinton ordered the Treasury to do so in a comprehensive fashion, thereby blocking access to Iranian, Iraqi, and Cuban assets held in the United States.[27] Thus, not only did the FSIA prohibit seizure of very valuable diplomatic properties to satisfy terrorism judgments, but Congress gave authority to the executive branch to prohibit the use of blocked terrorist state assets to satisfy civil judgments.

Even though federal district courts are very willing to incorporate international human rights norms into civil litigation against terrorist states, they are reluctant to broadly interpret Congressional policy on state immunity in the FSIA. They are also hesitant to override the executive's national security and diplomacy concerns related to the seizure of a foreign state's diplomatic property. The *Flatow* court adjudicating the Iranian property issue did find it interesting that the Clinton administration did not fully support Flatow's attempts to collect the liability award from Iran. As the court put it, "despite its public proclamations of support for efforts to being state sponsors of terrorism to justice, the Clinton administration has intervened to forestall plaintiff Flatow's ability to satisfy his judgment."[28] Indeed, the district court created quite a dilemma for Flatow and other litigants: "the Court regrets that plaintiff's efforts to satisfy his judgment against Iran have proven futile. Indeed, in light of his lack of success thus far, it appears that plaintiff Flatow's original judgment against Iran has come to epitomize the phrase 'Pyrrhic victory.' Yet, unless or until Congress decides to enact a law that authorizes the attachments plaintiff seeks, this Court lacks the proper means to assist him with such endeavors."[29] The court points out that for Flatow to collect his judgment against Iran, Congress will again have to modify the law of sovereign immunity to facilitate the seizure of diplomatic properties held by Iran in the United States.

Several Senators introduced legislation to help Flatow and similarly situated plaintiffs to collect judgments from foreign states, and their proposed law explicitly allowed federal courts to attach diplomatic and consular properties and assets held in the United States but blocked by the president.[30] After extensive discussion between the House, Senate, and president, a different bill was adopted by both houses and signed into law by President Clinton in October 2000. Instead of amending the FSIA to remove immunity for diplomatic properties owned by terrorist states, Congress and the president approved a completely different strategy: Plaintiffs with outstanding judgments against terrorist states such as Cuba, Iran, and Iraq, would be able to collect part of their damage awards directly from the federal government.

Sections 2002 and 2003 of the Victims of Trafficking and Violence Protection Act are respectively entitled the "Payment of Anti Terrorism Judgments" and "Aid to Victims of Terrorism," and are collectively called the Justice for Victims of Terrorism Act.[31] The act specifically targets plaintiffs from the *Flatow* and *Alejandre* litigation, as well as Cicippio, Anderson, and others with outstanding judgments against Iran, Cuba, and Iraq. They may collect from the U.S. Treasury 110 percent of the compensatory (but not punitive) damages owed if they give up all rights to compensatory and punitive damages awarded by federal courts. Or, they may continue to pursue their claims as best they can. If the plaintiffs opt to collect compensatory damages from the federal government, the government can then seek to collect the damages from the liable state, and the statute mandates that resolution of damage awards should factor into attempts to normalize diplomatic relations with terrorist states. The law also provides that the president will liquidate Cuban government properties located in the United States in order to pay the *Alejandre* plaintiffs, and the Secretary of the Treasury will pay judgments against Iran out of rental proceeds accumulated from the Iranian diplomatic properties and from other U.S. funds such as the Iran Foreign Military Sales Account.[32] The act is limited in scope, however, and applies only to those litigants that received final judgments by July 20, 2000, or had filed suit on one of five specific days.[33] Thus, only a certain group of successful plaintiffs are entitled, by statute, to compensation.

Interestingly, Congress still included a national security waiver provision in the legislation that allows the president to prevent attachment and seizure of foreign-owned property in the interest of national security, provided the state was on the list of terrorist states maintained by the State Department.[34] Although the statute offers no guidelines concerning how the national security waiver is to be used, Congress clearly stated its intent in how the president is to exercise this authority:

> When a future President does make a decision whether to invoke the waiver, he should consider seriously whether the national security standard for a waiver

has been met. In enacting this legislation, Congress is expressing the view that the attachment and execution of frozen assets to enforce judgments in cases under the Anti-Terrorism Act of 1996 is not by itself contrary to the national security interest. Indeed, in the view of the Committee, it is generally in the national security interest of the United States to make foreign state sponsors of terrorism pay court-awarded damages to American victims, so neither the Foreign Sovereign Immunities Act nor any other law will stand in the way of justice. Thus, in the view of the committee the waiver authority should not be exercised in a routine or blanket manner, but only where U.S. national security interests would be implicated in taking action against particular blocked assets or where alternative recourse—such as vesting and paying those assets—may be preferable to court attachment. Future Presidents should follow the precedent set by this legislation, and find the best way to help victims of terrorism collect on their judgments and make terrorist states pay for their crimes.[35]

President Clinton issued a broad waiver, per the statute, in November 2000 to block all attempts to seize foreign-owned diplomatic properties and other assets to satisfy civil judgments.[36] Thus, while the civil cases specifically defined in the statute will receive at least some compensation, it is unlikely that damage awards from future civil lawsuits will be satisfied unless Congress again changes the law, or the executive stops blocking access to assets and properties that can be sued to satisfy damage awards. It may well be, though, that states other than Iran, Cuba, and Iraq may be sued, and indeed the September 2002 lawsuit naming the Republic of Sudan as a sponsor of terrorism invokes a state that has not been sued in the federal courts before in the context of terrorist activities. Whether the president will grant access to Sudan's assets in the United States to satisfy a civil judgment is speculation at best.

Conclusion

Civil litigation against terrorist states is one front in the ongoing war against global terrorism. By holding rogue states accountable to expanding norms of international human rights law that prohibit torture, kidnapping, hostage taking, hijacking, and extrajudicial killing, measures of justice are achieved and the wrongdoing of states in the global community is publicly highlighted. As the Seventh Circuit Court of Appeal put it in the *Boim* case discussed above, going after states and organizations that fund and sponsor terrorist activities and making them financially accountable to their victims will have some impact on the flow of money, arms, and other material resources to terrorists.

Federal courts initiated the process of using civil litigation to remedy violations of international human rights law in *Filartiga v. Pena-Irala,* and Congress responded by giving the *Filartiga* ruling a secure statutory footing in the Torture Victim Protection Act. Indeed, District Judge Royce Lamberth points out in the *Flatow* case that by making international norms part of federal criminal law, Congress has a much larger purpose in mind:

> Congress created jurisdiction over and rights of action against foreign state sponsors of terrorism. By creating these rights of action, Congress intended that the Courts impose a substantial financial cost on states which sponsor terrorist groups whose activities kill American citizens. This cost functions both as a direct deterrent, and also as a disabling mechanism: if several large punitive damage awards issue against a foreign state sponsor of terrorism, the state's financial capacity to provide funding will be curtailed.[37]

To facilitate this policy of using civil lawsuits to hold terrorist states accountable, Congress not only expanded federal law to include international law prohibitions against terrorist activities, but it also removed barriers to litigation caused by immunity doctrines in federal courts. That sovereign states are generally immune from litigation is a well-settled tenet of international law based on the sovereign equality of states in the international system. By removing the immunity of states for terrorist activities, Congress responded to the inability of federal courts to hold states accountable in cases such as *Saudi Arabia v. Nelson* and *Smith v. Libya,* and also indicated to the world community that U.S. federal courts were open to adjudicate disputes arising out of state-sponsored terrorist activities.

However, there are several significant pitfalls to Congress's policy on civil litigation against terrorist states. To begin with, the political compromise between Congress, the president, and terrorist victims in the Victims of Trafficking and Violence Protection Act in which the civil judgments for some litigants are satisfied by payments from the federal government sets up a federal compensation scheme for some victims of terrorism, but not others. To be sure, an unlimited federal fund was established to compensate victims of the September 11, 2001 terrorist acts, and as such may well pose a good alternative to litigation in federal courts. Victims of other terrorist acts who cannot claim compensation from the September 11 fund, and instead choose to sue organizations and states that sponsor terrorism, may find themselves in the same position of the *Flatow* and *Alenjandre* plaintiffs. They may receive large damage awards that go uncollected until either the executive branch facilitates seizure of foreign-owned properties and assets or Congress again appropriates money to satisfy civil judgments.

Congressional appropriations to satisfy civil judgments against terrorist states greatly undercut the purpose of civil litigation, which is simply to hold rogue states financially accountable for their terrorist acts. If civil litigation is to act as a "direct deterrent" to terrorist states as well as deprive them of the financial resources for sponsoring terrorism, then it makes little sense for Congress to spend taxpayer money for civil judgments as they arise. Moreover, by allowing the executive branch to block the collection of civil judgments by prohibiting the seizure of a foreign state's diplomatic properties and assets held in the United States, Congress effectively subordinates the satisfaction of civil judgments to the national security and diplomacy

John C. Blakeman

concerns of the executive branch. To be sure, allowing the executive to block attachment of assets increases the president's flexibility in foreign affairs and also means the threat of seizure of another state's assets can be a diplomatic bargaining chip. Congress fully recognizes that the executive must have suitable powers to fight the war on terrorism, and limiting the president's control over some foreign-owned assets located in the United States will seriously hamper his ability to conduct foreign affairs. Yet, by still granting a broad power to the president to block access to terrorist state property and assets, Congress ensures that while civil lawsuits against rogue states will proceed, and may well be successful, satisfaction of large judgments will ultimately depend on the executive branch's understanding of, and responses to, larger global events. By making the collection of civil judgments against terrorist states dependent on national security concerns and larger global events, the use of civil litigation to "imperil the flow of money and discourage the financing of terrorist acts" by rogue states is dramatically undermined.

Notes

1. *Burnett et al. v. Al Baraka Investment and Development Corporation, et al.,* complaint filed in federal district court, District of Columbia, August 15, 2002, available at http://news.findlaw.com/hdocs/docs/terrorism/burnettba81502cmp.pdf. See also *Ashton et al. v. al Qaeda Islamic Army,* complaint filed in federal district court, Southern District of New York, September 3, 2002, available at http://news.findlaw.com/hdocs/docs/terrorism/ashtonalq90302cmp.pdf.
2. International legal definitions exist for these specific categories of conduct and do not need to be discussed here. However, extrajudicial killing is essentially state-mandated killing without benefit of a judicial process; extrajudicial killing is also termed summary execution.
3. William P. Hoye, "Fighting Fire with . . . Mire? Civil Remedies and the New War on State-Sponsored Terrorism," *Duke Journal of Comparative and International Law* 12 (winter 2002): 146.
4. *Boim v. Quranic Literacy Institute and Holy Land Foundation for Relief and Development,* 291 F. 3d. 1000, 1021 (7th Cir., 2002).
5. See Anthony D'Amato, "The Alien Tort Statute and the Founding of the Constitution," *American Journal of International Law* 82, no. 1 (1988): 62–67.
6. *Dolly M. E. Filartiga and Joel Filartiga v. Americo Norberto Pena-Irala,* 630 F.2d 876, 890 (2nd Cir.1980).
7. *Tel-Oren v. Libyan Arab Republic,* 726 F.2d 774 (1984).
8. Of course, torture and extrajudicial killing committed in the United States would fall under applicable state and federal laws.
9. H.R. Rep. No. 367, 102d Cong., 1st Sess., pt. 1 (1991), reprinted in Beth Stephens and Michael Ratner, *International Human Rights Litigation in U.S. Courts* (Irvington-on-Hudson: Transnational Publishers, 1996), 248–50.
10. S. Rep. No. 249, 102nd Cong., 1st Sess. (1991), quoted in ibid., 257.
11. *Saudi Arabia v. Nelson,* 507 U.S. 349, 361 (1993).
12. *Smith v. Socialist People's Libyan Arab Jamahiriya,* 886 F. Supp. 306 (E.D. N.Y. 1995); affirmed by 2nd Circuit, (101 F. 3d 239 1996), cert. denied, 520 U.S. 1204 (1997).

13. *The Schooner Exchange v. M'Faddon and Others*, 11 U.S. 116, 134 (1812).
14. *Argentine Republic v. Amerada Hess Shipping Corp.*, 488 U.S. 428, 434 (1989).
15. The State Department currently (May 2002) lists the governments of Cuba, Iran, Iraq, North Korea, Syria, Libya, and the Republic of Sudan as sponsors of terrorism. See the State Department Report to Congress, "Patterns of Global Terrorism," 2001, available at http://www.state.gov/s/ct/rls/pgtrpt/2001/.
16. Pub. L. No. 104–208, § 589, codified at 28 U.S.C. § 1605 note. "An official, employee, or agent of a foreign state designated as a state sponsor of terrorism . . . while acting within the scope of his or her office, employment, or agency shall be liable to a United States national or the national's legal representative for personal injury or death caused by acts of that official, employee, or agent for which the courts of the United States may maintain jurisdiction under section 1605(a)(7) . . . for money damages which may include economic damages, solatium, pain, and suffering, and punitive damages if the acts were among those described in section 1605(a)(7)."
17. *Alejandre v. Republic of Cuba*, 996 F. Supp. 1239, 1248 (S.D. Fla., 1997).
18. Ibid., 1252.
19. *Flatow v. Islamic Republic of Iran*, 999 F. Supp. 1 (D.D.C. 1998).
20. Ibid., 61. The Civil Liability for Acts of State Sponsored Terrorism Law is referred to as the "Flatow Amendment" to the FSIA, since it was passed in part to facilitate the Flatow litigation against Iran.
21. *Cicippio v. Islamic Republic of Iran*, 18 F. Supp.2d 62 (D.D.C. 1998).
22. *Anderson v. Islamic Republic of Iran*, 90 F. Supp.2d 107 (D.D.C. 2000).
23. *Eisenfeld v. Islamic Republic of Iran*, 2000 U.S. Dist. LEXIS 9545 (D.D.C. July 11, 2000).
24. *Daliberti v. Republic of Iraq*, 146 F. Supp.2d 19 (D.D.C. 2001).
25. *Alejandre v. Cuba,* supra note 14, 1252.
26. *Flatow v. Islamic Republic of Iran*, 76 F. Supp. 2d 16, 23 (D.D.C. 1999). See also *Flatow v. Islamic Republic of Iran*, 74 F. Supp. 2d 18 (D.D.C. 1999), in which Flatow asked a court to attach Iranian funds held by the U.S. Treasury in accordance with the Iran–United States Claims Tribunal that decides disputes arising out of the 1979 Iranian Revolution. The Clinton administration successfully blocked access to those funds, too.
27. Presidential Determination No. 99–1, 63 Fed. Reg. 59,201 (Oct. 21, 1998).
28. *Flatow v. Islamic Republic of Iran*, supra note 26, 20.
29. Ibid., 32.
30. See "Bill to Modify the Enforcement of Certain Anti-Terrorism Judgments, and For Other Purposes," S. 1796 § 1 (3) (A), 106th Cong. (1999).
31. Victims of Trafficking and Violence Protection Act of 2000, P.L. 106–386; 114 Stat. 1464; § 2002–2003.
32. Ibid., § 2002 (b) (1) and (2).
33. The eligible recipients are those who "as of July 20, 2000, held a final judgment for a claim or claims brought under section 1605(a)(7) of title 28, United States Code, against Iran or Cuba, or the right to payment of an amount awarded as a judicial sanction with respect to such claim or claims; or (ii) filed a suit under such section 1605(a)(7) on February 17, 1999, December 13, 1999, January 28, 2000, March 15, 2000, or July 27, 2000." The specific dates correspond to lawsuits filed by other plaintiffs such as Terry Anderson, David Daliberti, and others whose litigation may not have been finalized.
34. See 23 U.S.C. §1610 subsection (f)(1).
35. H.R. Conf. Rep. No. 106–939.

Chapter 5

The Needs of the Many:

Biological Terrorism, Disease Containment, and Civil Liberties

David B. Cohen

Alethia H. Cook

David J. Louscher

The liberty secured by the Constitution of the United States to every person within its jurisdiction does not import an absolute right in each person to be, at all times and in all circumstances, wholly freed from restraint. There are manifold restraints to which every person is necessarily subject for the common good. . . . Real liberty for all could not exist under the operation of a principle which recognizes the right of each individual person to use his own [judgment], whether in respect of his person or his property, regardless of the injury that may be done to others.

—Justice John Marshall Harlan, Jacobson v. Massachusetts *197 U.S. 11 (1905)*

Introduction

Although in the minds of most Americans the 9/11 terrorist attacks signified a watershed event in American history, the less well-remembered anthrax attacks of autumn 2001 represent an omen of potentially more devastating bioterror threats on the American horizon. In an unprecedented bioterrorist attack, letters containing a powder composed of *Bacillus anthracis* (anthrax) were dropped in a mail depository in New Jersey and sent to the corporate offices of the *Sun* tabloid in Florida, the *New York Post*, the offices of CBS News anchor Dan Rather, NBC News anchor Tom Brokaw, and the U.S. Senate offices of Tom Daschle (D-SD) and Patrick Leahy (D-VT).[1] In the wake of these attacks, five individuals were dead, including a photo editor at the *Sun*, two postal workers in Maryland, a hospital supply worker in New York City, and a ninety-four-year-old woman in Connecticut. The latter four deaths resulted from mail that was cross-contaminated by the packages bearing the anthrax bacterium or because the victims worked in a mail-sorting facility in which the contaminated mail was processed. Seventeen others were treated for anthrax-related illness, Congress shut down, the U.S. mail system was in disarray, and millions of dollars were spent cleaning up federal buildings contaminated with anthrax spores.[2] A mild panic ensued within the country as public health authorities and physicians were besieged with requests from patients for information about anthrax as well as antibiotics that would protect them from the bacterium.[3] As of this writing, the perpetrator(s) of America's first major act of biological terrorism are unknown and remain at large.[4]

Anthrax is just one of a wide assortment of biological agents that can be used to terrorize or kill. The Centers for Disease Control and Prevention (CDC) in Atlanta lists on its website the sixteen biological agents that are most likely to be used as weapons of terror.[5] The U.S. Army Medical Research Institute of Infectious Diseases (USAMRIID) details thirteen biological agents in its seminal handbook (also known as the "Blue Book") on medical management of biological weapons casualties.[6] These lists are certainly not exhaustive. Compounding the threat of bioweapons is the highly mobile nature of modern society. The effects of the anthrax attack stretched along the East Coast, infecting victims as far north as Connecticut and as far south as Florida. Perhaps more frightening, if this particular attack had utilized a highly communicable pathogen such as smallpox or pneumonic plague, the results could have been unimaginable, resulting in death and panic in the United States not seen since the deadly influenza outbreak of 1917–18.[7]

The anthrax attacks are an important wake-up call to an American public that, until recently, had not confronted the realities of biological terrorism. The attacks further energized ongoing governmental attempts to prepare for such a contingency. U.S. policymakers during the cold war were understandably worried about the potential for a nuclear war—the threat of biological weapons was a much lower priority when considering the potential devastation associated with an all-out nuclear confrontation between the superpowers.[8] Given hindsight, considering the lethality of biological weapons and the relative ease with which they can be acquired/produced, this may have been a mistake.

The balance of this chapter will examine the challenges to conventional views of individual civil liberties posed by responses and planned responses to biological attacks on the nation. As the anthrax attacks illustrate, a biological attack is an imminent threat to the United States and is an ideal instrument for terrorists. The variety of biological agents and forms of delivery make response planning a very difficult task. Among the instruments for mitigation are isolation, quarantine, and vaccination; however, these tools can be problematic when considering American notions of civil liberties.[9] The Model State Emergency Health Powers Act (Model Act) is assessed to gain insights into the dilemmas. The recent responses of various countries to severe acute respiratory syndrome (SARS) provide further lessons. The authors conclude that the Model Act and the SARS experience indicate that disease-containment strategies must be more disease specific than provided for in current plans and training exercises.

Biological Weapons in History

Unlike nuclear weapons, biological weapons have been used throughout the centuries with little hesitation.[10] In 1346, Tartar forces attacking the city of Kaffa (now the city of Feodosia, Crimea) catapulted plague-ridden corpses over the walls of the city in hopes of causing a plague epidemic.[11] British forces used smallpox as a weapon to emasculate Indian forces that were loyal to the French during the French and Indian War (1754–1767).[12]

The twentieth century is rife with examples of the use of biological weapons and the devastation associated with them. In fact, the 2001 anthrax attacks were not the first deliberate use of biological weapons on American soil. During World War I, German saboteurs attempted to infect U.S. horses, cattle, and animal feed headed for Allied forces in Europe with glanders.[13] Japan had an extensive biological weapons program operating in occupied Manchuria from 1932 to 1945. Known as Unit 731 and composed of more than 3,000 scientists and 150 buildings, Japan's biological weapons program resulted in the deaths of over 10,000 prisoners and the attack of at least 11 Chinese villages using weapons such as plague, cholera, anthrax, and other pathogens.[14] Even after completion of the 1972 Biological Weapons Convention (BWC), signatory nations such as the Soviet Union and South Africa continued to produce biological weapons on a grand scale.[15] In fact, during the 1970s, 1980s, and 1990s, South Africa unleashed biological weapons to promote the interests of apartheid in the Rhodesian civil war as well as in other sub-Saharan African states such as Namibia and Mozambique. South Africa's apartheid government also contemplated utilizing biological weapons as both a tool of mass destruction and as a means of individual assassination within South Africa and across the globe as the African National Congress and Nelson Mandela gained in power.[16] The Soviet Union's secret biological weapons program never shut down and in fact increased following the 1972 BWC. The 1979 incident at Sverdlovsk (now Ekaterinburg, Russia), in which anthrax escaped from a biological weapons production plant killing sixty-six residents, exposed a program that many experts suspect continues to this day.[17]

To the present day, a number of countries persist in their efforts to acquire/produce biological weapons, including such pariah states as Iran, Libya, Syria, North Korea, and, until recently, Iraq.[18] Equally (and perhaps more) important are the efforts of rogue groups to acquire a biological weapons capability. Groups such as the Aum Shinrikyo doomsday cult in Japan and Al Qaeda have engaged in efforts (including an Aum Shinrikyo mission to Africa in an attempt to acquire Ebola) to gain such a capacity.[19] It is likely that a great many more terrorist organizations are seeking such weapons.

For a host of reasons, biological agents are ideal instruments for terrorists or for nations that wish to launch a surreptitious attack on the United States. First, many such agents are indiscriminate in effect and many require no or only limited technologies for deployment. Also, an attack has a low threshold for success and major strategic consequences may be obtained with minimal cost. Many agents have high latency, can be easily spread (often by the victims themselves), and may be difficult to diagnose or treat. Particularly troubling is that detection of an attack may be slow, and as a consequence, mitigation strategies may only be evacuation and isolation— responses that will only enhance the intended terror. Prevention, deterrence, and defense strategies are extremely difficult and costly, and, in fact, there are so many varieties of agents available, and so many different ways each of these agents may be released, that most response strategies or plans may not be appropriate.

From a civil liberties standpoint, biological weapons pose a vexing problem to American policymakers, especially when one considers the great challenges of controlling a potential epidemic and ensuring the public's safety in the wake of a biological attack. During the mitigation phase of a biological incident, the personal liberties of individual American citizens and the needs of the various levels of government to protect the public will no doubt clash. Examining this potential conflict between the rights of the individual and the needs of the many will be the purpose of the rest of this chapter. Before examining the specific civil liberties/public health issues, the nature of the biological weapons threat must be more fully examined.

Biological Agents

Biological terrorism poses several unique challenges to governments that wish to protect their populations from epidemic disease. First, unlike other kinds of terrorist strikes, it may be days or weeks before the country is aware that it is under attack. With a chemical, nuclear, radiological, or conventional event, there will be a discernable event that alerts the public and emergency response personnel that an attack is underway (e.g., an explosion, bodies lying on the ground, fire, high radiation levels). With a biological attack the timetable for identifying the event will be significantly expanded. Diseases most likely to be used in a bioattack have incubation periods of anywhere between one and twenty-four days.[20]

After the disease becomes symptomatic there may be additional delays. Many biological agents resemble the flu in the early stages. Infected individuals may not seek medical attention because they underestimate the severity of their condition. Furthermore, once patients visit their physician or hospital there are additional potential sources of delay: Medical personnel may diagnose the patients as having the flu and send them home; patients may arrive at a variety of different hospitals and physicians' offices throughout the city, making it difficult to establish that there was an intentional bioterror attack rather than an isolated case of the disease; and hospitals, medical offices, and clinics may not communicate effectively with national authorities.[21] These factors may increase the impact of the biological attack as infected individuals go about their daily lives potentially spreading the disease throughout the community or across the globe.

An additional complicating factor of biological terrorism for governments to address is the panic and fear that accompany such events. Individuals may not know if they have been exposed and many may fear they were exposed. It may take weeks for officials to determine where the biological agent was actually released. Even if an individual was not in the area of the attack, the fear of contact with victims may keep people at home.[22]

Evidence of the panic that would ensue can be found in a recent naturally occurring epidemic of meningitis. In the spring of 2001, three students in Alliance, Ohio were diagnosed with meningitis. Panic ensued. About 5,800 school employees and students were vaccinated at school. Officials had to turn away some parents and other adults who wanted to get the shot.[23] Another 37,000 fearful citizens lined up to receive antibiotics just in case they had been infected.[24] During this incident, baseball and softball games, other athletic events, and various extracurricular activities were cancelled in the surrounding areas.[25] Schools closed, parents kept their children at home, and local physicians and pharmacies scrambled to keep up with the public demand for their services.[26] This public reaction to three cases of a disease that is not communicable through casual contact hints at the mass hysteria that may ensue in the face of any biological terror event.[27]

The challenge to local, state, and federal authorities during such public panic will be to restore calm. They will need to find ways to inform the public about the situation without worsening the fears of the people. Officials will also have to manage the masses of people that will rush to hospitals or medical offices in search of treatment.[28]

Finally, biological terrorism poses a significant threat in that there are a wide variety of agents that may be used. Each has its own symptoms, progression, mortality rate, and appropriate treatment. Hospitals that want to prepare for a biological terrorist attack are challenged in deciding what kinds of medicines will be best to stock and in what quantities to stock them. Antibiotics that would save individuals from plague may not have any impact on anthrax. A vaccine for smallpox will be of no use if terrorists choose to use Ebola or some combination of different diseases.[29] When public health services are facing constant funding shortfalls and running at 80 to 90 percent capacity, expenditures for supplies to respond to a potential biological terrorist attack are difficult to justify.

Government interactions with the public will also vary based on the kind of agent used. Each potential biological agent poses unique challenges to policymakers and emergency responders. Noncommunicable agents will require minimal imposition on citizens' conventionally accepted rights as government agencies attempt to decontaminate private property and individuals. It may also require that government agencies intrude into the daily lives of citizens as they conduct a criminal investigation into the source of the contaminant and the perpetrators of the act.

However, the implications of the intentional dissemination of a communicable biological agent is much more significant. When a disease is communicable, issues of isolation, quarantine, and possibly vaccination—perhaps by force—are practically inevitable. This may take the form of asking potentially infected individuals to stay at home, locking infected individuals in or out of hospitals, restricting the movement of individuals in or out of cities or states with large infected populations, and requiring vaccination of the population. One expert has noted that:

> Large-scale biological attacks highlight the conflict between the normal civil rights consideration affecting interference with civil liberties, the law enforcement priorities necessary to obtain evidence and convictions, the need to take every possible measure to prevent follow-on attacks, the need to provide immediate emergency services, and long-standing problems in using U.S. intelligence assets to support defense and response inside U.S. territory when it may involve U.S. citizens.[30]

Compelling a terrified population to comply with these regulations will require officials to impose significantly on the civil liberties of the few in order to protect the health of the many.

Disease Containment and Civil Liberties Issues

Federal, state, and local governments have engaged in training exercises to better respond to a bioterror incident. Many of these simulation exercises have exhibited events quickly spinning out of control leaving a trail of panic, death, and gridlock, while government efforts to control the epidemic through traditional public health actions such as quarantine, mandatory vaccination, and travel restrictions proved to be inadequate in forestalling a health epidemic.[31]

Despite the growing number of exercises, most government officials and first responders lack practical experience in responding to a biological weapons attack. However, laudable efforts have been initiated to generate a nationwide set of procedures.[32]

The Model State Emergency Health Powers Act

The CDC, in cooperation with the Center for Law and the Public's Health at Georgetown and Johns Hopkins Universities, authored a document designed to bring more coherence to state public health laws and regulations: The Model State Emergency Health Powers Act. Originally released October 23, 2001, the revised version of the Model Act (December 21, 2001) has been used by thirty-seven state legislatures that have introduced legislation reforming state public health laws.[33] As of November 1, 2002, twenty-one states had passed legislation based on the Model Act.[34]

The purpose of the Model Act is to provide states with a framework for legislation that will make decision making more efficient following a biological event. Many state public health laws had not been updated since the turn of the last century. Furthermore, because public health laws in the various states have often varied widely, an efficient multistate response in the aftermath of a bioterrorist incident would be problematic where state health laws result in substantially different methods of response. Because of modern travel, diseases often spread quickly as infected individuals travel between states and countries.[35] Thus, some uniformity among state public health laws is needed in order to respond to public health crises more effectively.

Perhaps one of the greatest challenges for coordinating a response to a biological weapons attack is determining jurisdiction. Traditionally, states, and through them local governments, have "police powers" to "promote the public welfare by restraining and regulating private individuals' rights to liberty and uses of property."[36] This power is derived from the Tenth Amendment and at the core of the police power is the states' responsibility to promote public health.[37] Though responsibility for public health had historically rested with the states, in the twentieth century, the federal government increasingly encroached upon those powers.[38]

A major challenge for public health authorities in the event of a biological attack will be to sort out lines of authority and jurisdiction. A communicable biological agent that threatens to cross state lines is surely as much a federal concern as it is a concern of the state where the attack initially occurred, as well as of the state that will be impacted by the spread of the disease. It is also a state and federal crime and, depending upon the nature of the perpetrator(s), may be an act of war as well.[39]

Because of the nature of biological weapons, civil liberties will no doubt be curtailed in the aftermath of an attack. At the core of the Model Act reside issues of great relevance for personal liberties—issues such as isolation, quarantine, and vaccination. The following assesses those issues and outlines many of the civil liberties dilemmas posed by a biological attack.

Isolation, Quarantine, and Compulsory Vaccination

Although there are a number of passages in the Model Act with which civil libertarians could take exception, perhaps no section is more controversial or debated than Article VI: "Special Power During a State of Public Health Emergency: Protection of Persons." It is here that the tactics of isolation, quarantine, and vaccination are explicated. The Model Act defines *isolation* as: "the physical separation and confinement of an individual or groups of individuals who are infected or reasonably believed to be infected with a contagious or possibly contagious disease from non-isolated individuals, to prevent or limit the transmission of the disease to non-isolated individuals."[40] It defines *quarantine* as: "the physical separation and confinement of an individual or groups of individuals, who are or may have been exposed to a contagious or possibly contagious disease and who do not show signs or symptoms of a contagious disease, from non-quarantined individuals, to prevent or limit the transmission of the disease to non-quarantined individuals."[41] Thus the difference between isolation and quarantine is whether individuals are thought to have been *infected* with a contagious disease versus individuals thought to have been *exposed* to a contagious disease. Regardless, isolation and quarantine involve mandatory confinement and separation of individuals from uninfected/unexposed individuals.

"The history of pestilence is the history of quarantine," and throughout history, the tactics of isolation, quarantine, and vaccination have been used in order to control health epidemics.[42] Perhaps at no time will these tactics be more important than when facing the potential devastation unleashed by a single biological weapon. The courts have acknowledged local, state, and federal governmental powers to isolate, quarantine, and forcibly vaccinate potentially exposed populations. The landmark 1905 U.S. Supreme Court case of *Jacobson v. Massachusetts* recognized the authority of state and local governments to vaccinate, quarantine, and isolate citizens, even against their will, if done for the common good of the population. The case involved an individual who refused a smallpox vaccination during a 1902 outbreak in the city of Cambridge, Massachusetts. The Court ruled that although the U.S. Constitution does guarantee individuals certain autonomy over their own individual health, when faced with the risks of spreading a communicable disease, governments do have authority to curtail individual liberties for the benefit of the public's health. As Justice Harlan stated, "upon the principle of self-defense, of paramount necessity, a community has the right to protect itself against an epidemic of disease which threatens the safety of its members."[43] The Court further noted that:

> There is, of course, a sphere within which the individual may assert the supremacy of his own will and rightfully dispute the authority of any human government, especially of any free government existing under a written constitution, to interfere with the exercise of that will. But it is equally true that in every well-ordered society charged with the duty of conserving the safety of its members the rights of the individual in respect of his liberty may at times, under the pressure of great dangers, be subjected to such restraint, to be enforced by reasonable regulations, as the safety of the general public may demand.[44]

Jacobson has since been cited as the legal justification for public health legislation that curtails liberties for the larger good in a variety of public health settings from quarantine of AIDS carriers in prisons, to control of tuberculosis, to the passage of mandatory childhood vaccination laws.[45] Later courts have continued to rely on *Jacobson* to support state/local authority in public health regulations; only in cases where isolation/quarantine/vaccination decisions were made based on race or ethnicity were governmental actions found to be unconstitutional.[46]

In the event of a bioterrorist incident, especially one involving a communicable agent, public health officials will move quickly to control its spread through the traditional methods of isolation, quarantine, and vaccination. However, there is no one-size-fits-all instruction manual on how to mitigate a biological attack. Rather, response needs to be tailored in a disease-specific fashion, and planning should be made in such a way that response to a biological weapons attack is flexible enough to adapt to changing and unforeseen circumstances. In some cases, large-scale isolation, quarantine, and vaccination may be appropriate; in others, it may do more harm than good.

Learning from SARS

The spring 2003 outbreak of severe acute respiratory syndrome (SARS) provides public health communities and policymakers with an amazing opportunity to learn about the challenges that may be posed to American civil liberties in the event of a bioterrorist incident. SARS began in Guangong Province of China in November of 2002. By April 2003, it had spread throughout the world, causing thousands of cases of the illness and hundreds of fatalities. China, Hong Kong, Singapore, and Canada all had serious outbreaks of the disease. How these nations responded provides valuable lessons for consideration of civil liberties issues in a biological attack.

SARS is a useful case study to examine the potential impact of a bioterror incident. It is a communicable disease that has a two to seven day incubation period and initially exhibits flu-like symptoms.[47] These characteristics are shared with many known bioterror agents. As of April 2003, the Centers for Disease Control and Prevention published a mortality rate for the disease of 5.9 percent; however, by May 8, 2003, the World Health Organization established a 15 percent mortality rate for SARS—particularly frightening when compared with the 1918–19 Spanish influenza outbreak which killed more than 20 million people in 18 months with a mortality rate of 3 percent.[48] There is some question about the way that the disease is spread. Some individuals (dubbed "super-spreaders") produce an abundance of the virus and are highly contagious; however, most people contracting the disease are only moderately contagious and infect people only with whom they have close contact, including medical personnel.[49] In some cases, there is evidence that the disease may linger for as long as twenty-four hours on infected surfaces, and up to four days in human waste.[50]

Governmental Response to SARS

China has been criticized for concealing the spread of the disease and the extent of its impact on that country from November of 2002 through April of 2003. In January 2003, China acknowledged that there was an epidemic, but little effort was made to stop the spread of the disease within China or throughout the rest of the world. In fact, as late as April 7, the Chinese government was claiming that the disease was contained and life in China was normal.[51] Quarantine in China was not discussed extensively until the end of April 2003. At that time it was announced that 4,000 people living in Beijing alone were ordered to quarantine themselves. That action caused incidents of hoarding among those who felt that the government was preparing to initiate martial law.[52] By May 1, the quarantine figure had risen to 11,000 individuals, including workers and patients at 128 medical facilities around Beijing.[53] In a truly remarkable challenge to civil liberties, the Chinese government announced on May 16, 2003 that the death penalty would be a possible punishment for violating quarantine or "deliberately spreading" SARS.[54]

Through April 2003, Hong Kong suffered the second-highest number of cases and fatalities. In late March, a quarantine of 1,080 people who were believed to have had close contact with infected individuals was ordered. People were ordered to stay in their homes and were informed that failure to do so could bring a fine of approximately $650 and six months' imprisonment.[55] Members of the Amoy Gardens apartment complex's Block E, where the disease had produced an inordinate number of patients, were initially quarantined at home but were later moved to government-owned resorts so that their apartments could be disinfected. They were moved under armed guard.[56] Those under quarantine were required to stay at home and report in at regular intervals about their health. Once the quarantine was enacted, the government had to initiate a search to find families that had left the Amoy Gardens Block E complex in anticipation of the quarantine. Regional missing person units were given the task of finding the families that had fled. In part, this difficulty may have resulted from Hong Kong's announcement of a quarantine three days prior to its actual implementation. In all, 113 families from Block E left in advance of the quarantine order. Most of those families gave themselves up voluntarily, but fifty-eight required special efforts by the government to locate them.[57]

Of the known actions to try to control the spread of the disease, those taken by Singapore likely are the most objectionable to traditional American notions of civil liberties. Individuals placed under quarantine in Singapore were initially asked to enter quarantine for the good of society. Once an individual violated that quarantine order, the government's efforts to control the spread of disease became more invasive. As the disease progressed, Internet-linked cameras were issued to supervise those under quarantine. Those with the cameras were expected to turn on the camera at specific intervals and report their health status to monitors. Violators were charged $2,840 for the first offense and $5,663 for the second.[58] Electronic bracelets normally used to monitor individuals who were under house arrest were also imposed on those who did not comply with the orders. In spite of such penalties, several people violated home quarantine. By April 23, Singapore announced that prison isolation was ordered for repeat offenders.[59] Finally, thermal-imaging scanners were used at all major entry points to detect the presence of fever in individuals. A goal of Singapore authorities was to distribute digital thermometers to all school children and households so that every resident could monitor his or her temperature daily for the foreseeable future.[60]

Canada experienced more incidences of SARS than any other country outside of Asia. By April 20, 2003, Canada had quarantined 10,000 and placed 1,500 Toronto residents in home isolation. Canada also took an extraordinary step in the case of a public health official who had come into contact with an infected individual and failed to comply with the quarantine order. The Ontario Superior Court of Justice issued what is known as a Section 35 order, which authorized police to forcibly escort the individual to a mandatory quarantine in a secure hospital. The order also carried a fine of $5,000 for each day the man remained at large.[61] In another case, an employee of Hewlett-Packard continued to go to work in spite of receiving a quarantine order. After he became symptomatic and infected another worker, all 200 employees at the firm had to be quarantined.[62] Toronto authorities also considered the use of electronic monitoring devices for those who break the quarantine.[63] Public health officials placed at least one person under police guard in the hospital and hired private security firms to check on those in isolation.[64] In another major move, Ontario health officials purchased a full-page ad in all major newspapers requesting that anyone with even one symptom of the disease quarantine him or herself for at least a few days until the symptoms had passed. Tony Clement, Ontario's health minister, was quoted as saying "This is a time when the needs of a community outweigh those of a single person."[65]

The impact of the disease on the United States has been relatively limited, with only thirty-seven reported cases, most of whom traveled to Asia or cared for someone with the disease.[66] As of this writing, no Americans have died of the disease. However, on April 4, 2003, President Bush signaled the seriousness of the disease's spread when he signed Executive Order 13295, which revised the U.S. list of quarantinable diseases to include SARS. This marked the first time that the list had been expanded since the addition of Ebola in 1983.[67] However, primarily due to the slight impact on the United States, the national response has been rather limited and has included voluntary cancellation of business and educational trips to Asian locations, the screening of patients entering the U.S. from Asian locations, and voluntary quarantine of a relatively small number of people. Some states have taken a more aggressive response to the issue of quarantine even in advance of the SARS epidemic. In December 2002, Washington state passed regulations that allow for mandatory quarantine for those who are exposed to infectious diseases or mandatory isolation for those who are symptomatic. In such cases, police are required to support public health officials and will need no court order to do so. The new regulations actually served to address civil rights concerns about the existing state laws, which some believed violated the due process rights of individuals.[68]

Lessons From SARS

Several important conclusions relevant to a potential bioterrorist attack can be drawn from the above case studies. First, it must be recognized that SARS provides us with insight into the potential impact that fear of a spreading disease may have on a society.[69] In fact, the fear of disease may have a greater impact than the disease itself. SARS is frightening because it is an incurable new disease that is rapidly traversing the globe. Smallpox, Marburg virus, Ebola, and other potential biological agents may be expected to have a comparable impact. Interestingly, the impact of SARS has been geographically limited as compared to common, endemic diseases such as influenza, which kills about 36,000 globally each year, and malaria, which kills approximately 3,000 African children daily.[70] As of this writing, SARS had killed fewer than 1,000 people; however, the impact of the disease on the international economy and individuals' perceptions of their safety is undeniable.[71]

SARS also illustrates that the vast majority of individuals will voluntarily comply with quarantine and isolation orders. As one man in Singapore stated, "it is no longer a matter of privacy. It is a matter of national security."[72] Only a very small proportion of those quarantined have violated the order. When violations have happened, they have largely been based on economic worries (e.g., individuals felt the need to continue working) or on health concerns.

Civil liberties issues are clearly evident in each country where SARS has been spreading. The institution of quarantine, whether voluntary or forced, necessarily infringes on the liberties of the individual. Isolation of individuals who are obviously ill or showing symptoms is rarely problematic. However, placing people under quarantine merely because they have been exposed to someone who has the disease, or someone who was around someone with the disease, just in case they caught it, is far more problematic.[73] For instance, a flight attendant in Singapore was harshly criticized by a neighbor who thought she should put herself under quarantine because she sometimes flew to Hong Kong. The flight attendant declared, "She has no right to demand that I be quarantined as I'm not sick. I have a job to do and a rice bowl to keep. If SARS goes on for the next six months and I stop work because of it, how do I feed my children?"[74] Such reactions may be common in a bioterror incident. It is difficult to convince people that they should disrupt their lives, stay home from work, and cut themselves off from society just in case they have contracted the disease. For this reason, it may be necessary that government intervene with more forcible options than voluntary quarantine.

Toward a Disease-Specific Containment Strategy

It is clear that subnational governments and public health officials are not well prepared to encounter an attack with biological agents. Funds allocated by Congress to improve preparedness at the subnational level are only slowly reaching state and local planners. In many cases, cities and states cannot afford to devote significant time or other resources to develop plans or exercise those plans without assistance from Washington, D.C.[75]

While the Model State Emergency Health Powers Act may help states prepare for a bioterror incident, it does not provide sufficient structure for state plans. Furthermore, it pays insufficient attention to the diversity of biological agents that may be used and the differing efforts that would be required to contain the spread of such diseases. Instead, the Model Act provides a one-plan-fits-all strategy that is inconsistent with the wide variation in disease characteristics.[76]

A different approach is required to become more prepared to encounter diverse agents. The recommended approach would be guided by the characteristics of specific diseases. Some diseases such as smallpox would require isolation, quarantine, and vaccination, and perhaps other intrusive measures to halt the spread of the disease. Others, such as Ebola or Marburg, require isolation of infected individuals but have no quarantine requirement. Finally, others such as anthrax or cholera require neither quarantine nor isolation but have a significant requirement for decontamination.

The authors propose a nationally sponsored plan that would identify for states and localities the differing requirements for specific types of agents that may be used. What is recommended is a "policy pack" that could be implemented piecemeal and broken down into parts, depending upon the specific disease that was spreading. A direction guide would be provided that would instruct the localities on what response measures were required for each disease. For instance, if smallpox were used in a terrorist attack, the local response officials could turn to the appropriate page and find which elements of the policy will be relevant to smallpox. They would be directed to gather the policies on inoculation, isolation, quarantine, and communicating with the public. Had the disease instead been anthrax, they would be directed to the sections for decontamination, distribution of antibiotics, and communicating with the public.

The challenge of developing a response plan that can be implemented across states is striking a balance between providing too much autonomy and providing too much guidance and direction. States need to have the freedom to draft and implement response plans that are appropriate to local conditions, including population demographics, existing medical infrastructure, and the number of personnel that are trained to assist in the response effort. The recommended approach would allow policymakers to achieve that kind of balance.

In terms of civil liberties, the plans would require the participation of first responders, public health officials, and other legal authorities from cities and states to assist in planning for quarantine breakers and the potential need for mass quarantine. While it is unlikely that public health officials would intentionally plan to violate civil liberties, providing legal representation to the planning process would help protect against inadvertent violation.[77] Furthermore, criminal justice structures of states and cities would be called upon to control potentially hysterical populations in the aftermath of a bioterror event. Informing them of the plans after the tragedy occurs could cause a breakdown in public order and, at a minimum, complicate their participation in response efforts.[78]

The nature of disease containment requires government to intervene in the lives of its citizens. A major bioterror incident would necessitate government action to protect society from the actions of the few individuals that would likely attempt to go about their daily lives even if they had been contaminated with a truly terrible disease. Today, American government at all levels is unprepared to face and mitigate the consequences of such activities. Careful planning before such an event is the only hope to avoid significant panic, public disorder, and a public health epidemic. Given the American sense of civil liberties, it is likely that public health authorities in the United States would encounter resistance to attempts to quarantine, isolate, and forcibly vaccinate individuals in the interest of public health. A strong and adaptable policy pack that anticipates the potential ways that such efforts may impinge upon American notions of civil liberties will aid officials in coping with the terror that would doubtless ensue.

Chapter 5

1. For our definition of bioterrorism or biological weapons attack, we borrow from Gostin et al.: "the intentional use of a pathogen or biological product to cause harm to a human, animal, plant, or other living organism to influence the conduct of government or to intimidate or coerce a civilian population." See Lawrence O. Gostin et al., "The Model State Emergency Health Powers Act: Planning For and Response To Bioterrorism and Naturally Occurring Infectious Diseases," *Journal of the American Medical Association* 288, no. 5 (August 7, 2002): 622–8.
2. For example, it took well over a year and $100 million to clean up two mail processing facilities in Brentwood, D.C. and Hamilton, NJ. The Brentwood project alone was "the most ambitious reclamation of a biohazardous building in U.S. history." See Manny Fernandez, "A Patient Assault on Anthrax," *Washington Post*, 18 December 2002, p. A1. See also Daniel B. Jernigan et al., "Investigation of Bioterrorism-Related Anthrax, United States, 2001: Epidemiologic Findings," *Emerging Infectious Diseases* 8, no. 10 (October 2002): 1019–28 and Thomas V. Inglesby et al., "Anthrax as a Biological Weapon, 2002: Updated Recommendations for Management," *Journal of the American Medical Association* 288, no. 17 (May 1, 2002): 2236–52.
3. Joshua A. Mott et al., "Call-Tracking Data and the Public Health Response to Bioterrorism-Related Anthrax," *Emerging Infectious Diseases* 8, no. 10 (October 2002): 1088–92.
4. Previous acts of biorelated domestic terrorism have been perpetrated on U.S. soil, but not to the magnitude seen with the anthrax attacks of 2001. For example, in 1984, a religious cult intentionally contaminated a number of salad

bars with *Salmonella* in The Dalles, Oregon, in an attempt to impact the November 6 local elections. Though a total of 751 individuals were afflicted with gastroenteritis following the attack, no one died and details of the attack did not emerge for years. For details see Judith Miller, Stephen Engelberg, and William Broad, *Germs: Biological Weapons and America's Secret War* (New York: Simon and Schuster, 2001) and Thomas J. Torok et al., "A Large Community Outbreak of Salmonellosis Caused by Intentional Contamination of Restaurant Salad Bars," *Journal of the American Medical Association* 278, no. 5 (August 6, 1997): 389–95.

5. "Biological Diseases/Agents List," Centers for Disease Control and Prevention. Available at http://www.bt.cdc.gov/Agent/agentlist.asp.
6. Mark Kortepeter et al., eds., *USAMRIID's Medical Management of Biological Casualties Handbook*, 4th ed. (Fort Detrick/Frederick, MD: U.S. Army Medical Research Institute of Infectious Diseases, February 2001). Available at http://www.usamriid.army.mil/education/bluebook.html.
7. See Gina Kolata, *Flu: The Story of the Great Influenza Pandemic of 1918 and the Search for the Virus that Caused It* (New York: Touchstone, 1999).
8. Christopher J. Davis refers to this oversight as "nuclear blindness." See Christopher J. Davis, "Nuclear Blindness: An Overview of the Biological Weapons Programs of the Former Soviet Union and Iraq," *Emerging Infectious Diseases* 5, no. 4, (July-August 1999): 509–12.
9. The Federal Emergency Management Agency defines mitigation as "To cause something to become less harsh or hostile, to make less severe or painful." Available at http://www.fema.gov/doc/fima/how1_appendix_a.doc (retrieved April 24, 2003).
10. For a comprehensive list of the use of biological weapons in history, see "Chronology of State Use and Biological and Chemical Weapons Control," *Center for Non-Proliferation Studies, Monterey Institute of International Studies*. Available at http://cns.miis.edu/research/cbw/pastuse.htm (retrieved January 21, 2003).
11. This did, in fact, result in the conquest of Kaffa, as well as perhaps the second plague pandemic (known more commonly as the Black Death) as a result of ships carrying plague-infected refugees and possibly rodents to major Mediterranean ports such as Constantinople, Genoa, and Venice. See George W. Christopher et al., "Biological Warfare: A Historical Perspective," *Journal of the American Medical Association* 278, no. 5, (August 6, 1997) and Kortepeter et al., *USAMRIID's Medical Management of Biological Casualties Handbook*. See also Norman F. Cantor, *In the Wake of the Plague: The Black Death and the World It Made* (New York: Perennial, 2001).
12. One particular incident involved the British Army purposely giving two smallpox-tainted blankets and a handkerchief to a delegation of Delaware Indians at Fort Pitt in an attempt to spread the disease among the native peoples. See Jonathan B. Tucker, *Scourge: The Once and Future Threat of Smallpox* (New York: Grove Press, 2001), Christopher et al., "Biological Warfare: A Historical Perspective," and Kortepeter et al., *USAMRIID's Medical Management of Biological Casualties Handbook*.
13. Christopher et al., "Biological Warfare: A Historical Perspective," and Kortepeter et al., *USAMRIID's Medical Management of Biological Casualties Handbook*.
14. Christopher et al., "Biological Warfare: A Historical Perspective," and Tom Mangold and Jeff Goldberg, *Plague Wars: The Terrifying Reality of Biological Warfare* (New York: St. Martin's Griffin, 1999).

15. The official name for the BWC is the "1972 Convention on the Prohibition of the Development, Production, and Stockpiling of Bacteriological and Toxin Weapons and on Their Destruction."

16. Mangold and Goldberg, *Plague Wars*.

17. Christopher et al., "Biological Warfare: A Historical Perspective," and Kortepeter et al., *USAMRIID's Medical Management of Biological Casualties Handbook.* See also Ken Alibek and Stephen Handelman, *Biohazard* (New York: Delta Trade Publications, 1999).

18. For a comprehensive list of the current possession of biological weapons, see "Chemical and Biological Weapons: Possession and Programs Past and Present," *Center for Non-Proliferation Studies, Monterey Institute of International Studies.* Available at http://cns.miis.edu/research/cbw/possess.htm (retrieved January 21, 2003). See also the "Unclassified Report to Congress on the Acquisition of Technology Relating to Weapons of Mass Destruction and Advanced Conventional Munitions," Central Intelligence Agency. Available at http://www.cia.gov/cia/publications/bian/bian_jan_2002.htm (retrieved January 21, 2003).

19. For examination of Aum Shinrikyo efforts, see David E. Kaplan and Andrew Marshall, *The Cult at the End of the World* (New York: Crown Publishers, 1996), pp. 96–97. For evidence of Al Qaeda's attempts, see such articles as Michael Gordon, "U.S. Says It Found Qaeda Lab Being Built to Produce Anthrax," *New York Times*, 23 March 2002 and Bill Gertz, "U.S. Says Al Qaeda Exploring Russian Market for Weapons," *Washington Times*, 8 October 2002.

20. Terry Gander, ed., *Jane's NBC Protection Equipment, 1996–97* (Alexandria, VA: Jane's Information Group Inc., 1997).

21. Jeff Nesmith, "Nation Ill-Prepared for Warfare against Germs," *Palm Beach Post*, 31 August 1998; Laurie Garrett, "The Nightmare of Bioterrorism," *Foreign Affairs* (2001): 77; and Scott Nance, "Expert: Government Should Build Complex Chem-Bio Warning Network," *Defense Week*, 24 June 2002.

22. E.g., see Harry C. Holloway et al., "The Threat of Biological Weapons: Prophylaxis and Mitigation of Psychological and Social Consequences," *Journal of the American Medical Association* 278, no. 5 (August 6, 1997): 425–7.

23. Tracy Wheeler and Andale Gross, "Thousands Vaccinated Against Meningitis," *Akron Beacon Journal*, 11 June 2001.

24. Cheryl Powell and Dave Ghose, "About 37,000 Line up for Drugs to Prevent Meningitis," *Akron Beacon Journal*, 7 June 2001.

25. Andale Gross, "Many Stark Sports Groups Cancel Practices, Games," *Akron Beacon Journal*, 7 June 2001.

26. Andale Gross and Barbara Galloway, "Disease Scare Alters Everyday Life," *Akron Beacon Journal*, 5 June 2001.

27. Additional evidence of this tendency toward hysteria can be found in the anthrax attacks of 2001, in the reaction to West Nile Virus when it entered the U.S. in 1999, and in the international response to SARS in early 2003.

28. E.g., see Holloway et al., "The Threat of Biological Weapons."

29. In fact, many biological weapons have no antitdote or vaccine that prevents or cures them. These include a class of genetically modified (GM) weapons that have been manipulated by biological weapons scientists to increase virulence, morbidity, and other characteristics. Included in this class of genetically modified weapons are so-called chimeras or biococktails, which combine two distinct weapons (e.g., smallpox and Ebola), as well as genetically modified

variants of standard biological weapons (e.g., GM smallpox strains that are resistant to the smallpox vaccine; anthrax strains which are highly antibiotic resistant). See Mangold and Goldberg, *Plague Wars*; Miller, Engelberg, and Broad, *Germs*.

30. Anthony Cordesman, "Biological Warfare and the 'Buffy Paradigm,'" Center for Strategic and International Studies, September 29, 2001, p. 33. Available at http://csis.org/burke/hd/reports/Buffy012902.pdf.

31. Some scenario-based training exercises include: the "Dark Winter" simulation of a smallpox attack on the U.S. staged by the Johns Hopkins Center for Civilian Biodefense Studies in June of 2001 and "TOPOFF," which was a series of exercises held by the Department of State and Department of Justice in May 2000 and May 2003 to better train top U.S. government officials to respond to a weapons of mass destruction attack.

32. For our purposes, *public health system* will be defined as "the organized system of federal, state, and local governmental authorities with primary responsibility for the health of the community." See Lawrence O. Gostin, "The Resurgent Tuberculosis Epidemic in the Era of AIDS: Reflections on Public Health, Law, and Society," *Maryland Law Review* 54 (winter 1995) 45.

33. For a copy of the Model Act, see "The Model State Emergency Health Powers Act," *Center for Law and the Public's Health, Georgetown and Johns Hopkins Universities*. Available at http://www.publichealthlaw.net (retrieved January 21, 2003).

34. See "The Model State Emergency Health Powers Act: State Legislative Activity," *Center for Law and the Public's Health, Georgetown and Johns Hopkins Universities*. Available at http://www.publichealthlaw.net (retrieved January 21, 2003).

35. The recently discovered Severe Acute Respiratory Syndrome (SARS) provides a good example of the rapidness with which disease spreads in modern society. Beginning November 16, 2002, China reported the first cases of an atypical pneumonia that sometimes results in death, now known as SARS, to the World Health Organization (WHO). By February 2003, SARS had spread to several other Asian countries and by March had traveled to North America. According to the WHO, as of May 8, 2003, 7,053 cases of SARS had been reported, resulting in 506 deaths, and was present in 33 countries including China (4698); Hong Kong (1661), Singapore (204), Canada (146), Taiwan (131), Vietnam (63), and the United States (63). Since the disease has a mortality rate of 15 percent and has spread to other continents in a short period of time, SARS shares many characteristics with known bioweapons. In comparison with smallpox, a highly communicable disease with a 30 percent mortality rate and a known weaponized disease, SARS represents the tip of a very alarming iceberg in terms of global spread of disease. For current information about SARS, see both the CDC (www.cdc.gov) and WHO (www.who.int) websites.

36. James G. Hodge, Jr., "Implementing Modern Public Health Goals through Government: An Examination of New Federalism and Public Health Law," *Journal of Contemporary Health Law & Policy* 14 (fall 1997): 100.

37. Hodge, "Implementing Modern Public Health Goals through Government," p. 101–2.

38. Beginning with the Federal Maternity and Infancy Act of 1922, the monopoly that states held on public health powers began to crumble. It is no surprise that following the tenure of President Franklin D. Roosevelt, the Supreme Court and Congress would reinterpret the national government's role in public health, via

the Commerce Clause, thus granting the federal government "national police powers." The federal government, through grants, regulations, and the creation of federal public health agencies such as the Centers for Disease Control and Prevention and Food and Drug Administration, among others, now impacts many areas of the public health that were once the sole province of the states, including air and water quality, food and drug safety, consumer product safety, occupational health and safety, and disease control, research, and epidemiology. See Hodge, "Implementing Modern Public Health Goals through Government," pp. 106–7.

39. George J. Annas, "Bioterrorism, Public Health, and Civil Liberties," *New England Journal of Medicine* 346 no. 17. (April 25, 2002): 1337.
40. "The Model State Emergency Health Powers Act," *Center for Law and the Public's Health*, p. 10.
41. "The Model State Emergency Health Powers Act," *Center for Law and the Public's Health*, p. 11.
42. John A. Gleason, "Quarantine: An Unreasonable Solution to the AIDS Dilemma," *University of Cincinnati Law Review* 55 (1986): 220.
43. *Jacobson v. Massachusetts*, 197 U.S. 11 (1905).
44. *Jacobson v. Massachusetts*, 197 U.S. 11 (1905).
45. E.g., see George J. Annas, "Control of Tuberculosis: The Law and the Public's Health," *The New England Journal of Medicine* 328 (February, 25 1993): 585–88; Gleason, "Quarantine"; James G. Hodge and Lawrence O. Gostin, "School Vaccination Requirements: Historical, Social, and Legal Perspectives," *Kentucky Law Journal* 90 (2001/2002); Paula Mindes, "Tuberculosis Quarantine: A Review of Legal Issues in Ohio and Other States," *Journal of Law and Health* 10 (1995/1996); Wendy E. Parmet, "Aids and Quarantine: The Revival of an Archaic Doctrine," *Hofstra Law Review* 14 (fall 1985); Kristine M. Severyn, "Jacobson v. Massachusetts: Impact on Informed Consent and Vaccine Policy," *The Journal of Pharmacy and Law* 5 (1995).
46. In the case *Wong Wai v. Williamson et al.* (103 F. 1 [1900]), the U.S. Circuit Court for the Northern District of California found that a mandatory vaccination program instituted by the board of health of the city and county of San Francisco, which targeted only Chinese residents of San Francisco, violated the equal protection clause of the Fourteenth Amendment. In a related case that followed, *Jew Ho v. Williamson et al.* (103 F. 10 [1900]) the same court found that a quarantine imposed based solely on race again violated the equal protection clause of the Fourteenth Amendment. Thus, though state and local governments are granted great leeway in terms of their authority to impose isolation, quarantine, and vaccination, that authority disappears if these measures are applied in a discriminatory fashion, at least concerning race, ethnicity, or religion. See also Parmet, "Aids and Quarantine."
47. "Preliminary Clinical Description of Severe Acute Respiratory Syndrome," *Morbidity and Mortality Weekly Report*. Available at www.cdc.gov/mmwr/preview/mmwrhtml/mm5212a5.htm (retrieved April 11, 2003).
48. The 15 percent mortality rate includes a 50 percent or greater chance of death in persons age sixty-five and older. "Frequently Asked Questions," Centers for Disease Control and Prevention. Available at http://www.cdc.gov/ncidod/sars/faq.htm (retrieved on April 24, 2003); Lawrence K. Altman, "W.H.O. Doubles Its Estimate of Death Rate From SARS," *New York Times*, 8 May 2003; Rob Stein and Ceci Connolly, "Estimated SARS Death Rate Rises to 15 Percent," *Washington Post*, 8 May 2003.

49. E.g., see M. A. J. McKenna, "Super-Spreaders Fan SARS Fears: Scientists Probe Why Some Infect So Many," *Atlanta Journal Constitution*, 27 April 2003 and Philip P. Pan, "A 'Superspreader' of SARS: How One Woman Touched Off Beijing Outbreak," *Washington Post*, 29 May 2003. See also Michael D. Lemonick and Alice Park, "The Truth About SARS," *Time* (May 5, 2003).

50. Rob Stein, "SARS Virus Revealed to Be a Tough Survivor," *The Guardian (London)*, 8 May 2003; "SARS—Experts Say Virus May Be More Contagious Than First Thought," *AFX News Limited*, 2 April 2003.

51. "SARS Spread Contained—Premier," *China Daily*, 7 April 2003.

52. John Pomfret, "China Seals Hospitals to Fight SARS," *Washington Post*, 25 April 2003.

53. Catherine Armitage and Glenda Korporaal, "Beijing Hospitals Sealed Off as Crisis Gets Worse," *The Australian*, 29 April 2003; "More Than 11,000 Quarantined in Capital," *South China Morning Post (Hong Kong)*, 1 May 2003.

54. Gady A. Epstein, "China Revives Intrusive Practices for SARS," *Baltimore Sun*, 20 May 2003 and "China Threatens the Death Penalty for Deliberately Spreading SARS," *Los Angeles Times*, 16 May 2003.

55. Cannix Yau and Michael Ng, "Tung Orders Quarantine," *The Standard*, 29 March 2003.

56. Matthew Lee and Cannix Yau, "300 Moved to Camps," *The Standard*, 2 April 2003.

57. Michael Ng, "Hung On For 58 Families," *The Standard*, 5 April 2003.

58. "Singapore Puts 740 in Home Quarantine," *China Daily*, 26 March 2003. See also Natalie Soh Wong Sher Maine, "Electronic Tag for Offender," *The Straights Times*, 13 April 2003.

59. Bertha Henson, "Government Draws Up Virus Battle Plan," *The Straights Times*, 20 April 2003.

60. Richard C. Paddock, "A Hotbed of SARS Warfare," *Los Angeles Times*, 8 May 2003

61. Michael Friscolanti and Mary Vallis, "Nine New Cases Appear; 23 Patients Released; Court Orders Two Suspected Carriers into Forced Isolation," *Ottawa Citizen*, 5 April 2003.

62. Betsy Powell, "Another 1,268 in Quarantine," *Toronto Star*, 10 April 2003 and Anita Manning, "In Crisis Mode," *USA Today*, 10 April 2003.

63. Erika Niedowski, "Toronto Sees Setbacks in SARS Battle; Some Refusing to Comply with Quarantine Orders," *The Baltimore Sun*, 14 April 2003 and Helen Branswell, "You Don't Want to Cause Panic . . . It's a Tough Time," *Toronto Star*, 17 April 2003.

64. Lawrence Altman, "Fearing SARS, Ontario Urges Wider Quarantines," *The New York Times*, 18 April 2003.

65. Altman, "Fearing SARS, Ontario Urges Wider Quarantines."

66. "Cumulative Number of Reported Probable Cases of Severe Acute Respiratory Syndrome," World Health Organization. Available at http://www.who.int/csr/sarscountry/2003_04_24/en (retrieved on April 25, 2003); U.S. Centers for Disease Control and Prevention, "Frequently Asked Questions." Available at http://www.cdc.gov/ncidod/sars/faq.htm#outbreak (retrieved on April 25, 2003).

67. Rob Stein, "Bush Puts New Disease on U.S. Quarantine List," *The Washington Post*, 5 April 2003 and M. A. J. McKenna and David Wahlberg, "Outbreak Patients Could Be Isolated," *The Atlanta Journal-Constitution*, 5 April 2003.

68. Carol Ostrom, "Trips to Asia Trigger SARS Jitters," *The Seattle Times*, 6 April 2003.

69. E.g., see Holloway et al., "The Threat of Biological Weapons."
70. E.g., see "Malaria is Alive and Well and Killing More Than 3,000 African Children Every Day," World Health Organization. Available at http://www.who.int/mediacentre/releases/2003/pr33/print.html (retrieved April 29, 2003).
71. For examples of articles on the economic impact of SARS, see Bayan Rahman and Mariko Sanchanta, "Japan Escapes SARS but Not Its Effect," *Financial Times*, 8 May 2003; Doug Struck, "Virus Takes Toll on Asian Dynamos," *Washington Post*, 26 April 2003. For information on the social and psychological consequences of bioterrorism, see Holloway et al., "The Threat of Biological Weapons."
72. Nawaz Marican, "Webcam Check on Singapore Suspects," *South China Morning Post* 22 April 2003.
73. See Annas, "Bioterrorism, Public Health, and Civil Liberties," p. 1337; Joseph Barbera et al., "Large-Scale Quarantine Following Biological Terrorism in the United States: Scientific Examination, Logistic and Legal Limits, and Possible Consequences," *Journal of the American Medical Association* 286, no. 5 (December 5, 2001): 2711–7.
74. Theresa Tan, "Fear . . . Anxiety . . . Optimism," *The Straits Times*, 7 April 2003.
75. E.g., see Dale Russakoff and Rene Sanchez, "Begging, Borrowing for Security: Homeland Burden Grows for Cash-Strapped States, Cities," *Washington Post*, 1 April 2003.
76. Barbera et al. argue that "political leaders . . . need to understand that a single strategy for limiting the spread of all contagious diseases is not appropriate and will not work." Barbera et al., "Large-Scale Quarantine Following Biological Terrorism in the United States."
77. Richard E. Hoffman, "Preparing for a Bioterrorist Attack: Legal and Administrative Strategies," *Emerging Infectious Diseases* 9, no. 2, (February 2003): 241–5.
78. Holloway et al., "The Threat of Biological Weapons."

Chapter 6

Terrorism, Security, and Civil Liberties:

The States Respond

Edward R. Sharkey, Jr.
Kendra B. Stewart

On September 11, 2001, while people all over the world sat stunned as they watched America under attack, state and local government workers were responding in ways that overwhelmed and inspired us. The first line of response to any major crisis is almost always at the local level. A catastrophe, like the attack on the World Trade Center, forces all levels of government to coordinate their actions and sometimes reevaluate their response. Although the majority of the focus since September 11 has been on how the federal government is responding to the acts of terrorism, the 50 state governments and over 80,000 local governments are also playing an integral role in planning, preventing, and recovering. This chapter examines the role of the states in this effort. We focus on two dimensions: how states are responding administratively, and how they are responding legislatively.

This chapter examines structural and legal changes and how these changes are affecting citizens' civil liberties. We only examine the fifty states—no local governments or U.S. territories. The conclusions drawn are based on both primary and secondary data collected by the authors and a number of independent organizations and federal agencies. In order to compliment the existing data and reports, we developed and conducted two surveys. The first was sent to all fifty state homeland security directors and attempted to capture information on duties, constraints, and the status of the homeland security offices. The second survey was sent to directors of the state chapters of the American Civil Liberties Unions (ACLU). Respondents were asked to identify areas in which the states had passed legislation and to give their opinion as to how state actions compare to federal actions regarding civil liberty restrictions.[1]

In general, if you had to summarize the response of the states to the events of September 11 in one word it would probably be "limited." ANSER Institute for Homeland Security Deputy Director Dave McIntyre claims this lack of response is due to an expectation of the states for clear guidance and direction from the federal government. He compares the state of the states to

Samuel Beckett's famous play, *Waiting for Godot*.[2] In this play, two men await in indecision and intellectual paralysis for Godot to arrive and tell them what to do. The play ends with Godot failing to arrive and a "sense of dread as the realities of life and the necessity for action overtake those waiting for Godot." McIntyre observes these same characteristics of indecision and failure to act in the federal, state, and local governments as they awaited the Bush administration's national strategy for homeland security. Before the plan was released, he accurately predicted that it would not likely "provide the level of detail and guidance the Godot-waiters desired." He pointed out that the Bush administration would likely stick to its guiding Republican values of decentralized, limited federal government providing guidance rather than details and incentives rather than mandates. McIntyre argues that this administration is "not going to reverse the long-term devolution of power down to the states that has (they believe) strengthened the country, and certainly strengthened the Republican leverage. . . . Those waiting for national guidance built on centralized power and a collectivist strategy are waiting for something that will not happen in this administration."

Our findings support McIntyre's observations. First, the federal government did hand down a plan that was probably not as detailed (or well-funded) as the states had hoped. Overall the states are in new territory—that of national security. Historically, as the federal government has taken on new policy areas, it has done so with broad and sweeping legislation that generally provides the states with funding attached to detailed expectations on program implementation. However, in recent decades we have seen an increase in the capacity of states to deal with their own problems coupled with a national sentiment for a smaller and more decentralized government. Power has been devolving to the states in areas in which they have the expertise to deal. The federal government appears to be approaching homeland security with this same attitude. Although the administration may think this is the appropriate response, the states may not all agree. They appear, in many cases, to still be waiting for Godot and looking to the federal government for some clearer guidance—and money. And why shouldn't they—after all, this is national security, and isn't that the jurisdiction of the *national* government?

The Office of Homeland Security is careful to point out the role they expect the states to play in their July 2002 report on state and local actions. They are looking for the states to "assume a key role in bridging federal and local efforts."[3] The office recognizes the local governments as first responders during times of crisis and has put the responsibility on the states to ensure that they will be included in developing and implementing statewide security plans. The Office of Homeland Security intends to provide a framework into which all of the states will fit their comprehensive programs.

As of November 2002, there is an effort by the federal government to establish a cabinet office of homeland security. House bill H.R. 5005 has passed the House and is being debated in the Senate, with the Lieberman

Amendment added as S. 4471. If this bill passes as written, the Department of Homeland Security (DHS) would be "responsible for coordinating activities with, and providing assistance to, state and local governments to ensure adequate preparedness for possible terrorist attacks."[4] Both the House and Senate bills propose an Office of State and Local Government Coordination within DHS to provide state and local governments with one primary contact and assist with the coordination and assessment of programs. Currently, agencies within the Departments of Defense, Health and Human Services, and Justice, and the Federal Emergency Management Agency (FEMA) all administer grants and training programs for state and local governments.[5] "This multiplicity of agencies offering assistance, and the subsequent shifting of agency responsibilities, have reportedly led to some frustration and confusion among state and local officials attempting to secure federal funds."[6] If passed, the bill would also require the Office of State and Local Government Coordination to appoint a liaison for each state to coordinate federal assistance, assess state and local needs, and provide training and information.[7]

Another question that is being explored is the role of the federal government in regards to setting standards. Currently FEMA has worked with other professional organizations to develop *voluntary* standards that it encourages the state and local governments to use for most emergency management functions. Thus far, the above-mentioned legislation does not address setting standards for training and equipment. Tom Ridge, Director of Homeland Security at the federal level, and FEMA both have expressed support for national standards, but federal grants to the states are not yet contingent upon satisfying standards.[8] FEMA is working to encourage states to adopt their own set of standards rather than wait for the federal government to impose national ones. A number of options are currently being debated regarding the approaches the federal government could take on emergency management and response standards, recognizing that mandatory standards could be prohibitively expensive to the states, even with federal assistance.[9]

Structural Responses

Overall the states have responded with planning and waiting. As is the case in most areas of state policy, there is great variation in the level of response that we are seeing. Table 6.1 below summarizes the organizational measures taken in each of the fifty states. In examining how states are dealing with homeland security we were interested in determining which branch of government has authority over homeland security, the background of the director/coordinator of homeland security, and what (if any) type of office or agency has been created.

In regards to authority, you will note in the second column that in the majority of the states the homeland security coordinators report to the governor. Thus far, only two state legislatures, Colorado and Iowa, have taken action to give the positions permanent homes. This means that the November 2002 election could lead to the replacement of twenty to thirty-six of the current homeland security directors. This begs the question: How much consistency and professionalism do we want in these positions? With the majority serving as political appointees, there appears to be a desire for politics, more so than permanency, to play a role in the selection of the state advisor.

The backgrounds of the homeland security advisors vary within a few distinct fields. According to John Nagy at Stateline.org, most of these positions are high-level policy advisors who command broad respect.[10] State adjutant generals (director of the National Guard) and emergency management directors were the most popular choices, followed by public safety and law enforcement personnel. A few elected officials (lieutenant governors and land commissioner) hold the post as well as a number of gubernatorial staffers. The majority of state homeland security directors see their role as that of coordinator.

The fourth column in the table represents new organizations created in the states since 9/11 to deal with homeland security issues. The majority of states have responded with task forces, councils, or blue-ribbon commissions (all categorized as "Council") to study, recommend, or advise the governor on homeland security issues. In general, the states that created an actual new stand-alone agency (with a budget) were states that were directly affected by the events of September 11, 2001. The term "office" refers to an organization that was created within an agency specifically to deal with homeland security. It is important to note that this column only indicates agencies created since 9/11, therefore a "None" does not mean that there has been no response, but that there is no *new* organization. A handful of states already had organizations in place to deal with terrorism and are designated with an asterisk (*). Other states categorized with "None" are in general relying on resources from an existing number of agencies. The current public sentiment toward smaller government has led most of the states to try to work within their existing organizations and budgets. Therefore, little new money or personnel have been permanently designated to homeland security. This is not to say that the states are doing nothing, but that they are making due with what they already have. Although a number are recognizing that in areas of health and technology the status quo is not good enough. However, budget shortfalls and a lack of public interest have kept states from appropriately preparing in these areas.

Based on self-reported responses compiled in the Office of Homeland Security report on *State and Local Actions for Homeland Security*, July 2002, states are responding in a number of ways. Efforts can be categorized into the following areas: training of first responders; strategic planning;

Table 6.1: Post-9/11 State Structural Responses

State	Authority	Director Background	Post-9/11 Organization
Alabama	Governor	Adjutant General	None
Alaska	Governor	Military	Council
Arizona	Governor	Governor's Staff	Council
Arkansas	Governor	Emergency Management	None*
California	Governor	Governor's Staff	None
Colorado	Legislature	Public Safety	Agency
Connecticut	Governor	Public Safety	Council
Delaware	Governor	Emergency Mgmt.	None
Florida	Governor	Public Safety	Council
Georgia	Governor	Public Safety	Office
Hawaii	Governor	Adjutant General	None*
Idaho	Governor	Adjutant General	Council
Illinois	Governor	Governor's Staff	None*
Indiana	Governor	Lt. Governor	Council
Iowa	Governor	Emergency Management	Council
Kansas	Governor	Adjutant General	None*
Kentucky	Governor	Adjutant General	Office
Louisiana	Governor	Governor's Staff	Council
Maine	Governor	Adjutant General	Council
Maryland	Governor	Governor's Staff	None*
Massachusetts	Governor	FBI	Office
Michigan	Governor	Public Safety	Council
Minnesota	Governor	Public Safety	Council
Mississippi	Governor	Emergency Management	Office & Council
Missouri	Governor	Military	Council
Montana	Governor	Emergency Management	Council
Nebraska	Governor	Lt. Governor	Council
Nevada	Governor	Emergency Management	Council
New Hampshire	Governor	Fire Marshal	Council
New Jersey	Governor	Asst. Attorney General	Office & Council
New Mexico	Governor	Public Safety	Office
New York	Governor	FBI	Agency & Council
North Carolina	Governor	Public Safety	Council
North Dakota	Governor	Emergency Management	None*
Ohio	Governor	Lt. Governor (Department of Public Safety also)	Council
Oklahoma	Governor (until 12/03)	Public Safety	Council
Oregon	Governor	N/A (no Homeland Security Position)	2 Councils

Table 6.1 (continued)

State	Authority	Director Background	Post-9/11 Organization
Pennsylvania	Governor	FBI	Office & Council
Rhode Island	Governor	Adjutant General	Council
South Carolina	Governor	Military	Council
South Dakota	Governor	Governor's Staff	Office & Council
Tennessee	Governor	Military	Council
Texas	Governor	Land Commissioner	Council
Utah	Governor	Public Safety	Council
Vermont	Governor	Governor's Staff	Council
Virginia	Governor	Public Safety	Agency
Washington	Governor	Adjutant General	None*
West Virginia	Governor	Public Safety	None
Wisconsin	Governor	Emergency Management/ Health and Family Services	Council
Wyoming	Governor	Adjutant General	Council

*A specific homeland security organization existed prior to September 11, 2001.

assessing potential targets; improving modes of communication; evaluating recovery capabilities; coordinating efforts of federal, state, and local agencies, and examining infrastructure, health, and agricultural areas of concern. In times of tight budgets, the states are feeling constrained as to how much they are able to do once they recognize how great their needs are in many of these areas.

The costs of antiterrorism measures in the states have been varied and staggering. The National Governor's Association (NGA) estimated the first-year state expenditures to be around $6 billion. This number is based on *expected* costs reported at the end of 2001. The exact number has been too difficult to capture since most states have not designated new funds specifically for homeland security and are relying on existing resources. The other problem lies in the lack of consistency in what the states are classifying as homeland security expenses. Some states are strictly counting direct costs, while others are looking at the indirect costs as well (such as the cost of covering state employees who were deployed with the national guard). There has yet to be an exact number derived at determining the cost of homeland security to the states. To assist the states in recouping some of their expenses, the NGA did ask Congress and the president for $4 billion to help states pay for protecting critical infrastructure, airports, power plants, and ports.[11] The federal government has provided some funding through grants for developing statewide plans and improving state health capabilities and facilities, but thus far this money has been limited. There are still a number of proposals being debated that would potentially distribute $3.5 billion to the states through FEMA block grants.

Legislative Responses

The states have passed a variety of resolutions and laws in response to the terrorist attacks on September 11, 2001. Early in the process, many scholars expressed concern about the potential for a widespread assault on basic civil liberties. Interestingly, the legislative reaction of the states has been measured, cautious, and not particularly egregious in terms of infringements on basic liberties. A discussion of state legislative activities in four areas (electronic surveillance, open access laws, identification cards, and laws promoting patriotism) follows.[12]

Electronic Surveillance Legislation

Electronic surveillance is arguably the most invasive technique available to law enforcement officials. A basic concern with this investigative tool involves the protection against unreasonable search and seizure provided by the U.S. Constitution's Bill of Rights. Specifically, the Supreme Court in *Katz v. United States* (1967) has established that the Fourth Amendment "protects people, not places" and that electronic surveillance is subject to the associated restraints.[13] Our understanding of these restraints is in a constant state of flux, but ongoing debates often involve the explicit requirements for both probable cause and a description of "the place to be searched."[14] In a broader sense, changes in our conception of the Fourth Amendment reflect our evolving struggle to find the appropriate balance between liberty and security.

Following the terrorist attacks, it was not hard to imagine the scales tipping in favor of the interests of order and officials moving quickly to improve their powers of observation. The public was insecure, politicians were desperate to act, and polls were registering overwhelming support for giving law enforcement enhanced authority. In fact, a Harris Poll conducted in September 2001 found large portions of the population favoring the use of facial-recognition technology (93 percent), increased camera surveillance in public places (63 percent), and efforts to monitor discussions in Internet chat rooms (63 percent).[15] The political environment, in other words, was positively oriented toward the development of legislation that empowered the law enforcement community. It was not surprising, then, when President George W. Bush signed the USA PATRIOT Act (2001) into law and dramatically expanded the surveillance capacities of the federal government.[16]

Despite the generous context, the willingness of the states to develop sweeping new eavesdropping powers has been relatively constrained. In fact, only a handful (See Table 6.2) have actually passed wiretapping legislation since the terrorist attacks, and many of the efforts do not raise significant concerns about civil liberties. In eight states (Arizona, Connecticut, Florida, New Jersey, New York, Ohio, Pennsylvania, and South Carolina) surveillance laws were expanded to include terrorist offenses. Other states increased the number of officials authorized to request a wiretap order. Virginia, for instance, now allows towns to initiate wiretap requests. In the past, cities and counties were the only political subdivisions of the state to have such capacity. Additionally, Arizona created new exceptions for liability in eavesdropping, and in California the list of items subject to monitoring expanded to include wire and pager communications.

There have been two sets of developments, however, that readily invite concern about Fourth Amendment protections. First, the state of Maryland approved legislation allowing for the use of "roving" wiretaps (see Table 6.2), which allow officials to track suspects as they use different forms of communication. Investigators could listen in, for instance, when a suspect uses a neighbor's telephone or creates a new mobile phone account. In the past, state authorities have generally been limited to monitoring individual telephone lines when gathering information. One possible concern with this "tool" is it might increase the likelihood that law enforcement officials will eavesdrop on the private communications of innocent people. Additionally, civil libertarian interests might argue that the flexible nature of roving requests runs counter to the Fourth Amendment's requirement for a precise description of the search.

Second, several states have passed laws that allow judges to issue search orders outside their normal jurisdiction (see Table 6.2). In Florida, judges with felony jurisdiction are able to authorize surveillance orders anywhere in the state. Georgia now has similar provisions and orders have statewide application when issued by a judge with jurisdiction over the associated case. The capacity of judges to monitor effectively the application of an order is one area of possible concern. Additionally, law enforcement officials might be more able to bypass "unfriendly" courts and submit requests to judges with desirable approval records.

Open Record and Meeting Restrictions

In response to the attacks, states also moved to consider legislation that might narrow open meeting and records laws. Proponents of such efforts undoubtedly felt that public information of value to future terrorists was simply too accessible and that tighter security measures would likely enhance levels of safety. A primary concern with this type of restriction is that access to governmental meetings and records acts as an important check on the behavior of public officials. To the extent we refuse access, citizens are less able to evaluate policy and hold responsible parties accountable for their actions.

By October 2002, at least twelve states had passed legislation involving some type of open meeting or record restriction (See Table 6.3). In eleven

Table 6.2: Post-9/11 Electronic Surveillance Legislation

State	Legislation	Description
AZ	SB 1427	Provides new exceptions for liability in eavesdropping, including cases where a provider believes that an emergency justifies the disclosure. (5/2/02)
CA	AB 74	Expands the definitions of the type of communications that can be intercepted to include wire and pager communications. (9/16/02)
CT	HB 5759	Allows state to pursue authorization to intercept wire communications in cases that appear to involve terrorist activity. (6/3/02)
FL	HB 1439	Allows the Department of Law Enforcement to intercept oral, wire, or electronic communications when investigating acts of terrorism or threatened use of destructive devices. (4/22/02)
	SB 1774	Substituted HB 1439. Permits a state judge having felony jurisdiction to authorize initial and ongoing interception of communications anywhere in the state. (4/22/02)
GA	SB 459	Search warrants for stored wire or electronic communications have statewide application when issued by a judge with jurisdiction over the criminal offense under investigation. (5/16/02)
LA	HB 53	Allows assistant district attorneys and assistant attorneys general to apply for surveillance requests. (4/23/02)
MD	SB 20	Permits a law enforcement officer to intercept oral communications after lawfully detaining a vehicle during a criminal investigation. (4/25/02)
	HB 1036	Provides an exception to the requirement that a specified description be provided in order to obtain a judicial order relating to wire, oral, and electronic communications (roving). (4/25/02)
NJ	AB 911	Expands wiretapping statutes to include violations of terror criminal provisions included in act. (6/18/02)
NY	S 70002	Anti-Terror Package (Special Session): Expands surveillance laws to include terrorist offenses. (9/17/01)
OH	SB 184	Expands surveillance laws to include terrorist offenses. (5/15/02)
OK	SB 1642	Expands the jurisdiction of courts to oversee the installation and use of eavesdropping devices. (5/8/02)

Table 6.2 (continued)

State	Legislation	Description
PA	SB 1109	Surveillance laws expanded to include activities involving weapons of mass destruction. (6/28/02)
SC	HB 4416	Grants the State Law Enforcement Division power to tap suspected terrorists' or criminals' telephone calls, e-mail, and other communications. (7/2/02)
VA	HB 41	Adds towns to the list of political subdivisions whose law-enforcement agencies are authorized to request a wiretap. Currently, only counties and cities are authorized. (1/9/02)
	SB 514	Includes granting the attorney general or his designee the authority to seek a wiretap for suspected terrorists and removes physical location and geographic boundary requirements from wiretap applications. (4/6/02)

cases (Alaska, Connecticut, Florida, Idaho, Louisiana, Maine, Michigan, Ohio, South Carolina, Utah, and Virginia), states approved new limitations on a citizen's capacity to access public records. For the most part, these involve classifying evacuation plans, emergency response plans, security plans and procedures, architectural drawings of state facilities, and public water works. Although most of these measures have common-sense appeal, there is often room for a state to remove from scrutiny information that is not vital to security concerns. In South Carolina, for instance, the Omnibus Terrorism Protection and Homeland Defense Act of 2002 protects all information regarding the "security plan" of a public body. Alaska, Florida, and Utah also have broadly stated provisions that may allow for abuse and unwarranted restrictions. Interestingly, Virginia has classified reports of diseases potentially caused by agents that hostile elements might use as weapons. This clearly sets up a classic struggle between the public's right to know and the state's obligation to ensure safety.

A second area of activity involves a narrowing of open meeting laws. In Florida, New Hampshire, Ohio, and Virginia the new measures specifically restrict the availability of access to meetings and the minutes of those meetings that might reveal security plans or threat assessments. Ohio simply allows for closed executive sessions to consider such matters, while New Hampshire offers exceptions for nonpublic meetings. Both Florida and Virginia embrace a rather significant narrowing of open meeting laws as part of their antiterrorist efforts. Unfortunately, citizens in these states and others that embrace similar restrictions may have an extremely limited capacity to understand how their state has chosen to prepare and respond to

Table 6.3: Post-9/11 State Legislation and Open Record and
Meeting Restrictions

State	Legislation	Description
AK	SB 238	Exempts from the category of public records certain records and information relating to state safety plans, programs, and procedures, and to systems, facilities, and infrastructure in the state. (6/21/02)
CT	HB 5627	Expands exemptions regarding security measures, security audit recommendations, and security plans for the future in government-owned or -leased properties. (2/28/02)
FL	SB 16	Provides exemption from public-records requirements for those portions of emergency-management plans that address response of hospitals to terrorism and from public-meeting requirements for any meeting that would reveal information contained in said plan. (2/4/02)
	SB 18	Information concerning the amount, type, or location of pharmaceutical materials maintained or directed by state agency is exempt from public-records requirements. (12/13/01)
	SB 20	Creates an exemption from disclosure for building plans, blueprints, schematic drawings, and diagrams of specific facilities and structures owned or operated by an agency. (4/22/02)
	HB 735	Provides exemption from public-records requirements for security-system plans and public-meeting requirements for those portions of any meeting that would reveal security-system plans. (2/4/02)
ID	HB 560	Exempts from public disclosure the records of buildings, facilities, infrastructures, and systems held by or in the custody of any public agency only when the disclosure of such information would jeopardize the safety of persons or the public safety. (2/6/02)
LA	HB 53	Louisiana Anti-terrorism Act extends exception to public record laws to include public water works records containing intelligence regarding terrorist related activity. (4/23/02)
ME	LD 2153	Adds an exception to the definition of "public records" in the freedom of access laws that would protect information concerning security plans or procedures of agencies of state government and local government. Previously, law only exempted information regarding identified law enforcement agencies. (3/7/02)

Table 6.3 (continued)

State	Legislation	Description
MI	HB 5349	Exempt from disclosure records or information regarding building, public works, and public water designs to the extent that they relate to the ongoing security measures of a public body; capabilities and plans for responding to a violation of the "Michigan Anti-Terrorism Act." (4/9/02)
NH	HB 1423	Addresses state or local government security issues under the right-to-know law and threats of biological or chemical substances. Extends exceptions for release of nonpublic minutes regarding terrorist threats or training. (5/3/02)
OH	SB 184	Exempts certain security-related information from the Public Records Law and to revises the Open Meetings Law provision allowing executive sessions to consider security matters. (2/4/02)
SC	HB 4416	Omnibus Terrorism Protection and Homeland Defense Act of 2002 provides that information regarding the security plan of a public body is not open to the public. (7/2/02)
UT	HB 283	Exempts records of governmental security measures and practices from the Government Records Access and Management Act. (2/1/02)
	SB 61	Modifies the Government Records Access and Management Act to provide that certain records related to explosives may be classified as protected. (3/15/02)
VA	HB 664	Reports of diseases by physicians and laboratory directors that may be caused by exposure to an agent or substance that has the potential for use as a weapon will be held confidential and not subject to the Freedom of Information Act. (1/10/02)
	HB 700	Plans to prevent or respond to terrorist activity; engineering and architectural drawings; operational, procedural, tactical planning or training manuals; or staff meeting minutes or other records, the disclosure of which would reveal surveillance techniques, personnel deployments, alarm or security systems or technologies, or operational and transportation plans or protocols, are exempted freedom of information requirements. (4/6/02)

possible terrorist attacks. With no access to existing plans, threat assessments, or the discussions that officials might have, citizens are left with little to ensure preparedness except faith. A fundamental check on the actions of government is undermined as public entities increasingly cloak themselves in secrecy in an attempt to achieve security.

At least two states have actually improved existing open record laws. Pennsylvania approved legislation in June 2002 that increased the public's access to records and made the government more accountable for handling requests for information. Specifically, the changes to the law require the state to respond to requests within ten days, mandate written explanations when requests are rejected, and provide penalties for violations. In the past, the state could refuse or simply ignore requests without the risking any negative consequence. Similarly, New Jersey passed a law in January 2002 that requires the state to respond to requests for information within seven working days.

Driver's License Requirements

In the wake of September 11, states also began to examine how they were managing the issuance of identification cards. This is largely a result of the high-profile discovery that many of the nineteen terrorists involved in the attacks were carrying state-issued forms of identification. Several obtained these documents using false identities while others used their own names. This scenario certainly encouraged consideration of reforms and increased awareness of the important role that issuing agencies might play in law enforcement endeavors.

One of the more common legislative remedies involves tying the expiration of a person's driver's license or identification card to the expiration of those documents that allow them to be in this country (See Table 6.4). In fact, at least eight states (Florida, Iowa, Kentucky, Louisiana, New Jersey, Ohio, South Carolina, and Virginia) have approved new laws that tie termination dates to that of legal presence. However, Kentucky's new law actually limits the validity of a state-issued card to no more than one year, but noncitizens would be eligible to apply for renewal. Mississippi has considered similar legislation, but these efforts to set a one-year expiration date failed early in 2002. Most of the other states listed in Table 6.4 have set limits of two to four years.

The second general area of activity involves changes to the requirements necessary to obtain a driver's license or identification card (See Table 6.4). For the most part, the changes have made the requirements more stringent. In Colorado and Florida the new laws prohibit the use of identification cards from other states that may issue cards to persons who are not lawfully in the United States. Ohio has forbidden cards that it issues to noncitizens for use in obtaining licenses in other states. The new law in Iowa requires foreign nationals to show Immigration and Naturalization Service (INS) documents to get a state identification card. In the past, only a social security number or

Table 6.4: Post-9/11 Driver's License Restrictions

State	Legislation	Description
CO	SB 112	Requires an applicant for a driver's license or identification card to provide further proof that he or she is lawfully in the United States if the applicant submits to the division of motor vehicles within the department of revenue, as proof of age or identity, a driver's license or identification card from a state that issues licenses or identification cards to persons who are not lawfully in the United States. (1/25/02)
CT	HB 5759	Allows the motor vehicles commissioner, within available appropriations, to require that new license and permit applicants be fingerprinted. (6/03/02)
FL	SB 520	Requires all changes of names and addresses by foreign nationals to be done in person rather than by mail. Expiration of identification is limited to two or four years, or expiration of documents, whichever is shorter depending on classification. Requires country of birth on application. Licenses and identification from other states is only valid if document requirements are similar to Florida. (5/15/02)
IA	SF 2192	Foreign nationals are required to show Immigration and Naturalization documents (rather than a work permit or social security card) to obtain a license. Licenses and cards issued to foreign nationals temporarily present in the United States shall only be issued for the length of time the foreign national is authorized to be present, not to exceed two years. (4/04/02)
KY	HB 188	Driver's license will expire when visa expires or after one year, whichever is shorter. (4/9/02)
	HB 189	Requires all new applicants and persons initially renewing a commercial driver's license (CDL) to undergo a state and national criminal background check. Allows a nonresident to be issued a CDL instruction permit and CDL. (4/5/02)
	HB 190	Requires all persons applying for a license to run a commercial driver training school, or be an instructor at the school, to undergo a state and national criminal history background check; requires applicants to submit fingerprints to the state police.

Table 6.4 (continued)

State	Legislation	Description
LA	SB 89	Creates the crime of operating a motor vehicle without lawful presence in the United States and provides for the issuance and cancellation of driver's license to alien students and nonresident aliens. (4/16/02)
NJ	SB 2708	Fixes driver's license and identification card expiration to end of legal presence in the United States. Director may refuse to grant a license if there is reason to suspect any identification documents are false until they are verified. (1/8/02)
NM	HB 135	Other documents may be accepted during the application process instead of social security number. (2/28/2002)
OH	SB 184	Makes all licenses issued to temporary residents nonrenewable and may not be relied upon to obtain a license in another state. Nonrenewable license expires on same date as legal presence document. (2/4/02)
SC	HB 4670	Driver's licenses issued to persons who are not lawful permanent residents of the U.S. will expire on same date as legal presence document. Allows persons with valid Immigration and Naturalization, Department of Justice, or Department of State documents to obtain or renew identification. (5/28/02)
VA	HB 415	Requires applicants for driver's licenses and special identification cards to submit documentary proof of their name, date of birth, and Virginia residency. Incorporated by HB 638.
	HB 14	Requires legal presence in the United States to obtain a license or identification card and ties expiration date to the date of legal presence. Incorporated by HB 638
	HB 638	Prohibits the use of immigration visas and written statements for proof of Virginia residency. Allows for individuals under the age of 19 to show proof of their parent's residency as proof of their own. (4/7/02)

work permit was required. Similarly, Virginia now disallows the use of immigration visas and written statements as evidence of Virginia residency. Interestingly, Florida requires all name and address changes by foreign nationals to be completed in person. Lastly, Kentucky now requires all new applicants for a commercial drivers license (CDL) and those seeking to run a CDL school to undergo a state and national criminal background check.

Iowa's new law has managed to raise serious civil liberties concerns. Once the bill was passed, the Iowa Department of Transportation interpreted the law as authorizing the creation of cards that single out noncitizens by marking their licenses in red capital letters: "Nonrenewable—Documentation Required."[17] The Iowa Civil Liberties Union has compared the new rule to a "Scarlet Letter" or the Star of David, which was used by the Nazis to identify Jews. A similar situation has developed in Minnesota. Specifically, after the state legislature rejected an effort to reform management of identification cards, Minnesota Department of Transportation officials chose to develop new administrative rules to address basic security concerns. They created a requirement to stamp noncitizen licenses with their visa expiration date and the words "Status Check." As in Iowa, civil libertarian groups are concerned about the consequences of categorizing portions of the population that might be particularly susceptible to discrimination.[18]

Although most activity has leaned toward the creation of more stringent requirements, a few states have actually opened the opportunity of having valid identification to new groups of noncitizens. New Mexico, for instance, now allows for a range of identification documents, like passports, when applying for a driver's license or identification card. In the past, applicants were required to have a social security number and, subsequently, many contract workers and international students were not eligible. South Carolina has actually redefined residency to include all legal noncitizens, and the legislature in California has sent a bill that eliminates an existing requirement for a social security number to the governor for consideration.

Encouraging Patriotism

The emotional and political context created by the terrorist attacks also supported the development of legislative attempts to promote patriotism in the states. In some cases, states embraced new requirements regarding either the pledge of allegiance in educational facilities or the display of the national flag. In other instances, laws were passed involving the posting of the national motto "In God We Trust" in public buildings. These initiatives were often desirable because they both appeared to cater to popular sentiment and did not involve significant appropriations. Overall, at least fifteen states passed what we might identify as patriotic legislation (See Table 6.5).

Of the general areas of activity, the new laws involving the pledge of allegiance and the national motto raise the most obvious concerns about

Table 6.5: Post-9/11 State Legislation Promoting Patriotism

State	Legislation	Description
AZ	SB 1055	Associations shall not prohibit the outdoor display of the American flag on a person's property if the flag is displayed in a respectful and honorable manner. (4/29/02)
CT	HB 5425	Requires boards of education to develop a policy allowing for time each school day for students to recite the pledge of allegiance. Does not require any person to recite the pledge. (6/7/02)
IL	SB 1634	Requires public high schools to lead students in the pledge every day. (7/3/02)
IN	SCR 3	Indiana General Assembly strongly encourages all public schools in Indiana to teach the Pledge of Allegiance and to conduct Pledge ceremonies on a regular basis. (2/4/02)
MI	HB 5091	Encourages all state agencies and units of local government to post the motto "In God We Trust" in or on public buildings. (12/20/01)
MS	SB 2321	Pledge of allegiance required every day during the first hour of class. Participation is voluntary.(7/02)
MO	SB 718	Requires the pledge to be recited at least once a week in public schools. (7/02)
	SB 918	Exempts displays of the U.S. flag from statutes and ordinances. (2/4/02)
NH	HB 1446	The New Hampshire School Patriot Act II instructs school districts to authorize a period of time during the school day for the recitation of the pledge of allegiance. Pupil participation shall be voluntary and students may silently stand or remain seated but must respect the rights of those pupils participating. (5/18/02)
RI	HR 7404	Resolution that encourages all homeowner associations and landlords to obey the law and allow residents and tenants to exercise their lawful right to display the flag of the United States. (2/7/02)
SD	SB 94	The right to post the United States flag shall not be limited or infringed upon in any public school classroom, public school building, at any public school event, or on any public school uniform. The right to recite the pledge of allegiance to the flag of the United States shall not be limited or infringed upon, and the national anthem may be sung during any school day or school event. (2/27/02)

Table 6.5 (continued)

State	Legislation	Description
TN	SB 2599	Requires the daily recitation of the pledge of allegiance in each classroom in the school system in which a flag is displayed. Districts are encouraged to have a flag in each classroom. Pupils not participating may silently stand or remain seated but shall be required to respect the rights of those pupils electing to participate. (7/3/2002)
UT	HB 79	All public schools shall post the motto "In God We Trust" in a prominent location. (3/18/02))
VA	SB 608	All public schools shall post the motto "In God We Trust" in a prominent location. (5/17/02)
VT	SJR 90	Urging that all schools and classes open each day with a pledge to the flag. (2/4/02)
WA	SB 6389	Authorizing placement of U.S. flags on school buses. (3/12/02)

civil liberties. Of the states listed in Table 6.5, nine approved legislation regarding the recitation of the pledge of allegiance. The new standards in Connecticut, Illinois, Mississippi, New Hampshire, and Tennessee require primary and secondary schools to lead students in the pledge every day. The other states set a weekly mandate (Missouri), encourage pledge ceremonies (Indiana and Vermont), or declare that the right to recite will not be limited (South Dakota). In each case, participation is voluntary.

The pledge of allegiance is of interest because of the recent ruling by the United States Court of Appeals for the Ninth Circuit declaring the pledge of allegiance unconstitutional. In *Newdow v. U.S. Congress,* the court found on June 26, 2002 that the words "under God" violated the First Amendment's prohibition of state endorsement of religion. Specifically, the opinion declared that when Congress added the phrase in question to the pledge in 1954, they infringed upon the provision that prohibits the passage of a law respecting the establishment of religion.[19] Under incredible public pressure, the author of the opinion (Alfred T. Goodwin) suspended his own ruling so that the entire Ninth circuit could review the case.[20] Regardless, for the time being the pledge has become a rather controversial topic that raises civil libertarian concerns.

The activity regarding the national motto also raises concerns about the role of the state in religious matters. The phrase "In God We Trust" was approved as the national motto in 1956.[21] More recently, many groups have recently advocated displaying the motto in public schools as an "acceptable" display of both patriotism and religious heritage.[22] A clear precedent was set prior to September 11, when Mississippi passed a law on March 23, 2001 stating that all public schools "shall" post the motto in each classroom, cafeteria, and auditorium. Following the attacks, both Virginia and Utah passed laws requiring each public school to post the phrase in a prominent location. In Michigan, state agencies and units of local governments are now encouraged to display the statement. One concern with these developments is that it represents an attempt to undermine the separation of church and state. In the case of schools, opponents could view it as compelling a captive audience of children to read a statement of religious doctrine.

The remaining pieces of patriotic legislation listed in Table 6.5 involve attempts by states to encourage the display of the national flag. Arizona now prohibits local associations from denying persons the opportunity to fly the flag on their property if it is done in a "respectful and honorable" manner. Similarly, the state of Missouri exempted the display of the flag from local provisions. Other states simply encouraged schools to display the flag in classrooms (Tennessee) or reminded landlords and homeowner associations that tenants and residents have an existing right to fly the flag (Rhode Island). Lastly, the state of Washington approved a new law allowing U.S. flags to be placed on school buses. These efforts do not represent relevant civil libertarian concerns.

Conclusion

Overall, we found that the response of the states to the terrorist attacks was limited. Any expectations involving sweeping programmatic attempts to enhance homeland security have largely gone unmet. Similarly, concerns about unwarranted infringements on basic civil liberties by state governments have generally not materialized. Despite the remarkable nature of the event, states have chosen to respond with very few dollars and a great deal of caution.

A partial explanation of this outcome rests on the fact that many states operated within severe financial constraints. In fact, at least forty-three states experienced budget shortfalls during the 2002 fiscal year that together total nearly forty billion dollars.[23] New spending on homeland security efforts would, as a result, often take place within the context of a deficit and likely involve raising taxes, shifting resources, or relying on federal dollars. Additionally, the midterm election magnified the significance of fiscal choices and, to the extent voters oppose efforts to raise more revenue or shift resources, further discouraged more ambitious endeavors.

Ultimately, the states chose to dedicate a small portion of their budgets to homeland security and relied heavily on federal dollars. Specifically, of the 6.1 billion dollars state and local units will spend in this regard, 4.8 billion will come from the federal government. The remaining 1.3 billion dollars represents only one-tenth of one percent of state and local expenditures for the year.[24] Not surprisingly, eighty percent of the homeland security offices we surveyed feel their ability to respond has been substantially limited due to monetary constraints.²⁵ Other factors mentioned as limiting response include: the lack of coordination/direction from the federal government, lack of public concern over the perceived threat, lack of national standards, lack of personnel, and the lack of personnel with necessary expertise.

In regards to civil liberties, the legislative actions of the states were measured and cautious. To be sure, a few states have approved laws in the policy areas we examined (electronic surveillance, open-access laws, identification cards, and laws promoting patriotism) that raise serious civil libertarian concerns. These actions represent exceptions to a more common approach characterized by constraint. Interestingly, eighty percent of the American Civil Liberties Union affiliates we surveyed felt that state responses were less aggressive than they expected. Additionally, ninety percent viewed federal actions as more threatening to civil liberties than state efforts.²⁶

Overall, the aftermath of September 11, 2001 has left the states struggling to create new structures to deal with homeland security, coordinate the efforts of all the levels of government, and make citizens feel safer, with virtually no new money in a very short time span. According to John Nagy at Stateline.org, state budget constraints, the slow pace of the federal government in providing funds and guidance along with agency turf battles and neglected public health systems have left little room for creative thinking and cutting edge initiatives in this area.²⁷ He points out that this does not mean that states are not getting things done, but that the name of the game is keeping up, rather than getting ahead.

Notes

1. The survey instruments can be found at http://www.coop.eku.edu/KendraStewart/WebPages/index.htm. Because of time and space limitations, you will not find a conclusive list of all the responses in each of the states. However, you will find several tables summarizing state responses and references as to where you can locate more detailed information. We are also not attempting to evaluate the effectiveness of any of these programs or policies. Program evaluation requires in-depth analysis and data collection that extends over a period of time. Although this analysis would be both beneficial and interesting, it would be incomplete due to the short amount of time most of these state programs have been around.
2. Dave McIntyre, *Waiting for Godot's Strategy,* ANSER Institute for Homeland Security, May 13, 2002. Available at http://www.homelandsecurity.org/hls/commentary/HLSCommentary19May2002.htm.
3. Office of Homeland Security, *State and Local Actions for Homeland Security,* July 2002, p.1. Available at http://www.whitehouse.gov/homeland/stateandlocal.
4. Ben Canada, CRS Report RL31490, *Report for Congress: The Department of Homeland Security: State and Local Preparedness Issues,* August 14, 2002.
5. Ben Canada, CRS Report RL31227, *Terrorism, Preparedness: Selected Federal Assistance Programs,* March 13, 2002.
6. Ben Canada, CRS Report RL31490, p. 3.

7. Ibid.
8. Ibid.
9. Ibid.
10. John Nagy, "State Anti-Terrorism Chief Plays Unclear Role," Stateline.org, September 11, 2002. Available at http://www.stateline.org/stateline/?pa= story&sa=showStoryInfo&id=259023.
11. Stateline.org, The Pew Center on the States, "State of the States 2001." Contact Stateline.org for a hard copy.
12. Throughout the research process, we relied heavily on the various state legislative websites to track the status and final text of the bills we were tracking. In addition, Statescape's website (statescape.com) and the National Conference of State Legislature's report, entitled *Protecting Democracy: America's Legislatures Respond* (April 2002), served as valuable resources.
13. *Katz v. United States,* 389 U.S. 347 (1967).
14. U.S. Constitution, Fourth Amendment.
15. Taylor Humphrey, *The Harris Poll no. 49,* October 3, 2002. Available at http:// www.harrisinteractive.com/harris_poll/index.asp?PID=260.
16. Charles Doyle, CRS Report RS21203, *Report for Congress: The USA PATRIOT Act,* April 2002.
17. William Petroski, "Licenses Denoting Citizens Criticized," *Des Moines Register,* 15 August 2002.
18. Sheryl Jean, "Driver's License Rules Spur Suit," *St. Paul Pioneer Press,* 22 July 2002, p. B1.
19. *Newdow v. United States,* 292 F.3d 597 (9th Cir. 2002).
20. David Greenberg, "The Pledge of Allegiance" *Slate,* 28 June 2002. Available at http://slate.msn/?msn.com/?id=2067499.
21. "National Motto," 36 U.S.C. Sect. 186 (1954).
22. To date, the federal judiciary has supported the constitutional legitimacy of the national motto. Please see *Aronow v. United States,* 432 F.2d 242 (9th Cir. 1970).
23. Darrell Preston, "States, Cities Spend Less on Security Than Expected, Fed Says," *Bloomberg News,* 9 September 2002.
24. Ibid.
25. All fifty state Homeland Security Directors surveyed with a 40 percent response rate.
26. All fifty state ACLU directors surveyed with a 25 percent response rate.
27. John Nagy, "Security Push Discourages Innovation," Stateline.org, October 23, 2002. Available at http://www.stateline.org/stateline/?pa=story&sa= showStoryInfo&id=266675.

zation will be significantly interrupted. Critical policy authority and decision making will shift to the federal government—a sort of reinvigorated
centralization—as a result. To consider the potential for such a reinvigoration
of federal authority it is useful to think about two key dimensions of any
policy domain, including one like transportation policy. First, September 11
has altered the *political* imperatives surrounding the distribution of authority in a federal system in that arguing for greater federal authority is now
politically tenable in a broader variety of policy domains. Second, the
attacks made clear a *management* imperative for greater coordination of
policy action and response, which likely means enhanced authority for the
federal government to direct subunit governmental action. Both of these are
possible given the introduction of a security dimension into policy areas
where that link was previously perceived to be less obvious.

It is apparent on its face that greater centralized authority in the federal
government has important consequences for American politics. Among the
most salient questions is: What does the exercise of expanded federal
authority—in response to perceived security threats—mean for civil liberties
in the United States? The question is relevant to any number of policy
domains, transportation being only one of many. But because we are
witnessing shifts in the locus of key decision making from state and local
authorities and the private sector to the federal government, it is useful to
tease out what changes in administrative authority will likely mean for
important aspects of citizens' public lives. Generally speaking, under conditions of war and crisis, democratic governments, sometimes in systematic
fashion, limit civil liberties and rights. In the United States, the public has
traditionally accepted such infringement on civil liberties as a necessary cost
that citizens must bear as a consequence of an immediate threat or crisis.
Immediately following September 11, national security concerns trumped
civil libertarian protections in most major public opinion polls, as most
social segments quickly rallied behind President Bush's war on international
and domestic terrorism. Such a rally effect supporting the federal government's ability to use expanded authority carries with it the risk that
inconsistent governmental treatment for certain categories of individuals
and dissenting groups could viewed as acceptable in regulating air travel.[2]

In this chapter, we address the issue of reinvigorated federal authority and
what that might mean for the related issues of public management and civil
liberties in the United States. We do so by examining one aspect of the most
immediate legislative response to September 11, the creation of the Transportation Security Administration (TSA). Examining the creation of the TSA
and how it is designed to function in terms of securing U.S. airports speaks to
the related concerns of the management of a more centralized administrative
authority and its consequences. The chapter is organized into three main
sections. We begin by discussing public management trends in the pre–
September 11 context in order to demonstrate how the creation of the TSA
speaks to broader issues of authority distribution in the U.S. system. We then
examine increased federal centralization of transportation security as a

security response to the public's demand that the federal government prevent terrorism. Here we contend that because of newly perceived security threats, there exists a discernible propensity for administrative centralization. In the next section, we analyze the implications of the TSA and the public's demand for increased security at U.S. airports. In doing so, we tackle the subject of what the exercise of increased federal authority might mean for the civil liberties of the air traveling public.

Devolution, Privatization, and Reinvention

Three linked trends in public policy and administrative management provide a backdrop to the airport screeners debate alluded to in the introduction, and to our assessment of transportation policy and civil liberties in the wake of September 11. While the federal government's presence in the national economy and other aspects of society steadily increased with the panoply of New Deal and Great Society programs, centralized federal authority has waned over the past several decades. The election of Ronald Reagan placed a great deal of political emphasis on states' rights and the devolution of federal authority; promoting limitations on federal authority was a key part of that administration's policy agenda.[3] A combination of service delivery privatization and "contracting out" became more prevalent since economic and budgetary crises at all levels of government in the 1970s and 1980s.[4] Perhaps more important, placing significant constraints on government activity in terms of direct service provision emerged as a broader philosophic movement.[5] This can be seen in part by a managerial reform movement emphasizing a less hierarchical and more "customer-friendly" federal bureaucracy that became a major governmental reform initiative of the Clinton administration, which was not otherwise ideologically opposed to activist government.[6] These trends have created pronouncements of a "new public management" paradigm where, above all else, government authority is more diffused among subunits of the central government, with less distinguishable lines of governmental and private authority in the conduct and provision of public program outputs and benefits.

The devolution of federal authority has continued steadily over the past two decades or more in a wide variety of program areas. This shift in policymaking authority has been an explicit policy choice that in part reflects the philosophical perspective that state and local government is more appropriately situated to deal with most policy questions.[7] This argument earned greater resonance as state governments' administrative capacity improved.[8] Noting the devolution trend of the past several decades serves our purposes since it is, at its core, defined by a shift in the locus of policymaking authority from federal officials to state and local officials.

Related to the devolving of policymaking authority to state and local government is the issue of privatization of government service delivery. Technically, while privatization might only be used to define a government activity that is given over wholly to the private sector (load shedding), it is more popularly used to indicate that the "provision of a public good or service is assigned, usually by contract, to a third party."[9] A discussion of such a privatization trend at all levels of government is beyond our scope here. However, the key point is that the idea of "contracting out" has gained considerable popularity since privatization is a more efficient mechanism of service delivery.[10] Contracting service delivery, along with devolved authority, points to both a further diminution of direct federal control over policy implementation choices and a blurring of governmental and nongovernmental authority in the conduct of a public policy.

Finally, the third linked trend is the so-called "reinvention" movement—the reconfiguration of management practices at the federal government.[11] The Clinton administration's National Performance Review (NPR) gave voice to a largely customer service–oriented logic of running the federal government. The basic principles of the NPR were: streamlining (i.e., cutting back on) federal regulations; enhancing customer service by gathering information on client preferences and competing for business when possible; promoting bureaucratic entrepreneurship by decentralizing decision making, decreasing supervisory personnel, and giving more authority to lower-level employees, and, finally, reducing the scope of government activity by reducing duplication, reengineering programs to reduce costs, etc. The general thrust of the reinvention movement is a decentralizing one; rigid hierarchy creates an ineffectual, nonresponsive, and even a moribund bureaucracy. The logic of the reinvention movement is that to cope with such problems it is necessary to reshape authority patterns, missions, and task patterns toward more flexible and responsive, and hence ultimately more effective, organizations.

Together these three trends in public management and policymaking authority distribution have created a model where the central government's raison d'être is characterized, or conceived of, as primarily being a "service-coordinating" entity with limited direct program control.[12] Of course the federal government has always had limits on its capacity for direct service provision and has typically relied heavily on state and local government units to implement and administer policy goals and programs. However, by the late 1990s, and certainly prior to September 11, the argument for an even greater decentralization of bureaucratic authority at the expense of the central government had gained a great deal of currency. In essence, the more direct engagement flowing from the New Deal model of governance was argued to be obsolete. The new public management perspective argues that central governments (or any government unit for that matter) should be and are increasingly oriented toward assisting in the management and distribution of society's resources with minimal administrative formalism and greater bureaucratic flexibility and partnership with the private sector.[13]

September 11 may ultimately prove to matter little to these interrelated trends, but we think there is a compelling reason to think that is not the case. Strictly from a public management perspective, the significance of the attacks lies with the idea that they suddenly and abruptly created a new centralizing imperative in both an administrative and a political sense. This is the case in areas like transportation policy that heretofore had not been seen as areas likely to produce calls for greater central government control. The critical issue is this: to the extent that a policy domain is now viewed as possessing a meaningful national security dimension, there will exist defensible political claims for greater authority exercised by the federal government. At the same time, the necessity of coordinated action to reduce certain types of redundancies and to minimize weak links in any integrated system of security precautions also creates an imperative for administrative actions directed by the federal government.

Initial responses to September 11 bear this out: Executive Order 13228, creating the Office of Homeland Security, and then subsequent legislative efforts to refashion that office as a department supports both this political and administrative logic of expanding federal executive authority (i.e., greater centralized authority in the federal executive branch). The creation of the Transportation Security Administration within the Department of Transportation likewise follows the same pattern. The TSA was created to produce greater centralized management capacity and clearer lines of authority in civil aviation security programs. The political dynamics of opposition to such was quickly overwhelmed by the perceived legitimacy of federal action to deal with terrorism as a primary—or the primary—national security concern. To the extent that terrorism endures as a tangible security threat, as the Bush administration would have Americans believe, then these twin imperatives provide a powerful counterpoise to the trends of new public management (i.e., flatter government bureaucracies that are considerably less formalized/routinized).

As our examination of air transportation security will show, the initial and likely enduring effect of September 11 is an important reinvigoration of federal authority in making and administering public policies. A major element in this reinvigoration has been the federal government's recognition of security as the primary motivation in this centralization imperative, which will be explained in the next section.

The Security Dimension as a Centralization Imperative

The introduction of national security concerns is highly salient to the broad domain of transportation policy, though previously this was not a major matter of emphasis in most issue-specific areas. For instance, in addition to airport security, the management systems in place for transportation issues like regulating hazardous materials (hazmat) transport or seaport surveillance and inspection heretofore were characterized by significant administrative fragmentation with relatively little emphasis on security considerations.[14]

Considering the security implications with respect to the management systems for such transportation issues, each with significant administrative authority fragmentation, points to an apparent need for greater coordination and hence an enhanced federal management role. Coordination is necessary in the hazmat transport area because the system in place does not possess sufficiently clear lines of authority among the various federal agencies involved and, in turn, among state and local governments that play a part in implementation.

It is important at this point to discuss how emergency situations are typically managed by drawing a clear distinction between consequence management and crisis management systems. Consequence management "addresses the effects of an incident on lives and property. It includes measures to protect public health and safety, treat persons injured, mitigate impacts, restore essential government services, and provide emergency relief. . . . "[15] The Federal Emergency Management Agency is oriented toward consequence management and is the lead federal agency in this regard in most disaster cases. However, consequence management should not be conflated with crisis management, which can be defined this way: "crisis management focuses on causes and involves activities to address the threat or occurrence of a terrorist incident. It is predominantly a law enforcement and intelligence function that includes measures to anticipate, prevent, and resolve a threat or act of an incident on lives and property."[16] This distinction is a critical one in terms of thinking about how to manage an administrative response to counteract terrorist threats. Consequence management is likely quite compatible with both the political and management orientation of a decentralized governance model (the new public management perspective). But on a practical management basis, crisis management likely will necessitate greater centralization in both standard setting and basic coordination of government activity at all levels. While consequence management at the federal level is reasonably well outlined, there is no apparent crisis management system (a prevention or security system) in place at present.[17] Given the reasonable potential of the hijacking of hazardous materials in transport to be used as a tool in a terrorist attack, this is a glaring policy deficiency. To remedy that will require greater delineation of security tasks among the respective government units by some authority within the federal government, whoever that might be. In other words, a clear management incentive exists for stronger central authority to ensure greater coordination among all government units involved in the *crisis management* aspect of transportation issues.

Such steps have yet to be realized, but we consider this a rather likely eventuality, especially given both the compelling logic of doing so and the direction of policy response since the attacks. The two immediate policy responses to the attacks, the passage of the Aviation Transportation Security Act and issuance of Executive Order 13228, intimate as much. Both responses reflect the logic of centralization necessary to confront policy challenges associated with external threats like potential terrorist attacks.

The Homeland Security Office was created for the expressed purpose of coordinating federal activities relevant to domestic security. Similarly, the TSA was created expressly as a centralizing tool since it is responsible for managing security issues in all modes of transportation. Both actions were designed to create stronger federal executive authority and capacity for dealing with a security threat. As such, whatever opposition existed to the politics of expanding federal authority was neutralized by public demand for concerted federal action.

The Bush administration initially opposed the idea but then reversed itself and announced that the president would ask Congress to create a cabinet office for the coordination of homeland security. Combining agencies such as the Secret Service, U.S. Customs, and the TSA into one cabinet department would serve to centralize security information systems and bureaucratic control over agency behavior. Tasks that were formally spread out among twenty-two federal agencies and eighty-eight congressional committees and subcommittees would be combined into one centralized command and control center. The proposal for the Department of Homeland Security suggests that it will have several main functions: "information analysis and infrastructure protection; chemical, biological, radiological, nuclear and related countermeasures; border and transportation security; emergency preparedness and response; and coordination of other parts of the federal government, with state and local governments, and with the private sector."[18]

However, the new cabinet secretary can receive only limited amounts of "raw" data without direct approval from the president. Whatever the results, it seems clear that Bush's proposal for the creation of a new cabinet department signals a move toward coordination and consolidation of security resources at the federal level. Whatever the practical merit of the move, it signals a shift toward greater federal authority. That the Bush administration abandoned its earlier opposition and quickly garnered House support suggests politically that ideological opponents of expanded federal authority have ceded considerable ground on the matter. Of course, our larger point is that security resources and security issues touch a vast array of public programs under current circumstances, such as the several policy areas alluded to above within the broader policy domain of transportation.

For instance, in terms of seaport security, initial responses to the threat of terrorism borne by September 11 display a shift to a stronger assertion of federal management practices. The newly created TSA in June 2002 awarded over $90 million in grants to enhance seaport security at some fifty-one ports. The TSA, along with the Maritime Administration (MARAD), specified and reviewed grant applications expressly on the basis of ameliorating the types of security deficiencies discussed above. Similarly, Captain William G. Schubert, the maritime administrator, in congressional testimony, outlined Department of Transportation (DOT) and MARAD's plan for exercising certain controls over both military and nonmilitary ports to promote port readiness.[19] This is not an entirely new activity but has increased in scope as a result the terrorist threat. This simply underscores how federal authority potentially can, and has, asserted itself as a means of addressing security issues within the broad transportation policy domain.

The Transportation Security Administration: Security Meets Liberty

The primary mission of the Transportation Security Administration is to "protect the nation's transportation systems to ensure freedom of movement for people and commerce."[20] By creating the new agency, the federal government was assuming direct responsibility for transportation security and safety, especially air travel. According to President Bush:

> A new team of federal security managers, supervisors, law enforcement officers and screeners will ensure all passengers and carry-on bags are inspected thoroughly and effectively. The new security force will be well-trained, made up of U.S. citizens. And if any of its members do not perform, the new Under Secretary will have full authority to discipline or remove them. At the same time, we will adopt strict new requirements to screen checked baggage, to tighten security in all other areas of airports, and to provide greater security for travelers by bus and by train.[21]

Organizationally, the TSA was placed within the Department of Transportation; its director assumes the formal title of undersecretary of transportation for security and serves for a period of five years. All transportation security activities are managed by the TSA director (undersecretary), who is advised by a Transportation Security Advisory Board (TSAB).

While the TSA is responsible for securing all modes of transportation, its main goal is protecting air travelers in the nation's over 400 major airports. It is entrusted with regulating two specific areas of private and commercial air travel: passenger screening and cargo screening. The TSA also possesses law enforcement powers with federal sky marshals and works through a newly established Transportation Security Network Program (TSNP) with other federal law enforcement agencies, such as the Federal Bureau of Investigation and the Bureau of Alcohol, Tobacco, and Firearms, to collect and analyze intelligence.[22] The duties of the TSA are broader than aviation security and its activities are more than screening as its job includes assessing threats to the national transportation system and preventing disruption by terrorists.[23]

Politically, as a new bureaucratic organization, the TSA must overcome two major hurdles if it wishes to be effective: 1) creating itself within the political framework established by the president and 2) devising a system for stopping terrorist threats to civil and commercial air transportation. At the outset, there was internal tension over the TSA's mission, with some officials skilled in law enforcement clashing with members of Congress, who demanded better customer service. TSA's first chief John W. Magaw and the

TSAB were frequently at odds with key members of Congress, the White House, and Magaw's boss, Secretary of Transportation Norman Mineta.[24] The considerable confusion over the TSA's responsibilities and obligations on the day of the most violent terrorist attack since September 11 (on July 4, 2002, when an Egyptian terrorist opened fire at the El Al counter of LAX, killing two persons) underscores how, after nearly a year of building a new federal agency to take over airport security, numerous constraints on improving security management still exist.[25]

For instance, while a handful of airports are beginning to see uniformed TSA screeners at checkpoints, the TSA is struggling to keep up with hiring, and many airports still use the same private screening companies that were in place a year ago. The government has ordered sophisticated bomb-detection machines to scan luggage, but the program quickly fell behind schedule. Early indications were that cargo security had not improved.[26] Although the federal government is developing a new computer system to identify people with "questionable backgrounds," it is dependent on antiquated software that assumes terrorists book flights by paying with cash, buy one-way tickets, or board flights just prior to takeoff.[27]

There is no question that the TSA has a difficult task to perform, as there are legitimate security concerns. To facilitate the process, and with its efforts directed at preventing further terrorist attacks, Congress assumed a completely new approach to aviation security with the TSA. Past proposals suggesting more active federal control over airport security that had been defeated by airline and/or airport interests have been adopted and are now enforced with deadlines.[28] For example, flimsy cockpit doors will be secured, all checked luggage scanned, airport screeners will be given financial incentives to do their jobs well, and attendants and pilots will get advanced training to deal with hijackers.[29]

The Preeminence of Security at U.S. Airports

Given the specific nature of the September 11 terrorist attacks, airport and airline security came under intense scrutiny with a central question being how best to regulate and reorganize aviation security. Prior to the passage of the 2001 Aviation Transportation Security Act, responsibility for civil aviation security was located within the Federal Aviation Administration's Office of Civil Aviation Security (CAS). The CAS Civil Aviation Security Strategic Plan, published in April 2001 prior to the terrorist attacks of September 11, enunciates "no successful attacks against U.S. civil aviation" as its goal for its strategic focus on airport and air carrier security.[30] Within the report, the CAS lists the establishment of standards and effective passenger and baggage screening methods as key strategies for achieving this goal. At the time the report was issued, the responsibility for implementing screening of passengers aboard civil airlines fell to the private air carriers themselves, and they generally hired private security firms to implement security screening. While Federal Aviation Regulations (FARs) govern the security of civil airlines and airports, much autonomy is given to individual airports and air carriers in implementing those regulations. The CAS office explains the decentralized system for providing security in the following manner:

> Generally, security FARs establish only broad standards or objectives, so to show specifically how security standards are to be met, airports and air carriers are required to design their own security program, or plan. The Office of Civil Aviation Security must approve the contents of a security program, and once the program is approved, airport and air carrier managers must carry out the mandatory program requirements or face enforcement action. As with a FAR, the security program has the force of law. Special Agents periodically conduct on-site assessments to ensure that the requirements of airport and air carrier security programs are being complied with.[31]

The events of September 11 called into serious question the effectiveness of air carriers in providing adequate passenger and baggage screening. In a report delivered to the Senate Committee on Governmental Affairs and the Subcommittee on Oversight of Governmental Management, Restructuring and the District of Columbia on September 25, 2001, Gerald L. Dillingham, director of physical infrastructure issues for the Government Accounting Office (GAO), suggested that the FAA's CAS initiatives for passenger screening were inadequate and required revision. Specifically, Dillingham noted that screening procedures for passengers and carry-on baggage manifested "significant, long-standing weaknesses" that compromised the security of civil aviation. These weaknesses had been audited by the GAO and the FAA repeatedly and displayed an increasing inability of airport screeners to detect weapons in carry-on luggage and on the persons of undercover agents who were testing the security apparatus. In fact, Dillingham reported "as tests become more realistic and more closely approximate how a terrorist might attempt to penetrate a checkpoint, screeners' ability to detect dangerous objects declines even further."[32] The GAO report highlighted high rates of turnover in screening personnel (averaging 126 percent from May 1998 through April 1999), which is exacerbated by the low pay screeners receive and the relative absence of benefits, to be one of several factors contributing to the poor performance of airline screeners. In addition, insufficient training and standards, combined with a high level of mundane, repetitive work, produce underqualified screeners.

The GAO report outlined a study directed through the House Committee on Transportation and Infrastructure's Subcommittee on Aviation, conducted prior to September 11, that queried airport and airline security personnel on their opinions regarding the best management structure for airport screeners. Four alternatives were identified: locating responsibility with airlines as the current system did, but with the implementation of new certification rules such as those mandated by the Federal Aviation Reauthorization Act of 1996 (for which the GAO noted the FAA had failed to issue final regulations); locating responsibility with individual airports; creating a federal agency to oversee and conduct a national screening program, or creating a federal corporation charged with these same duties but with greater flexibility and autonomy than a federal agency. GAO analysis of the responses suggested that security professionals favored the creation of a federal body to oversee screening because they felt it would increase both screener performance and accountability. However, the current system of airline responsibility, with new rules and certifications, also was seen as a way to increase screener performance. Overall, the GAO report indicated that security professionals in the industry viewed an increased role for federal oversight and coordination as beneficial.[33]

Thus, even prior to September 11, the inadequacies of a decentralized, airline-based system for passenger screening and airline security raised concerns and pointed to the need for stronger regulations at the least, and even perhaps suggested direct federal coordination as a viable policy option. The legislative debate in Congress that followed the events of September 11 highlighted the tension between stronger coordinated management and a type of "contracted-out" service-provision model. Indeed, while a consensus emerged that airport screening was deficient, if not dangerously inept, the core question over remedy focused on that very issue. Two ideological positions shaped debate over whether airport screeners remain employees of private firms hired by the airlines to implement the stricter regulations or whether the federal government would assume responsibility for screening passengers and their baggage at the nation's airports.

In October 2001, the Senate passed the Aviation Transportation and Security Act by a vote of 100 to 0. The act, among other things, provided for the federalization of airport screeners (i.e., the transfer of airport screening duties from airlines and private security firms to federal employees). However, in hindsight, the unanimous vote did mask the political and ideological disagreements that led to the Senate passage and the eventual adoption in the House. In October, CNN reported a pitched battle in the House between the Bush administration, Secretary of Transportation Norman Mineta, and House Republicans, who favored enhanced federal oversight of airport screeners, who would remain employees of private security firms, and House Democrats, who insisted that the federal government assume control over the security industry and directly manage airport screening with a federal workforce.

House Minority Whip Tom Delay underscored the ideological tenor of the security debate: "What the Senate passed is a nationalized system; what we hope to pass is a federalized system."[34] That distinction points to interpretation of federalism that requires a decentralized structure of management as opposed to one that sees "federalization" as an assumption by the federal government of the responsibility and authority to institute direct policy control.

The House passed a GOP version of airport security legislation that required federal oversight of private screeners in early November. After passing through conference committee, the compromised airline security legislation was approved in the House and the Senate on November 16 and signed into law by President Bush in a ceremony at Reagan National Airport on November 19. The major compromises in the legislation that emerged included federalization of airport screeners, meaning that all airport security screeners would be federal employees at the conclusion of a one-year transition period. However, a pilot program installed at five airports would continue to utilize private employees of security firms in an effort to collect data for comparison of the results of the federal and private programs. After three years, airports would have the option of requesting private screeners.

In addition to the question of federal control over airport security screeners and procedures, the passage of the Aviation Transportation Security Act further suggested a conflict between ideology and practical management in the creation of the TSA, located in the DOT, to oversee all transportation security. The TSA would assume the duties of the FAA's Civil Aviation Security Office in administering airport and airline security regulations as well as directly overseeing the newly created federal screening workforce.

As the implementation of the Aviation Transportation Security Act commenced in February 2002, John Magaw, the first chief of the TSA, suggested that a major benefit of the law and the agency it created was the increased coordination and concentration of oversight for airport security screeners. Magaw was even quoted as saying: "You had 60 companies all around the country doing slightly different things, and there was no one oversight or one advisory group, one controlling unit. Now you have that."[35]

At What Expense? The TSA and Profiling

Under the present state of affairs—a perception of ongoing and serious threats to national security—infringement of civil liberties is a potential consequence of the prosecution of the war on terrorism. The responsibilities and activities of the newly created TSA help illustrate this point. Through the TSA, the federal government has sought tighter security restrictions on certain segments of the traveling public via profiling practices and technologies. Its very creation was described by Homeland Security Adviser Tom Ridge and Attorney General John Ashcroft as a welcome shift in priorities for the federal government's approach to regulating travelers, from the prosecution of terrorist acts to the prevention of future attacks with particular profiling techniques.[36] Such a shift, however, carries with it the potential for profound changes to government and the nation—changes that seemingly might alter the boundaries of traditional civil liberties and common notions of law enforcement.

For the TSA, this means that making prevention a priority allows the federal agency to operate with an increased reliance on suspicion, a more frequent use of confidential information, and a more broadly cast policy of secrecy than before. It allows TSA personnel significant latitude in how they handle the arrest, imprisonment, and profiling of suspects. The TSNB has enabled TSA law enforcement agents to obtain and share information about suspected terrorists and potential plots. Expanded utilization of profiling techniques has allowed the TSA a significant degree of latitude in how it handles the tracking, arrest, and imprisonment. Nevertheless, this begs the questions: How well is the TSA protecting the law-abiding citizenry from actual terrorists, and what are the consequences of profiling suspects for individual rights and liberties?

The impact of profiling in the context of air travel security can be seen in individual cases as well as in the broad government policy directives issued in reaction to the September 11 attacks. In one case, the TSA and FBI detained Shakir Ali Baloch, a Pakistani-born Canadian, without formal charges for seven months until the government was able to carry out a deportation order issued two days after his arrest in Queens, when it was deemed he fit the profile of an Al-Qaeda terrorist. In the end, FBI agents and TSA officials cleared him of suspicions concerning his alleged terrorist connections. Another case involved Liban Hussein and his brother, who operated a small money-exchange business for travelers in Boston until December 2001, when the FBI and Treasury Department, acting on a tip by the TSA after Hussein traveled out of Logan airport, froze their assets and labeled them terrorists. Interestingly, there was no physical evidence to support the government's claim. Such cases are troubling reminders that government's sweeping powers to wage war on terror can entrap relatively powerless individuals simply on the basis of "fitting a profile."[37]

As the Bush administration accumulated expansive new transportation security powers, conducted secretive nationwide arrests, and created broad plans for domestic surveillance, several groups expressed concern over the risk that preventing terrorism poses to civil liberties. The American Civil Liberties Union (ACLU), the Center for National Security Studies, and the Center for Constitutional Rights have filed a series of lawsuits challenging the government's antiterrorism policies, particularly opposing the government's secrecy.[38] The TSNB program, for example, has promoted the extensive utilization of secret lists of suspected terrorist and criminal activities to facilitate the gathering of intelligence. The CIA, FBI, and TSA work together to compile the lists, which are used by the president, attorney general, and homeland security adviser to designate people and groups as terrorists.

In addition to lists, current TSA chief James M. Loy has endorsed the use of highly sophisticated tools capable of intruding on individual privacy at airports. The use of face-recognition technology in video cameras—first used at the 2001 Super Bowl in Tampa—placed at airport entrance and exit ways, terminals, and parking lots and garages, is proliferating with few public protests.[39] The cameras match faces in the crowd against photos of criminals and suspected terrorists. They have already been deployed at airports around the nation, including in Boston, Dallas, Fresno, and St. Petersburg-Clearwater. Loy and the TSA are encouraging airlines to install video cameras aboard planes. Jet Blue Airways plans on installing cameras on some of its planes to monitor passenger activity in the cabin from the cockpit. Eventually, the carrier wants to use the cameras to monitor planes in flight from the ground.[40] In August 2002, Boeing announced plans to offer video surveillance cameras near cockpit doors on new planes. Advanced communications technology has been deployed by law enforcement to eavesdrop on cellular communications. The TSA may also utilize sophisticated x-ray devices with biometric technology, which would allow its screeners to "see" through a person's clothing to check for hidden weapons. In fact, the FAA ordered five of these systems in October 2002 for testing.[41]

Furthermore, the TSA has strongly encouraged the airlines to institute a national ID card program and other types of "trusted traveler" or "smart traveler" cards for frequent fliers. Such cards would have photo and computer chips containing fingerprint data or other biometric data (physical and biological characteristics) that could be read at scanners.[42] The Passenger Access Security Solution, developed by a consortium including Electronic Data Systems, is one of the proposed "trusted traveler" or "smart traveler" systems. The system operates according to four principles. First, the traveler submits personal information on a web site or at an airline club. Second, the company that runs the system verifies information such as address, credit card, and employment through publicly available databases. Third, an approved traveler gives a fingerprint, has a retina scan, and is issued a "smart card" that carries the identifying marks to match the card to the user. Fourth, each time the card is used for a trip, the traveler's identity is confirmed, and then his or her name is run through law enforcement and security data bases.[43] A February 28, 2002 survey released by Travelocity.com found that 76 percent of frequent travelers would support such an identification program.[44]

Although the option of such a card might appeal to some groups who say they are discriminated against because they appear to fit the profile of a terrorist, not all support the idea. James Zogby, president of the Arab American Institute, raised two concerns echoed by others: First, the card violates First Amendment protections, and second, the holder of a card could still bring a weapon onto a plane. Arab Americans still face harassment at some airports and will be subject to potentially unconstitutional scrutiny with or without a card.[45]

Nevertheless, the reality is that the same technologies that make it harder for terrorists to hide make it harder for law-abiding citizens to protect their personal privacy. According to Michael Erbschloe of *Computer Economics,* "We're being watched, more and more every day, and that is going to continue to increase. . . . We'll be watched all the time."[46] Nothing has driven demand for high-tech security like the September 11 terrorist attacks. In post–September 11 America, people who would otherwise worry about their privacy while traveling are more willing to brush aside those qualms in exchange for a perceived sense of safety.[47] For example, a January 2002 poll by Zogby International found that 54 percent of Americans favor allowing telephone conversations to be monitored at airports and 80 percent favor allowing video surveillance in terminals and airport restaurants.[48]

Of course, the pertinent question is whether this technology will actually make us safer when traveling by plane. Some say no, that we are giving up our personal privacy and not getting all that much security in return.

According to the San Diego office of the ACLU, "It seems as if Big Brother's much more a welcome member of the family than he was prior to 9/11."[49] Face-recognition technology, for instance, is only as good as its database of people. A terrorist whose face is not in the database simply gets lost in the crowd. In the case of the September 11 attacks, only a handful of the nineteen hijackers were on terrorist wanted lists.

Whatever the technology in use, profiling is seen as the best remedy in this TSA-led security system. "Everyone gets all freaked out when they hear the term profiling," according to a spokesman for the American Association of Airport Executives. "Finding someone who intends to hijack or blow up a plane is like looking for a needle in a haystack, you've got to figure out how to make the haystack smaller."[50] The attributes that subject people to closer scrutiny are secret. Government officials have said that a large part of the system is based on ruling people out; if enough is known about travelers, from their travel history, for example, they are not profiled. While many people believe that a cause for suspicion would be paying cash for a one-way ticket at the last minute, it seems difficult to imagine that sophisticated terrorists would call attention to themselves that way.

Important to note here is that security experts do not trust this existing profiling system enough to make it the sole basis of security. Partly as a result, security checks have a randomness associated with them, with some people selected simply to give terrorists the idea that there is always a chance of being singled out. According to one TSA screener, "randomness adds an element of fairness," since the profiling system does not deliberately take race or religion into account, although this is sometimes a consequence for those who are searched.[51] While the breakdown of who gets searched is secret, the results have not always inspired public confidence in the system. Some of the threats to which airport security screeners pay the closest attention seem distinctly unthreatening to typical passengers. The current profiling system often hones in on the unlikely. In a widely publicized case, a World War II flying ace, on his way to give a speech at West Point, was stopped by a guard who said that his Medal of Honor was a sharp object and couldn't be carried on board. In another instance, an elderly member of Congress from Michigan with an artificial hip was made to strip to his underwear.[52]

Implications for Trends in Administration and Civil Liberties

In spite of long-term trends toward a new public management paradigm of greater administrative decentralization and bureaucratic entrepreneurship, the events of September 11 created imperatives for a more active federal management role in air transportation. In other words, because security was transformed into a primary consideration on a number of transportation-specific policy questions, both political and managerial dynamics made an expansion of federal policy authority necessary. One corollary to this expanded authority is the very real potential for an enduring contraction of individual liberties and rights of the traveling public in the name of security concerns. On the one hand, since homeland and national security are seen as appropriate functional tasks for the national government in the wake of September 11, the introduction of security concerns into transportation policy make that assertion of federal authority seem less problematic and more justifiable for the general public. This dynamic is likely to be sustained as long as terrorism remains a perceived threat. President Bush's rhetoric of a nearly permanent and total war on terrorism and his focus on the nation's threatened disposition is likely to maintain reinvigorated central government authority over transportation security into the future.

On the other hand, the utilization of security as a centralization imperative has already contributed to a transformation in the activities of the federal government and the traveling public. The TSA has been at the center of this nexus between greater federal centralization of air security and the increased utilization of profiling and surveillance. September 11 and the ensuing war on terrorism has produced a preoccupation with internal and external threats to security from particular groups within society, which are often targeted as security risks because of ethnicity, race, political beliefs, or religion. This has been fueled by the present societal tendency toward conformity, a major element in American political behavior in both critical and noncritical periods.[53] Common opinions driven largely by stereotypes and prejudice have been reflected in the TSA's security policies and profiling practices and are widely supported by the public. However, as sociologist Robert Nisbet has suggested, "No nation in history has ever managed permanent war and a permanent military Leviathan at its heart and been able to maintain a truly representative character."[54]

Interestingly, the current state of security preeminence in air transportation policy is in stark contrast to the steady expansion of rights and liberties that has dominated American politics and society since the Vietnam War. The post–September 11 environment that has contributed to public support for profiling by the TSA in particular, and civil rights contraction by the Bush administration in general, harkens back to the cold war, when an anticommunist consensus prevailed in U.S. society, producing significant intolerance toward alleged seditious groups.[55] The Vietnam War shattered this consensus as Americans began expressing a diverse number of opinions concerning domestic and international affairs. September 11 has certainly reversed this trend as the ability to exercise civil liberties has been limited, since it is combined with a nationalism that encourages government contraction of certain liberties. The specific events of September 11 generated a great sense of instability and fear among policymakers and citizens that has legitimized TSA profiling in the name of security.

We have suggested here that the events of September 11 have altered the conventional wisdom that central government authority was on an inevitable path to reformulation and reversed expanding rights and liberties. This is not to say by any means that the new public management paradigm is lost or that individual freedom of travel will return to their pre–September 11 orientation.[56] It is to say instead that insofar as air transportation policy has a security dimension, it is likely that federal executive authority will continue to be increased, with a potential for further governmental limitations on individual rights and liberties.

Notes

1. President George W. Bush, "President Signs Aviation Security Legislation," November 19, 2001. Available at http://www.whitehouse.gov/news/releases/2001/11/20011119-2.html. The specific provisions of the act are set forth in Public Law 107–71, "Aviation and Transportation Security Act of 2001," 49 United States Code 40101. The general goals of the act are twofold: 1) increase effective coordination for security operations, in the areas of policy enforcement, aviation operations, sea and land safety, technological development, information gathering, and strategic intelligence analysis; 2) promote effective management and policy development through rigorous training of new security personnel, streamlined inspection procedures, and tighter security regulations.
2. See Godfrey Hodgson, *America in Our Time* (New York: Vintage Books, 1976) and Jerel A. Rosati, *The Politics of United States Foreign Policy* (Fort Worth, TX: Harcourt Brace, 1999). Even more, during the present post-9/11 period, there exists a social and political propensity toward a state of paranoia and intolerance toward particular groups in conflict with democratic values. See Richard Hofstadter, *The Paranoid Style in American Politics and Other Essays* (New York: Alfred A. Knopf, 1965).
3. John D. Lees, "The Reagan Administration and Intergovernmental Relations: Decentralization and New Federalism," in John D. Lees and Michael Turner, eds., *Reagan's First Four Years: A New Beginning?* (Manchester, UK: Manchester University Press, 1988); Gillian Peel, "The Agenda of the New Right," In Dilys M. Hill, ed., *The Reagan Presidency: An Incomplete Revolution?* (New York: St. Martin's Press, 1990).
4. Irene S. Rubin and Bernard H. Ross, "Explaining the Growth and Contraction of Municipal Services," in B. Guy Peters and Bert A. Rockman, eds., *Agenda for Excellence 2: Administering the State* (New York: Chatham House Publishers Inc., 1996); E. S. Savas, *Privatization: The Key to Better Government* (New York: Chatham House, 1987).
5. Ronald C. Moe, "Managing Privatization: A New Challenge to Public Administration," in B. Guy Peters and Bert A. Rockman, eds., *Agenda for Excellence 2: Administering the State* (New York: Chatham House Publishers Inc., 1996).
6. Donald F. Kettl and John J. DiIulio, Jr., *Inside the Reinvention Machine: Appraising Governmental Reform* (Washington D.C.: The Brookings Institution, 1995).
7. Russell Hanson, "Intergovernmental Relations," in Virginia Gray, Russell L. Hanson, and Herbert Jacob, eds., *Politics in the American States* (Washington D.C.: CQ Press, 1999); Carl Van Horn, "The Quiet Revolution," in Carl Van Horn, ed., *The State of the States* (Washington D.C.: CQ Press, 1996).
8. Ann M. Bowman and Richard C. Kearney, *The Resurgence of the States* (Englewood Cliffs, NJ: Prentice-Hall Publishers, 1986)
9. Moe, "Managing Privatization," 135.
10. See Savas, *Privatization: The Key to Better Government.*
11. David Osbourne and Ted Gaebler, *Reinventing Government* (New York: Addison-Wesley, 1992); For more, see David Osbourne and Peter Plastrik,

Banishing Bureaucracy: The Five Strategies for Reinventing Government (New York: Addison-Wesley, 1996).

12. Donald F. Kettl, "The Transformation of Governance: Globalizations, Devolution, and the Role of Government," *Public Administration Review* 60 (2000): 488–497.

13. Donald F. Kettl, "The Global Revolution in Public Management: Driving Themes, Missing Links," *Journal of Policy Analysis and Management* 16 (1997): 447. Other scholars offer interesting critique of some foundational premises of the "new public management's" manifestation in the United States—the "reinvented government" model. For more, see Joel D. Aberbach and Bert A. Rockman, *In the Web of Politics: Three Decades of the U.S. Federal Executive* (Washington D.C.: Brookings Institution Press, 2000) and Moe, "Managing Privatization."

14. See: Brian J. Gerber, Susan J. Tabrizi, and Elizabeth A. Sanders, "Federalism and Administrative Management Imperatives in Transportation Policy: An Assessment of September 11th effects on Policy-Making Dynamics," paper presented at the 2002 annual meeting of the American Political Science Association, Boston, MA, August 29–September 1, 2002.

15. U.S. General Accounting Office, "Regulatory Programs: Balancing Federal and State Responsibilities for Standard Setting and Implementation," GAO-02-495, 2002, p. 5.

16. Ibid.

17. See "Robert T. Stafford Disaster Relief and Emergency Assistance Act," as amended 42 U.S.C. 5121, *et seq.* For more, visit http://www.fema.gov/rrr/frp/frpbpln.shtm.

18. Analysis for the Homeland Security Act of 2002. For more on the act, see the website http://www.whitehouse.gov/deptofhomeland/analysis/hsl-bill-analysis.pdf.

19. Captain William G. Schubert, Maritime Instructor, U.S. Department of Transportation, "U.S. Representative Christopher Shays (R-CT) Holds Hearing on Seaport Security," Capitol Hill Congressional Hearing of the House Government Reform Committee, Subcommittee on National Security, Congressional Witness Testimony, Washington D.C.: Federal Document Clearing House, July 23, 2002.

20. For more, please visit the website http://www.tsa.gov/agency/about_tsa_index.shtm.

21. President George W. Bush, "President Signs Aviation Security Legislation."

22. Greg Schneider and Sara Kehaulani Goo, "Twin Missions Overwhelmed TSA," *Washington Post*, 3 September 2002, 1.

23. See Public Law 107–71, "Aviation and Transportation Security Act of 2001," 49 United States Code 40101.

24. Schneider and Goo, "Twin Missions Overwhelmed TSA," 1.

25. The event led Mineta to replace Magaw with James M. Loy, the current TSA chief.

26. John Riley, "Taking Liberties," *Newsday*, 15 September 2002, 3.

27. Jason Roberson, "Screeners Handle 'Learning Curve,'" *Dayton Daily News*, 26 September 2002.

28. Natalie Morris, "Keeping Watch: Security Chiefs See No Problem Meeting Federal Deadline to Have Screeners in Place," *State Journal Register*, 15 September 2002, 49; Liz Fedor, "Baggage Screening System Preliminary Wins OK for Funding," *Minnesota Star Tribune*, 7 August 2002, 5B; Brian Williams,

"Airport's Federal Screeners Ready," *Columbus Dispatch,* 27 July 2002, 1D; Daniel Sforza, "Federal Screeners Take Posts at Airports," *Bergen County Record,* 14 August 2002, 1; Matthew L. Wald, "Traces of Terror: Transportation Security," *New York Times,* 19 July 2002, 14.

29. Schneider and Goo, "Twin Missions Overwhelmed TSA," 1.
30. See Federal Aviation Administration, *Civil Aviation Security Strategic Plan 2001–2004,* April 2001. Available at http://cas.faa.gov/pdf/ACSPLN.DOC.
31. See Federal Aviation Administration Office of Civil Aviation Security, External Security. Available at http://cas.faa.gov/esp.html.
32. U.S. General Accounting Office. "Aviation Security: Vulnerabilities in, and Alternatives for, Pre-board Screening Security Operations," GAO-01–1171T, September 25, 2001.
33. Ibid.
34. CNN, "Congress seeks agreement on airline security bill," October 31, 2001.
35. CNN, "Feds take control of airport security," February 17, 2002.
36. Riley, "Taking Liberties," 3.
37. Ibid. Schneider and Goo, "Twin Missions Overwhelmed TSA," 1.
38. Kathryn Balint, "Protection Versus Privacy," *San Diego Union Tribune,* 11 March 2002, E1; David McGuire, "Technology Versus Liberties," *Washington Post,* 25 September 2002, 1.
39. Matthew Wald, "At Airports a Search for Better Security," *New York Times,* 26 May 2002, 5.
40. Liz Fedor, "Airlines Push for Traveler ID," *Minnesota Star Tribune,* 29 June 2002, 1.
41. Wald, "At Airports a Search for Better Security," 5.
42. Steve Huettel, "Airlines Push Trusted Traveler Idea," *Saint Petersburg Times,* 26 April 2002, 1; Schneider and Goo, "Twin Missions Overwhelmed TSA," 1.
43. Fedor, "Airlines Push for Traveler Id," 1; Huettel, "Airlines Push Trusted Traveler Idea," 1.
44. Ibid. Wald, "At Airports a Search for Better Security," 5.
45. Wald, "At Airports a Search for Better Security," 5.
46. Riley, "Taking Liberties," 3.
47. Wald, "At Airports a Search for Better Security," 5.
48. Riley, "Taking Liberties," 3.
49. Fedor, "Airlines Push for Traveler Id," 1.
50. Huettel, "Airlines Push Trusted Traveler Idea," 1.
51. Ibid.
52. Wald, "At Airports a Search for Better Security," 5.
53. See Seymour Martin Lipset, *Political Man: The Social Bases of Politics* (Garden City, NY: Anchor, 1968); David Riesman, Nathan Glazer, and Reuel Denney, *The Lonely Crowd: A Study of the Changing American Character* (Garden City, NY: Anchor, 1953).
54. Robert Nisbet, *The Present Age: Progress and Anarchy in Modern America* (New York: Harper and Row, 1988).
55. For instance, cold war unity led to the Senate McCarthy hearings, the House Un-American Activities Committee investigations of Hollywood, and to loyalty oaths for government employees. For more, see David Caute, *The Great Fear: The Anti-Communist Purge under Truman and Eisenhower* (New York: Simon and Schuster, 1978); Stanley I. Kutler, *The American Inquisition: Justice and Injustice in the Cold War* (New York: Hill and Wang, 1982); Rosati, *The Politics of United States Foreign Policy,* chapter 17; Stephen J. Whitfield, *The*

Culture of the Cold War (Baltimore: Johns Hopkins University Press, 1991); and Daniel Yergin, *Shattered Peace: The Origins of the Cold War and the National Security State* (Boston: Houghton Mifflin, 1977).

56. In effect, the crisis management paradigm conflicts in some important ways with the new public management paradigm. That is not the case for disaster consequence management, which at this point ostensibly includes terror attack outcomes, which are treated like disaster responses. The two are in conflict because crisis management necessitates stronger central authority to perform necessary coordination. More importantly, that coordinating authority will likely need to be accompanied by greater capacity to set specific standards and be mindful of individual privacy. This is in contradistinction to a more entrepreneurial model of policy implementation. To be sure, this does not mean that all aspects of the new public management paradigm will be supplanted or, of course, that change will occur across many disparate policy areas. Contracting out and public-private partnerships are key tools of public service delivery that will not change. What will change is that on a number of issues where national security preparedness is germane there is now an imperative for the federal government to be a more—and not less—direct manager of policy activities.

Chapter 8

Terrorism, War, and Freedom of the Press:

Suppression and Manipulation in Times of Crisis

Kendra B. Stewart

L. Christian Marlin

Following the terror attacks of September 11, political comedian Bill Maher indicted American foreign policy as a contributory cause of the attacks on his late night forum for pop commentary, *Politically Incorrect*.[1] The next day, White House Press Secretary Ari Fleischer sounded a warning to Maher and others poised to join in his satirical vulgarity: "[t]here are reminders to all Americans that they need to watch what they say and watch what they do, and that this is not a time for remarks like that. There never is."[2] ABC, the network on which Maher's show appeared, cancelled *Politically Incorrect* effective May 2002. The National Coalition Against Censorship indexed several censorship moments post-9/11 on its Internet web site, as categorized by their relationship to art, entertainment, news and commentary, and even the workplace.[3] The purpose of this chapter is not to catalogue such incidents, but to expound upon their origins and effect.

Historically, in times of crisis in this country, "constitutional protections have taken a back seat to national security," although in hindsight Americans often regret these new assertions of government powers.[4] National leaders are now downplaying civil liberties concerns, such as freedom of the press, with the reassurance that any violations of them are the result of temporary wartime provisions that will end when the hostilities end. Others argue, however, that the president has already assured us that our present wartime status is unlike that of conventional wars and will likely not be resolved quickly. Top officials in the Bush administration, including Homeland Security Director Tom Ridge, have equated the war on terrorism to the war on drugs and crime.[5]

In September 2002, the Reporters Committee for Freedom of the Press issued a Homefront Confidential "White Paper" to assess the threat to the press of the government's responses to 9/11 and argued that "[t]he atmosphere of terror induced public officials to abandon this country's culture of openness and opt for secrecy as a way of ensuring safety and security."[6] Lucy

Dalglish, executive director of the group, concludes in her introductory remarks that, "[w]e believe the public's right to know is severely threatened in the areas of changes to freedom of information laws, war coverage and access to terrorism and immigration proceedings."[7] Overall, there have been three major areas in which we have seen changes in the federal government's relationship with the media after September 11, 2001. The first deals with access to government information and the interpretation of the Freedom of Information Act (FOIA) by the executive agencies. The second area where we have seen a difference is in the openness of administrative and judicial proceedings involving immigrants and suspected terrorists. Immigration and a number of other hearings were closed to the public and the press after September 11. Information regarding detainees, suspects, as well as material witnesses has also been kept private. And finally, the media's access to American troops overseas and to military battles has also changed.

Access to Information

Media access to the government's management of the events of September 11 suffered immediately following the attacks. The ground and air space surrounding the disaster areas in New York and Pennsylvania was closed off to the public as well as the press. Although access had been restricted, at least four media photographers disregarded the bans and landed in jail for trespassing. Access to the crime scenes was both limited and controlled. When the scenes were finally opened, reporters were angered by the government's interference with coverage of the aftermath of the terrorist attacks.

A related issue that arose in the following weeks surrounded the broadcasting of videotapes from Osama Bin Laden and his followers. The White House warned news executives that such videos could be used to scare the American people and to send secret messages to terrorists and urged them not to air any such videos. In an unprecedented decision, all five major networks agreed not to play unedited videos from Bin Laden or his followers.[8] The organizations also agreed to edit out language based on the federal government's suggestions.

In the days and weeks following September 11, 2001, a number of federal agencies began restricting access to information that had previously been public. Agencies removed public information from their websites if it related to infrastructure, security, or anything else the government deemed of potential interest to terrorists. For example, the Federal Aviation Administration removed information, such as security violations, from its enforcement files; the U.S. Geological Survey requested that all federal depository libraries destroy CD-ROMs with information on American surface water supplies; the Bureau of Transportation Statistics removed its National Transportation Atlas Databases and the North American Transportation Atlas from its website; and President Bush signed executive orders limiting access to former presidents' papers and allowing the secretary of Health and Human Services to classify information as "secret." A number of these events lead to the filing of lawsuits by both civil liberties organizations and members of the press.

This new interpretation of what constitutes public information in executive agencies stems from a change in the Department of Justice's classification as to how to determine if documents are open according to the Freedom of Information Act (FOIA). On October 12, 2001 Attorney General John Ashcroft issued a memorandum changing the federal government's policy regarding FOIA requests.[9] According to the Department of Justice,

> The Ashcroft FOIA Memorandum emphasizes the Administration's commitment to full compliance with the FOIA as an important means of maintaining an open and accountable system of government. At the same time, it recognizes the importance of protecting the sensitive institutional, commercial, and personal interests that can be implicated in government records—such as the need to safeguard national security, to maintain law enforcement effectiveness, to respect business confidentiality, to protect internal agency deliberations, and to preserve personal privacy.

In replacing the predecessor FOIA memorandum, the Ashcroft FOIA Memorandum establishes a new "sound legal basis" standard governing the Department of Justice's decisions on whether to defend agency actions under the FOIA when they are challenged in court. This differs from the "foreseeable harm" standard that was employed under the preceding rules and standards. Under the new standard, agencies should reach the judgment that their use of a FOIA exemption is on sound footing, both factually and legally, whenever they withhold requested information. Significantly, the Ashcroft FOIA Memorandum also recognizes the continued agency practice of considering whether to make discretionary disclosures of information, which are exempt under the act, subject to statutory prohibitions and other applicable limitations. It also places particular emphasis on the right to privacy among the other interests that are protected by the FOIA's exemptions.[10]

The Ashcroft Memorandum is representative of the federal government's current focus on protecting order over liberty. The problem is twofold. First, it is the discretion of an individual in an agency that determines who will get what information, rather than strict objective and consistent standards. And second, as Mark Gribben, the public affairs manager for the Michigan Press Association, points out, "I don't believe terrorists file FOIA requests."[11] In the end, it is likely that in its attempt to protect a variety of information that could assist potential terrorists, the government is keeping large numbers of environmentalists, educators, researchers, reporters, and other citizens from accessing documents that provide data important to their work.

Not only has the federal government been recently restricting information, but there have been claims that the Pentagon was intending to provide false information. Soon after September 11, 2001 the Department of

Defense established the Office of Strategic Influence to handle the public relations for the War on Terror. According to an article that appeared in the *New York Times* on February 19, 2002, this office was established to provide propaganda to the foreign press via e-mail and the Internet. One Pentagon official told the *Times* that the office intended to partake in "black" campaigns utilizing false information and covert activities to promote a more favorable opinion of the United States both domestically and abroad.[12] The practice of black campaigns is not new to the United States and was practiced by the Central Intelligence Agency (CIA) in the 1970s and led to the printing of false information in the American press. It is illegal for federal agencies to provide misinformation to American news organizations; however, it would be virtually impossible to prevent U.S. news outlets from carrying stories printed in the foreign press. After a blitz of bad press, the Department of Defense closed down the well-funded Office of Strategic Influence one week after the story initially ran in the *New York Times*.

Another controversial issue regarding free press surfaced when the Daniel Pearl video was aired on television. Daniel Pearl was a *Washington Post* reporter on assignment in Pakistan in January of 2002, when a Muslim extremist group kidnapped him. In the spring, the government received a video showing Daniel Pearl repeating a statement given to him by his captors and then being executed. The government edited and distributed the video to the American press. CBS aired a portion of the tape on May 14, 2002 and defended the broadcast as necessary to understanding the propaganda war that was being waged.[13] The White House responded by calling CBS and expressing concerns that the tape had been aired. Days later, the unedited version of the video began to spring up on a number of Internet sites. According to a company that hosts one of the sites, Prohosters.com, they were contacted by the FBI and instructed to remove the video from the site or risk being charged with obscenity. Prohosters temporarily removed the video but reposted it at the end of May 2002 with a warning that the video shows the "real (tragic though it may be) outcome of terrorists' actions."[14] Currently, a number of sites have the Pearl video posted with a warning of its graphic nature, and to date there have not been any further attempts by the federal government to encourage its removal.

Whenever government agencies begin to withhold information, we often witness problems with information leaking out to the press against orders. The events following September 11 were no different. A number of leaks occurred, including a classified document from the Department of Defense about an attack on Iraq, information from a Congressional panel's closed-door meeting with the National Security Agency, and e-mails regarding the John Walker Lindh case. The federal government launched an investigation to thwart the source of leaks, and federal agents interviewed thirty-seven lawmakers and over one hundred bureaucrats. The leaks have resulted in tighter control of reporters' access to government employees and their offices. For example, the Pentagon now requires an escort for all reporters visiting the Pentagon who do not work there full-time or visit at least twice a week. These new regulations have resulted in the arrest of one photographer and the seizure of his video for filming illegally on government property.

As of November 2002, one of the most serious threats to the press by the federal government has yet to be enacted. The Homeland Security Act will allow the newly created Department of Homeland Security to waive the whistleblower protections for its employees as well as refuse to release information under the FOIA. According to an article in the *Washington Times* by Audrey Hudson, this new bill would "eliminate the agency's responsibility to answer questions from the public."[15] The act is being publicly criticized for a number of other issues, including the Department of Defense's "grand database."

Though the much-maligned USA PATRIOT Act widened the scope of the equally maligned Foreign Intelligence Surveillance Act, and weakened fifteen privacy laws in the process, it enhanced Congress' oversight role of secret domestic government eavesdropping on individuals. A little known feature of the Homeland Security Act would eviscerate such minimal protections, providing substantial monetary support for an under-the-radar project within the Department of Defense's Defense Advanced Research Projects Agency's (DARPA) Information Awareness Office, headed by Admiral John Poindexter. The goal of the project: "Total Information Awareness," as achieved through a "virtual, centralized grand database" linking data elements concerning credit card purchases, magazine subscriptions, medical information, Internet habits, academic records, banking data, travel data, passport application data, driver's license information, bridge and road toll records, judicial and divorce records, private complaints made to government agencies, and camera surveillance.[16] Predictably, the press and civil liberties organizations have been very critical of the act.

Access to Hearings and Detainees

Members of the press have raised concerns about their access to various proceedings involving charges relating to terrorism. The federal government is attempting to keep various hearings and trials closed to the public and the press. Two months after the attack on the World Trade Center, President Bush signed a military order allowing suspected terrorist to be tried in a military court. The Department of Defense has set the guidelines for these trials, allowing them to be closed to the press at the discretion of the presiding officer. According to the Reporters Committee for Freedom of the Press, the rules that have been developed for the military tribunals do not conform to our country's standards of openness, which will likely lead to challenges by media organizations once trials begin in the military tribunals.

Ten days after the September 11 attacks, Chief Immigration Judge Michael Creppy at Immigration and Naturalization Service (INS) issued a memorandum closing "special interest" immigration hearings to the public. At least two lawsuits filed (in New Jersey and Michigan) have resulted in the "Creppy Memorandum" being declared unconstitutional, although these cases are currently under appeal. Both courts ruled that immigration proceedings could be closed, but only on a case-by-case basis, not through a blanket ruling. Not only have the hearings been closed, but also the INS has refused to release information on the hearings and deportations of hundreds of detainees. The Reporters Committee for the Freedom of the Press has estimated that at least 600—and possibly more than 750—immigration proceedings have taken place in secret, and the government has failed to release the identification of all but a few of the detainees.[17] A number of groups have filed a lawsuit resulting in the Washington, D.C. Federal District Court ordering INS to release the names of the detainees. To date, the press is still awaiting the identification of the detainees pending an appeal in which the judge has issued a stay.

The media has also been battling to gain access to hearings of material witnesses from September 11. A district judge in New York has ruled that all material witness hearings may be closed. Additionally, federal agencies are not releasing the number or identification of the material witnesses being held. Thus far, the records of only one case involving a material witness has been unsealed, but only after both sides were given the opportunity to redact information.

A number of cases have come up as a direct result of September 11 in which the press (and the public in general) has been denied access to information about federal detainees. Currently, two U.S. citizens are being held by the government and denied the right to obtain legal counsel or other outside assistance. The federal government has labeled these two detainees as "enemy combatants" without providing proof of this status to anyone outside of the executive branch. Thus far, a District Court in New York has ruled that more information must be reviewed before such a status can be granted, but an appeals court overturned this ruling. The press has been publicizing these cases, but to date has yet to gain access to the detainees.

In April 2002, approximately 500 suspects were transferred to Guantanamo Bay Naval Base in Cuba (Camp Delta) where the media has not had contact with or view of the detainees. When complaints surfaced about the poor living conditions and treatment at Camp Delta, reporters raised the issue of the lack of outside verification by the press. Overall, the government has been very cautious in allowing access or releasing information on anyone being held who is suspected of being linked to terrorist activities. The press has been vigilant in filing lawsuits to gain access, and the courts have been ruling on behalf of openness in a number of the cases, but the majority of these are still under appeal. Only time will tell whether or not the government is acting in accordance with the Constitution by withholding information and limiting access to federal detainees and court proceedings.

Access to the War on Terrorism

Due to the unconventional nature of this war, the media claims that there has been a "considerable lack of openness."[18] The press is at the mercy of the

Pentagon when it comes to covering the war in Afghanistan. A number of events have transpired without the presence of the media. The U.S. government argues this is a safety issue and that there are times when having reporters with troops can be a hazard to both the reporters and the men and women fighting. There is also the issue of national security and the fear that in order to get a good story the press will release information that could benefit the enemy. The press, on the other hand, argue that whenever the American government is acting on behalf of the American people, the public has a right to know what is going on. This is the job of the media in their role as government watchdog—to provide an independent assessment of the acts of government. This naturally contentious relationship between the government and the press has led to a growing distrust among the players and attempts by the government to limit reporters' access.

Reporters have publicly complained about their lack of access to military strikes and other events that have gone uncovered since the "War on Terror" began in September 2001. The Reporters Committee for Freedom of the Press has pointed out the following incidents in which the government either did not allow press coverage or has failed to provide information:

- Prior to October 7, 2001 U.S. troops were moved into Afghanistan without media presence. When the military strikes began, there were no reporters with troops in active combat.
- The Pentagon has refused to comment on an article in the *New Yorker* that reported a detailed account of a failed raid by U.S. Special Forces near Kandahar.
- The Department of Defense will not provide adequate information on a raid in Oruzgan, where it has been claimed that U.S. forces beat, shot, and murdered men before they were able to surrender.
- A number of other raids and victories have occurred without media coverage.
- A *Washington Post* reporter claims to have been told by a U.S soldier that he would be shot if he went near the scene of a missile strike in February 2002.
- In December 2001 members of the press were locked in a warehouse by Marines to prevent them from reporting on a stray bomb that killed American troops north of Kandahar. The only information they received on the event was filtered through the military.
- The Pentagon is not yet reporting the death toll for the number of lives lost in Afghanistan. The *New York Times* has reported that thus far ten Americans and several hundred Afghan citizens have lost their lives.[19]

What is perhaps most disappointing for reporters is that agreements that were reached during times of peace regarding media presence in war are no longer being upheld. In 1992, a post–Gulf War nine-point compromise was made between journalists and the Pentagon allowing open (rather than pooled—see below) coverage of war, press access to troops, and government-provided transportation and information centers for the press. It appears that the Pentagon has already failed to adhere to their end of the bargain, leaving the press out of the loop when it comes to covering military action. The media has historically not had much luck in forcing the Department of Defense to bring them along into battle. The courts have generally been leery about making the military provide access to troops in combat, fearing that this type of interference could be interpreted as the courts overstepping their bounds and upsetting the balance of power. Often suits filed by the press regarding the denial of military access are moot by the time they are heard because access is eventually granted, albeit, some argue, too late. By the end of February 2002, journalists were given access to troops in combat, although there are now reports of an unfriendly and hostile environment for the press in the field.

The Department of Defense will argue that there are issues of security that could be breached by allowing the press open access to all of its military decisions, movements, and battles. Reporters will put forward that it can be to the benefit of the military to have the press in battle to serve as independent observers of events and to verify military reports to the public. The media will also point out that journalists have traditionally kept secrets for the military during times of war and have a history of complying with the wishes of high-level military officials. However, the Internet has given rise to a new, less-ethical form of journalism where often the goal is to get the story out first rather than abide by the requests of government personnel. Due to the lack of standards that apply to various Internet news sources, other reputable news organizations have at times temporarily compromised their standards to report breaking stories before their competitors. The sheer number of news sources today has also increased competition among media outlets and leaves the military with more reporters to accommodate and answer to.

One other factor that has perhaps led to the government's continued attempts to limit access is the general lack of public concern surrounding these restrictions. According to a poll conducted by the Pew Research Center, the public thought better of the press in the weeks following September 11 than it did almost one year later.[20] In November 2001, 73 percent of survey respondents rated news organizations as highly professional. By July 2002, that number dropped to only 49 percent. The same percent rated that the media "stands up for America," in July, which was down from the November rating of 69 percent. The boost in public opinion of press coverage following the events of September 11 coincides with the government's most stringent limits on public information. The July 2002 poll demonstrates a decline in the public's opinion of the press's compassion, morality, fairness and accuracy in reporting. One thing that remained constant was that the public rated the media's coverage of the war on terrorism higher than its coverage of most other news. At a time when the president has higher public approval ratings than the press, it is easier for the government to garner public support for its decisions, even if they are eventually overturned in court. So although civil libertarians and members of the media may be upset over restrictions on the press, until the American people become overwhelmingly concerned, there is little hope that the government is going to guard liberty over order unless the courts order it.

Contemporary and Historical Legal Treatment of the Press

It is difficult, if not impossible, to view the dynamism of contemporary events without comparing those events to some measuring stick—some calibrating force. In the United States, the press is calibrated by its ever-fluctuating legal standing, as framed by constitutional jurisprudence. Because legal calibration is a social, subjective, function as much as it is a legal, objective one, the treatment of the press in times of uncertain national security has ebbed and flowed according to the U.S. Supreme Court's reflections of the popular contemporary fears carrying the day.

Some say the core of American leadership in the world is built on America's obsessions with self-criticism at home—newspapers, books, radio, television, movies, the Internet. A draft of the First Amendment, in fact, referred to the press as "one of the great bulwarks of liberty." The tradition of the press in the United States is that it both reflects the public view and informs the public view. In many ways, the public has "deputiz[ed] the press as the guardians of their liberty."[21] In a time of color-coded terror alerts, and in a nation captivated by the "what next?" horrors a global criminal terror syndicate might reap, there is increasingly less tolerance for more than one sheriff in town. Some ask the fundamental question: Do I want to deputize the pen or the gun in defense of my liberty?

Certainly, national security issues must be taken into account when answering any such question. The door to the government surely cannot remain perpetually open to the probing press. Then again, "[d]emocracies die behind closed doors."[22] "When government begins closing doors, it selectively controls information rightfully belonging to the people. Select information is misinformation. The framers of the First Amendment did not trust any government to separate the true from the false for us."[23]

Sedition and the Press

The Sedition Act of 1798 made it unlawful to publish "false, scandalous, and malicious" writings against the U.S. government, in its various forms, if the intent of such a writing was to promote the people's ill-will against the government. Though ten people were convicted under the Sedition Act of 1798, Thomas Jefferson pardoned each of them. Thereafter, legal challenges concerning the First Amendment and the press's freedom as protected within it were scarcely, if ever, pursued until the time of World War I and the projection of American military might abroad.

Supreme Court–level challenges to government suppression of the press in times of war that arose following World War I involved members of the "independent" or "underground" press, more than institutional versions of media with which we are most familiar today. In its 1918 term, the Court upheld multiple criminal convictions under the Espionage Act of 1917.[24]

One of those convicted, Charles Schenck, was general secretary of the Socialist Party. He was charged with and convicted of willfully conspiring to publish to men in military service information intended to create insubordination and obstruction among their ranks. The Schenck publication attacked conscription as a violation of the Thirteenth Amendment's proscription against slavery. Justice Oliver Wendell Holmes, who wrote the Court's opinion, argued that Schenck's writings might be permitted in times of peace, but that different standards applied in times of war. The distinction drawn by Holmes gave rise to a controversial jurisprudential test of acceptable speech limitations, the "clear and present danger test," which would protect speech unless the words expressed "so imminently threaten immediate interference with the lawful and pressing purposes of the law that an immediate check is required to save the country."[25]

The clear and present danger test, which tended to be used to uphold proscriptions on speech to the detriment of the speaker and the press, was an occasional, if not frequent, component of Supreme Court First Amendment decisions until the 1940s, even if it was not identified as such.[26] A version of the clear and present danger test, known as the "preferred freedoms test," was eventually adopted by the Court in a format that lead to today's strict scrutiny of government speech regulations, including those directed at the press.[27] The clear and present danger test, however, tended to be applied to isolated speech, not that marshaled forth by the mainstream, corporate media. It was applied readily to pamphleteers and radicals striving for attention. According to many, the conventional press, as we know it today, began its modern-day struggle with the government when an era of reporting on a scandalous government of scoundrels and deceivers began in the protest-rich time of the Vietnam War, Watergate, and so on.

National Security and the Press: The Government's Responsibility to Muzzle Its Own

The Court disfavors prior restraints on speech and the press—restraining the press from reporting information *before* it has actually reported such information. Since 1971, this principle has stood clear, as forcefully articulated in the infamous Pentagon Papers case. In that case, the U.S. government sued to restrain the *New York Times* from publishing portions of a putatively classified document, "History of U.S. Decision-making Process on Vietnam Policy."[28] A *New York Times* reporter obtained the report through a Pentagon source. The report was leaked.

The First Amendment's resonance throughout the Court's opinion is perhaps best captured by the core of Justice Black's portion of the opinion, with whom Justice Douglas joined, concurring:

> Only a free and unrestrained press can effectively expose deception in government. And paramount among the responsibilities of a free press is the duty to prevent any part of the government from deceiving the people and sending them off to distant lands to die of foreign fevers and foreign shot and shell. . . . The Framers of the First Amendment, fully aware of both the need to defend a new nation and the abuses of the English and Colonial governments, sought to give this new society strength and security by providing that freedom of speech, press, religion, and assembly should not be abridged.

The Court, in siding against restraining the *New York Times* from publishing either the report itself or stories relating to the report, articulated the strong social, legal, and historical traditions against prior restraints on speech of any kind and, particularly, that of the press. Perhaps more importantly, however, the Court placed the burden of securing the nation's sensitive communications squarely on that branch of the government making the case for the sensitivity of such communications—the executive branch. These elements of the case are found in the strongly worded concurrence of Justice Stewart, with whom Justice White joined:

> In the absence of the governmental checks and balances present in other areas of our national life, the only effective restraint upon executive policy and power in the areas of national defense and international affairs may lie in an enlightened citizenry—in an informed and critical public opinion which alone can here protect the values of democratic government. For this reason, it is perhaps here that a press that is alert, aware, and free most vitally serves the basic purpose of the First Amendment. For without an informed and free press there cannot be an enlightened people. . . . When everything is classified, then nothing is classified, and the system becomes one to be disregarded by the cynical or the careless, and to be manipulated by those intent on self-protection or self-promotion. . . . It is the constitutional duty of the executive—as a matter of sovereign prerogative and not as a matter of law as the courts know law—through the promulgation and enforcement of executive regulations, to protect the confidentiality necessary to carry out its responsibilities in the fields of international relations and national defense.

Justice Stewart rested punishment of the leak not on a prior restraint of the *New York Times* but on White House management of personnel under its authority and the Department of Justice's prerogative to enforce the laws of the United States. In this instance, perhaps both the leak (identified as Daniel Ellsberg) and perhaps even the *New York Times* itself ran afoul of the United States criminal code.[29] It is this second element of the Court's decision that may have led to unintended consequences: a press-permitted military siege of the press in times of war. This leads one to the question: Does the press manipulate and suppress itself?

The Persian Gulf War: An Integrated Media Becomes Estranged from Itself

While preparing to write this chapter, the authors spoke with members of the press in their various iterations. One former reporter was appalled at the suggestion of our chapter's title, that the government, in some way, was capable of manipulating or suppressing media. He stated, simply and staunchly, "[t]he government doesn't suppress the media, the media takes care of that themselves."

Criticism of the government's restrictions on media during the Gulf War abounded in the post–Gulf War 1990s. Criticism of the media was also pitched, the reverb of our reporter friend's admonition that the media is the only institution capable of doing itself in. The press was criticized as a tool for breeding a nationalistic fervor of a jingoistic bent[30] and reducing themselves to "the level of stenographers."[31] In an exhaustive review of media-critical and government-critical Gulf War information and reporting analysis, Marie Gottschalk concluded that, "[i]t is clear now and has been for some time that Americans were not informed of the war's major occurrences in a timely fashion; that the Pentagon consciously misled the media and the public; and that much of the media failed to cover a number of critical issues both before, during and after the war."[32]

In her indictment of the press, Gottschalk identifies as the most important factors leading to the media's Gulf War failure: "the absence of effective political parties or other mechanisms for the average American citizen to connect with the political process in a meaningful way; the emergence of an angry, volatile, and potentially bellicose public; the way in which technology is transforming how we relate to reality; and the elevation of image and the bottom line to sacrosanct positions in all walks of American life while values such as truth and integrity are demeaned as quaint anachronisms."[33] With the Gulf War, she says, "[t]he problem was not simply that the Pentagon and the president misled the media, but that the media generally swallowed without question whatever the military and the administration dished out."[34]

World War II, Korea, and Vietnam press access (in both geographic proximity and coverage substance) to the war zone itself was ensured by civilian authorities. In the 1983 invasion of Grenada, this responsibility was shifted to the military, which denied journalists access to the war zone during both the two-day military action and for two days there following.[35] This move could have been a nod to the Court's harsh criticisms levied against the executive in the Pentagon Papers case. If the executive was not going to police itself against press intrusion, the signal of the Pentagon Papers case was that, to be sure, the Court would not.

Enter pool reporting.[36] Pool reporting is a form of press control resurrected by the Reagan administration in the oft-lampooned assault on Grenada (the largest American military action since the Vietnam War) and had been a historic valve through which to compress the dissemination of information in critical wartime settings. Through the pooling mechanism, limited numbers of press obtain access to limited amounts of information on a limited timetable, and in limited servings by the government. It is the opposite of unilateral reporting, that romantic image of the lone reporter skipping through the perils of a war-ravaged urban landscape, images popularized by media coverage of unilateral reporters covering El Salvador, Beirut, Bosnia, and other hot spots around the globe to which American forces were mobilized on a small scale, if on any scale at all.

Critics of pool reporting tout examples by which pool reporting may have obscured potential atrocities committed in Panama by American or pro-American forces.[37] They also cite examples of press co-optation, whereby Pentagon-selected, press-adopted euphemisms for war like "collateral damage," "sorties" or "visits," "ordnance," and "softening" of the enemy obscure the harshness of more straightforward, less-spun terms for the same activity, such as civilian deaths, bombing raids, bombs, and blowing the enemy to bits.[38]

Finally, celebrity media critics such as Stephen Brill symbolize a new breed of reporter committed to reporting on the media itself and the corporate apparatus that drives media decisions. According to one such commentator "[a]s news organizations become bigger and bigger corporations, they behave more and more like the people they cover—that is, less and less willing to take risks."[39] Such arguments underpin continuing criticisms of the press's acquiescence to government-led efforts to influence its coverage and reporting. The media is a business. As such, it must report to stay in business. Secrecy is bad for the media business because it is a limitation on content. Beyond the civil rights and free press issues inherent in the post–September 11 media environment, business issues—the corporate profit motive—also resonate. For the corporate media business, secrecy compromises content and legitimacy—the ability of the press to deliver the goods it promises.

Secrecy Interests in the Mosaic: Post-9/11 Efforts to Protect Intelligence

In defending its secrecy measures following September 11, the government offers its compelling interest in national security and the prevention of terrorism. Everyone agrees that the government maintains a compelling interest in preventing terrorism. It is an interest each American shares, personally. As a result, it is a natural extension of reasoning to acknowledge that the government, likewise, has a compelling interest in its antiterrorism investigations and prosecutions. Again, each American shares this interest— or should. It is the secrecy surrounding such investigations and prosecutions that draws the ire of the media and some individuals.

In support of its secrecy efforts, the government argues that bits of pieces of information take on relevance greater than their parts when made available to terrorist elements by the press, and that such bits and pieces could be assembled into a broader picture detrimental, if not absolutely dangerous, to government efforts. This phenomenon has been described as the "mosaic" intelligence process, whereby small pieces of a larger puzzle have independent and collective relevance well beyond what could be discerned by the media or any average (noncriminal) recipient of such information.[40] This theory of mosaic intelligence has been offered by the government in support of its secret immigration hearings.

We have already heard something about restricted access to immigration hearings and, particularly, those hearings relating to accused terrorist immigrants. Legally speaking, the press's first hurdle in gaining access to immigration proceedings is, in part, due to the interplay of press rights and the rights, or lack thereof, of immigrants. For example, noncitizens hoping to enter the United States, who have no ties to the United States, are not "persons" under Fifth Amendment's due process of law protections.[41] As a result, any process they received, no matter how minimal, even secret, is legally considered due process of law.[42] "Whatever the rule may be concerning deportation of persons who have gained entry into the United States, it is not within the province of any court . . . to review the determination of the political branch of the Government to exclude a given alien."[43]

But the relative lack of rights of the object of any such proceedings, the immigrant, is balanced by the relative strength of rights of the press, in limitation of the government's rights, in presenting coverage of those proceedings. The Bill of Rights is most often cited for what it *grants* nongovernmental institutions and individuals—the press, religion, each of us. The Bill of Rights, however, is written not as a *grant* of rights but as a limitation on the power and authority of government. The Bill of Rights is premised upon the general notion that "Congress shall make no law" abridging the freedom identified. Here, we are concerned with abridgements of press freedom. The Bill of Rights is written in the negative, not the positive. The resulting limitations on the legislative, whose laws are deployed by the executive, are then left to the judiciary to construe. In the case of secret immigration trials, some have argued that the press is fighting for access and coverage as much in defense of its special status in American constitutional law as it is to protect streams of content that are integral to its business survival.

Judging contemporary events, as they unfold, against legal standards developed during differing historical contexts, does not provide for informed critical analysis. It is, however, one of the few avenues available for present-day observers to express their views of the developing course of history. Civil libertarians who vocalize mistrust or criticism of the government's treatment of civil liberties and institutions of liberty, such as the press, are sometimes labeled obstructionist, disloyal, and harmful to the Republic. Sometimes their critical views of the government, however, do not extend to the institutions they seek to protect, such as the media or the press, itself. The freedoms we exalt in times of crisis are not independent of the coordinate institutions that operate symbiotically in the functioning of freedom. The government must respect the free press. The press must fight for its freedom and respect itself. The government and the press are equally responsible for ensuring that the people get what they are told they have been promised, an unencumbered press.

Notes

1. September 17, 2001, *Politically Incorrect*, American Broadcasting Company (ABC).
2. Fleischer's comments are available at the White House website, http://www. whitehouse.gov/news/releases/2001/09/20010926-5.html
3. Ibid.
4. American Civil Liberties Union, *Insatiable Appetite: The Government's Demand for New and Unnecessary Powers After September 11*, April 2002, p. 15. Available at http://www.aclu.org/SafeandFree/SafeandFree.cfm?ID= 10623&c=207.
5. American Civil Liberties Union, *Insatiable Appetite*.
6. The Reporters Committee for Freedom of the Press, *Homefront Confidential*, 2d. ed., p. 1. Available at http://www.rcfp.org/homefrontconfidential.
7. The Reporters Committee for Freedom of the Press, *Homefront Confidential*, p. 2
8. Ibid.
9. The Ashcroft FOIA memorandum is available at the Department of Justice website, http://www.usdoj.gov/oip/foiapost/2001foiapost19.htm.
10. Ibid.
11. Murphy, Kathleen, "War on Terror Restricts Information Flow," Stateline.org, August 28, 2002. Available at http://www.stateline.org/print_story.do? storyId=256975.
12. James Dao and Eric Schmitt, "Pentagon Readies Efforts to Sway Sentiments Abroad," *New York Times*, 19 February 2002.
13. Dan Rather's statement available at http://www.cbsnews.com/stories/2002/05/ 14/attack/main509059.shtml.
14. Available at the Prohosters website at http://www.prohosters.com/pearl/.
15. Audrey Hudson, "Security Bill Bars Blowing Whistle," *Washington Times*, 22 June 2002.
16. William Safire, "You Are a Suspect," *New York Times*, 14 November 2002.
17. The Reporters Committee for Freedom of the Press, *Homefront Confidential*, p. 5.
18. The Reporters Committee for Freedom of the Press, *Homefront Confidential*, p. 1.
19. The Reporters Committee for Freedom of the Press, *Homefront Confidential*, pp. 2 – 3.

20. The Pew Research Center, "News Media's Improved Image Proves Short-Lived," August 4, 2002. Available at http://people-press.org/reports/display.php3?ReportID-159.
21. *Detroit Free Press et al. v. Ashcroft et al.* (Electronic Citation) 2002 FED App. 0291P (6th Cir.) August 26, 2002.
22. Ibid. at 4.
23. Ibid. *Kleindienst v. Mandel,* 408 U.S. 753, 773 (1972) (quoting *Thomas v. Collins,* 323 U.S. 516, 545 [Jackson, J., concurring]).
24. *Schenck v. United States,* 249 U.S. 182 (1919), *Frohwerk v. United States,* 249 U.S. 204 (1919), and *Debs v. United States,* 249 U.S. 211 (1919).
25. *Abrams v. United States,* 250 U.S. 616 (1919).
26. *Gitlow v. New York,* 268 U.S. 652 (1925) (the Court endorsed punishment of "incitement" by Gitlow, leader of a left-wing section of the Socialist Party, even though Holmes derided the majority's misapplication of the "clear and present danger" test); *Whitney v. California,* 274 U.S. 357 (1927) (Fourteenth Amendment due process and California's Criminal Syndicalism statute).
27. *Terminiello v. Chicago,* 337 U.S. 1 (1949); finally adopted by the Court in *Brandenburg v. Ohio,* 395 U.S. 444, 447 (1969).
28. *New York Times Co. v. The United States,* 403 U.S. 713 (1971).
29. 18 United States Code ("U.S.C.") Section 797 makes it a crime to publish certain types of drawings or photographs of military installations; Section 798 criminalizes knowing and willful publication of classified information concerning cryptographic and other intelligence activities and information; Section 793(e) criminalizes any unauthorized possessor of a document relating to "National Defense" willfully communicating such document to any other unauthorized recipient, or willfully retaining the document, failing to deliver it to a U.S. officer otherwise entitled to receive it.
30. Colman McCarthy, "When the Media Danced to Jingo Bells," *Washington Post,* 17 March 1991.
31. John R. MacArthur, *Second Front: Censorship and Propoganda in the Gulf War* (New York: Hill and Wang, 1992), p. 196.
32. Marie Gottschalk, "Operation Desert Cloud: The Media and the Gulf War," *World Policy Journal* 9 (summer 1992): 449–86, at p. 450.
33. Ibid.
34. Ibid. p. 451.
35. Ibid. p. 456.
36. For an excellent review of pool reporting's structure and function, see Mark Thompson, "With the Press Pool in the Persian Gulf," *Columbia Journalism Review* (November-December 1987): 40–45 (commenting on the American press pool covering the U.S. Navy's first escort of American-flagged Kuwaiti oil tankers during the Iran-Iraq War).
37. Marc Cooper, "Missing the Story: The Press and the Panama Invasion," *Nation* (June 19, 1990): 850–54; Michael Massing, "New Trouble in Panama," *New York Review of Books,* 17 May 1990.
38. Gottschalk "Operation Desert Cloud," p. 462.
39. Christopher Georges, "Confessions of an Investigative Reporter," *Washington Monthly,* March 1992, 37–43; quoting Bill Kovach of Harvard's Nieman Foundation and former editor of the *Atlanta Journal and Constitution.*
40. *J. Roderick MacArthur Found. v. FBI,* 120 F. 3rd 600, 604 (D.C. Cir. 1996); see also *CIA v. Sims,* 471 U.S. 159, 178 (1985) (recognizing the validity of this model of intelligence gathering). "[E]ach individual piece of intelligence infor-

mation, much like a piece of jigsaw puzzle, may add in piecing together other bits of information even when the individual piece is not of obvious importance in itself." *Halperin v. CIA*, 629 F. 2d 144, 150 (D.C. Cir. 1980).

41. See *Kwong Hai Chew v. Colding*, 344 U.S. 590, 598 (1953).
42. See *Shaughnessy v. United States ex. rel. Mezei*, 345 U.S. 206, 212 (1953).
43. *United States ex. rel. Knauff v. Shaughnessy*, 338 U.S. 537, 543 (1950).

Chapter 9

At What Price?

Security, Civil Liberties, and Public Opinion in the Age of Terrorism

Susan J. Tabrizi

The attacks of September 11 left in their immediate wake death, destruction, fear, anger, confusion, and despair. However, as the smoke literally began to clear, President George W. Bush described the response of the United States in terms of resolve and justice. Speaking to a joint session of Congress, Bush proclaimed: "Tonight we are a country awakened to danger and called to defend freedom. Our grief has turned to anger, and anger to resolution. Whether we bring our enemies to justice, or bring justice to our enemies, justice will be done."[1]

Resolve, however, was not all that Bush and Congress would ask of the American people—they would ask for vigilance and would provide in return increased security. The question remains: At what cost would Americans receive this security? Was an infringement of civil liberties necessary to achieve it? Would Americans be willing to give up some measure of civil liberties in exchange for peace of mind and freedom from fear? Security was on everyone's mind; the question was whether the government could deliver. Clearly, the American public was asking for security, but at what price?

This chapter reviews public attitudes regarding civil liberties and national security in the post–September 11 environment. What were the reactions in the immediate aftermath of 9/11? Did the public anticipate a restriction of civil liberties? What were they willing to give up? Where would they draw the line? What effect would time and distance have on the public's opinion about security and civil liberties?

The debate over civil liberties in the United States is neither new nor resolved. During the struggle over the ratification of the Constitution, the federalists and the anti-federalists clashed over the inclusion of a bill of rights in the document.[2] The anti-Federalists, led by an anonymous writer adopting the pseudonym "John De Witt," argued against increasing the power of the federal government and feared that doing so would pose a grave danger to the natural rights of citizens.[3] De Witt contributed to the debate in a series of essays that appeared in the Boston *American Herald* from October to December 1787. In the second of these essays, De Witt argues that while citizens give up certain rights to government in order to enter into society, those rights that are retained by the people must be explicitly set forth in a bill of rights. To do otherwise is to rely on a vaguely understood implication that those reserved rights exist and consist of agreed upon protections. This, for De Witt, is too dangerous an assumption in the face of a powerful central government.[4] In other words, an explicit bill of rights is essential in order to assure that government cannot encroach upon the freedoms of the people.

At the same time, Alexander Hamilton, James Madison, and John Jay composed a series of essays in support of the newly drafted Constitution of the United States known as *The Federalist Papers*.[5] Writing in response to anti-Federalist charges regarding civil liberties, Alexander Hamilton, in *Federalist #84*, argues that including a bill of rights into the new constitution would be more dangerous than relying on the fact that reserved rights were understood. A tyrannical government could easily infer that those rights not specifically included in the bill of rights were not guaranteed to the people. In other words, writing into the constitution the specific rights reserved to the people inferred that those rights not delineated were not protected. Given that it would be impossible to list all rights guaranteed to the people, a bill of rights would jeopardize liberty by suggesting that the rights included there exhausted those the people were guaranteed. The Constitution, as written, already included prohibitions against government encroachments. Article II, Section 9 states that people cannot be imprisoned without being charged with a crime except in extreme circumstances of "rebellion or invasion" where protection of "public safety may require it" (also known as the right to habeas corpus). It also forbids punishment for crimes without trial (bills of attainder) and forbids Congress from passing *ex post facto* laws that make an act illegal after it has been committed. Hamilton also noted the Constitution's prohibition of titles of nobility, guarantee of trial by jury and other inherent proscriptions that served to make the Constitution a bill of rights in its own regard. Hamilton warned that to create a separate bill of rights that listed specifically what government may not do would be to prohibit it from doing things it never had the right to do in the first place and therefore would be dangerous, as government would then claim that those rights not guaranteed in the constitution could be violated.[6]

Despite Hamilton's arguments in *Federalist #84*, as a political compromise to secure ratification of the Constitution, the Federalists eventually acquiesced to the demands of the anti-Federalists to include a bill of rights as the first amendments to be passed after adoption. Ironically, federalist James Madison authored those ten amendments that have come to be known as the Bill of Rights. Despite Hamilton's fears, this listing of civil liberties provides the basis for the people's freedom in the U.S. This of course does not mean that the Bill of Rights is completely inclusive in its specificity. A right to privacy, so dear to the hearts of most Americans, appears nowhere in the original words, but the Supreme Court in *Griswold v. Connecticut* (1965) and later in *Roe v. Wade* (1973) applied this right, as implied by the First, Third, Fourth, and Fifth Amendments, to issue historic rulings in those cases.[7] However, at the same time, the Bill of Rights has not proven to be absolute or universally applicable, as violations have occurred throughout U.S. history. Thus, the Bill of Rights, what it means, what it protects, and what it implies, continues to evolve. Times of war put special pressure on civil liberties.

Civil Liberties in Times of War

The public's relationship to the debate over civil liberties in times of war and crisis is, unfortunately, not novel in regard to the case of the September 11 terrorist attacks. Repeatedly, when national security was at stake, American's have been asked, if not required, to relinquish some of their liberty.[8] During the Civil War, Abraham Lincoln found it necessary to suspend the right to habeas corpus guaranteed in Article I, Section 9 of the Constitution, which indicates that an individual's right not to be imprisoned unless formally charged with a crime "shall not be suspended, unless when in Cases of Rebellion or Invasion the public Safety may require it."[9] During World War I, the Congress passed the Espionage and Sedition Acts, which allowed government to punish people for communicating information that put national security at risk but also allowed punishment for criticism of the government and antiwar speech. Famously, during World War II the government justified the internment of Japanese Americans in camps as a necessary step to guard national security. During the Vietnam era, antiwar protest leaders were tried for conspiracy.[10] Restrictions of civil liberties are historically not uncommon in times of war. The question is, would Americans see restrictions in the wake of September 11 as a reasonable price to pay for assurances of security?

Public Notions about Civil Liberties after September 11

The events of September 11 had an unprecedented impact upon the nation. People from coast to coast were left wondering what life would be like in the wake of these devastating terrorist attacks. Pollsters were out in force attempting to discern what the public's reaction was and where it would lead in the weeks and months to come as the country recovered from the shock of the immediate impact.[11]

One of the indicators of the public's interpretation of the significance of September 11 comes in the form of a simple question asking people what they think is the most important issue facing the country. This question appears in many forms in most public opinion surveys at one time or another and serves to indicate what issues are on the minds of the public. For example, in early September 2001, the Harris Poll reported that while taxes, healthcare, and the economy were the top issues the public considered important, not one in particular was dominating public attention.[12] In November of 2001, two months after the attacks, it was clear that everything had changed. National Public Radio, the Kaiser Family Foundation, and the Kennedy School of Government reported that the September 11 attacks and the related war on terrorism were seen overwhelmingly as the most important issues for government to address in November 2001. The war in Afghanistan and the economy came in second and third, leaving traditional domestic issues such as healthcare and taxes, and other staples such as education, social security, crime, poverty, etc. on the back burner of public concerns.[13] In January 2002, the Pew Research Center found that compared with domestic issues, the war on terrorism dominated what the public saw as the priorities for George W. Bush's agenda (with 52 percent saying the Bush's priority should be the war on terrorism and 33 percent saying domestic issues in a question that asked which of the two should dominate); 13 percent said both while 2 percent either refused to answer or said they did not know).[14] The same question asked in August of 2002 suggested that public opinion had changed. When asked to choose between domestic issues and the war on terrorism one year later, Americans reorganized their priorities for Bush's agenda by balancing their concerns. Now, while 43 percent in the Pew survey said the war on terrorism should dominate and only 29 percent favored domestic issues, fully 22 percent said that *both* issue areas deserved Bush's attention, up from 13 percent six months earlier.[15] As public opinion changes and as the immediacy of September 11 fades, it appears that the priorities of the nation will change as well. Terrorism and security, however, appear to have lasting salience.

Security Versus Rights?

Much of the speculation in the weeks and months after September 11 had to do with the extent to which the new focus on security would affect the freedoms of the people. With the passage of the USA PATRIOT Act in November 2001, law enforcement powers were expanded to aid in the detection and deterrence of terrorist acts. Many, including the American Civil Liberties Union, argued that the PATRIOT Act was an impermissible affront to civil liberties. Could an acceptable balance be struck? Writing for *Insight on the News* in October 2001, conservative political columnist Paul Weyrich called the post–September 11 political environment "a significant test for Bush" and warned that if Bush could navigate the perils of fighting a war on terrorism without abandoning a commitment to the Constitution and its protection for civil liberties, he would be revered. If, on the other hand, he allowed the Constitution to fall to the pressures of demands for security, he would be reviled.[16] Similar criticism appeared from the political left. Bruce Shapiro, writing for the liberal magazine *The Nation,* concluded in October 2001 that the Bush administration's efforts to increase the authority of law enforcement in the name of security had the potential to pose serious threats to Constitutional protections in terms of privacy and rights of suspects and those accused of crimes.[17] Did the American people agree? Was September 11 likely to pose a threat to their civil liberties? Would they be asked to consider a tradeoff between security and civil liberties?

An NPR/Kaiser/Kennedy School poll conducted November 20–25, 2001, found that people were evenly split in terms of their anticipation of whether they thought the average American would have to surrender some of their civil liberties in order to fight terrorism (51 percent versus 46 percent). However, when asked if they would have to give up their own rights and liberties in this fight, 58 percent of those polled believed that they would.[18]

Clearly, while Americans seemed to be concerned about the implications of the potential tradeoff for the country as a whole, they were much more concerned about the effect it would have on their own lives.

In December of 2001, CBS News, in conjunction with the *New York Times,* asked members of the public how concerned they were about losing some of their civil liberties. In other words, were the tradeoffs that the NPR/ Kaiser/Kennedy School asked about causing concern among members of the public with regard to the sanctity of their civil liberties? CBS/*New York Times* reported their poll results in terms of the aggregate response and response by partisan groups. They found that the majority of people were concerned that their civil liberties were in jeopardy in the wake of the September 11 attacks (65 percent). Democrats (44 percent) and Independents (33 percent) were more concerned than were Republicans (23 percent), perhaps reflecting a trust in the sitting administration's ability to balance the impending tradeoff.

In the same survey, CBS/*New York Times* couched the tradeoff in another way: Would the government be tough enough on terrorism or too tough on civil liberties? Asking the survey participants "Which concerns you more right now—that the government will fail to enact strong anti-terrorism laws, or that the government will enact new anti-terrorism laws that excessively restrict the average person's civil liberties?" The survey found that Americans were evenly split between the two (43 percent saying the government would fail to act and 45 percent saying they would restrict civil liberties). Again, however, the results suggested that Republicans were more concerned that the government would fail to act while Democrats, and to a lesser extent Independents, were worried that civil liberties would be threatened.[19]

Would this concern for civil liberties persist? As the events of September 11 began to fade, would Americans be less concerned about the potential tradeoff between civil liberties and security? Would they be more or less willing to make the tradeoff in favor of civil liberties?

In January 2002, four months after the devastating attacks in New York and Washington and the failed hijacking that ended in destruction in Pennsylvania, a CNN/Gallup/*USA Today* poll found that 47 percent of those surveyed said that "the government should take all steps necessary to prevent additional acts of terrorism in the United States even if it means basic civil liberties would be violated" while 49 percent said that "the government should take steps to prevent additional acts of terrorism but not if those would violate basic civil liberties."[20] By June, however, the view of the public had changed. They were clearly less torn in the tradeoff between security and civil liberties; civil liberties were more of a concern. In response to the same question, CNN/Gallup/*USA Today* now found that only 40 percent were willing to prevent terrorism at the cost of civil liberties if necessary where 56 percent would only allow steps to be taken that fought terrorism without violating civil liberties.[21] Time and distance had changed perspective.[22] Americans, still wary of the threat of terrorism, were growing more concerned about potential threats to their civil liberties. In April 2002, a CBS News poll reported that 72 percent of Americans believed that "Americans will have to give up some of the personal freedoms in order to make the country safe from terrorist attacks."[23] By June 2002, the American public was split: 46 percent said that it would be necessary to give up civil liberties to fight terrorism, 46 percent said it would not, and 8 percent remained unsure according to a *Newsweek* magazine poll.[24]

The Price: Privacy and Speech?

Even if Americans were willing to acknowledge that they would be asked to surrender some civil liberties for security, and even if many were concerned that that tradeoff would be at the expense of civil liberties they cherished, what were Americans thinking would be the specific costs they would pay? Would their privacy be endangered? Would they be restricted in their speech? Where exactly would the tradeoff between civil liberties and security rest?

In their early November 2001 survey about civil liberties, the NPR/Kaiser/Kennedy School poll asked participants how concerned they were about the invasion of their personal privacy. Sixty-two percent said that they were very or somewhat concerned. Interestingly, however, 67 percent said that they did not think that the federal government was a threat to their personal rights or freedoms.[25] Perhaps some elements of personal privacy were things participants were willing to give up in exchange for security. But when asked about whether or not it would be ok for government agencies to monitor phone calls and e-mail correspondence by ordinary Americans in order to reduce the threat of terrorism, 65 percent of respondents to the December CBS/Gallup/*New York Times* poll answered that listening in was not something they were willing to allow.[26] Fox News echoed these results with a poll in late November 2001 that showed that 52 percent of adults polled opposed allowing the government to step up the monitoring of private communications.[27] While a healthy minority of Americans was willing to give up this type of privacy, the majority was not, even if terrorism prevention was part of the bargain.

The skepticism about invasion of privacy did not necessarily hold for those who were suspected of committing terrorism, however. The CBS/*New York Times* poll asked if it was a good idea for government to abandon prohibitions against listening in on conversations between attorneys and their clients who were in jail for criminal cases and 64 percent responded that it was a bad idea; however, this prohibition did not hold for conversations between those suspected of terrorism and their lawyers. When asked, "do you think it is a good idea or a bad idea for the government to listen in on conversations between suspected terrorists in jail and their lawyers?" Seventy-two percent responded that it was a good idea.[28] Clearly, protections of this sort rested on circumstance in early December 2001, because the population was wrestling with the tradeoff between civil liberties and security. An ABC News/*Washington Post* poll conducted in late November 2001 found very similar results, with 73 percent of those asked saying that they thought it should be legal "for the federal government to wiretap conversations between people who are being held on terrorism charges and their lawyers."[29] Civil liberties were not absolute.

One of the freedoms dearest to Americans is the right to free speech. Guaranteed in the First Amendment, this right is not absolute either, but it is generally held to be sacrosanct in terms of measuring the vitality of democracy. Would Americans hold this right to speech above the need for security in the face of a tradeoff? Would speech be a victim of the need to maintain order and safety in the new post–September 11 world?

Tolerating disagreeable speech is often touted as the cornerstone of democracy. Free speech is so important to the exchange of ideas that citizens are generally very supportive of the abstract principle that freedom of speech should be protected at all costs. The NPR/Kaiser/Kennedy School poll asked participants if they agreed that restricting freedom of speech was dangerous; 77 percent agreed (47 percent strongly agreed).[30] This was a strong endorsement of the principle of free speech in the recent wake of a devastating attack. But free speech and democratic tolerance in general are complicated issues. Academic researchers have concluded that, generally, Americans are willing to endorse free speech in abstract terms such as these but are often less generous when specific groups (particularly hated groups) or incidents are associated with the free speech issue.[31] The NPR/Kaiser/Kennedy School study echoes these observations. Individuals who support terrorists or who blame terrorism on U.S. actions in the world received less consideration when it came to free speech. According to respondents in the early November 2001 study, 57 percent felt that individuals who suggested terrorism could be blamed on U.S. actions in the world should be allowed to make a speech at a college but only 33 percent thought they should be allowed to teach in the public schools and only 35 percent agreed they should be allowed to work in the government. When confronted with the subject of individuals who actually express support for terrorists, clearly a hated group among members of the U.S. mass public, 61 percent felt that they should not be allowed to make a speech at a college and overwhelming majorities agreed that they should not be allowed to teach in the public schools (85 percent) or work in the government (90 percent).[32]

The ideas of supporting terrorists or blaming the United States for terrorist attacks might be so harsh that we can reasonably expect the American people to draw the line of tolerance decisively at that point. But what kind of speech can individuals engage in? How critical of the government can citizens be without stepping over the line in the sand between democracy and tolerance on the one side and danger and intolerance on the other?

In early December of 2001, Americans were split in their answers to this crucial question about free speech and the post–September 11 world. The CBS/*New York Times* poll reported that 50 percent of Americans believed that it was okay to criticize the government, even if it was damaging to the national interest; 44 percent said it was not.[33] This conflicted response reinforces the tenuous nature of freedom of speech in times of crisis. It represents a less-than-ringing endorsement of the sanctity of free speech in times of war.

President Bush enjoyed record approval ratings in the aftermath of September 11, a spellbinding rise from mediocre scores hovering around 50 percent just days before the tragedy. Government officials seemed wary to criticize the president's plans for retaliation against Al Qaeda and the Taliban in Afghanistan. New security measures coming out of Congress and expanded provisions for law enforcement such as the USA PATRIOT Act were not unchallenged but in the end passed easily through the public viewfinder. Was Bush insulated from the potential for criticism? Would the American people reject criticism of their leader in time of war and uncertainty?

The CBS/*New York Times* poll asked about public criticism of the president and found that despite high approval ratings and a temporary lull in partisan rancor, the American public still believed that it was permissible to disagree with and criticize Bush on domestic issues (73 percent said it was okay to criticize the president's proposals publicly) and even on military issues (56 percent said it was okay to criticize his military decisions).[34]

Overall, then, freedom of speech seemed to survive September 11 relatively intact, with the important exception of those who questioned the U.S. responsibility in the attacks and those who would support the terrorists in their cause. Even a freedom so revered as free speech has limits. September 11 seemed to prove that that limit could be found with enemies of the people.

Singled Out: Racial Profiling and Noncitizen Rights

Asking Americans if they wanted increased security seems to be a silly question; of course they did. The important thing to consider is the mechanisms by which that security would be delivered. We have already seen that the American people were wary about the extent to which new security concerns would overshadow their civil liberties. And yet, those concerns were balanced by a general rejection of restrictions on privacy or free speech for their fellow citizens, with important exceptions for anyone suspected of terrorist activities; that suspicion was focused no more strongly than on Arab Americans and noncitizens of Arab descent. Should we be more suspicious of these groups within our society? Was racial profiling of Arab people acceptable? Should noncitizens be afforded the same civil liberties as citizens? Would Americans be as generous with freedom for those who resembled the terrorists of September 11 as they were for non-Arab members of their community?

Racial profiling is an issue most often associated with young black men and disproportionate incidents of traffic stops targeting this demographic, otherwise referred to as the "driving while black" syndrome by those who charge police discrimination. But after September 11, the backlash against Arab Americans, and indeed "foreign-looking" Americans who were not Arab at all, raised concerns about racism and targeted violence. This anger and suspicion was channeled through the justice system and recast the issue of racial profiling into a possible necessary evil to combat terrorism. The American public seemed torn about the use of such measures. In November 2001, a Fox News/Opinion Dynamics poll found that 58 percent of those asked agreed that "allowing police to stop and search anyone who fits the general description of suspected terrorists" was an allowable way to fight terrorism.[35] In the same poll they asked, "As part of the war on terrorism, the federal government wants to question 5,000 Middle Eastern immigrants on the basis of their religion or nationality. Some local officials have refused to perform the questioning, suggesting the government needs to show more cause to question the visitors. Do you approve or disapprove of the government questioning these individuals?" to which 67 percent answered that they approved.[36] A similar question asked in the CBS/*New York Times* poll in early December found similar support (61 percent) for interviewing "young Middle Eastern men who are legal residents of the United States, based on their age and the country they come from."[37] Forty-one percent of participants said that such interviewing violated the civil rights of these legal residents while 52 percent did not think it was a violation. Democrats were much more likely to believe that this practice was a violation of civil rights than were Republicans (48 percent compared with 28 percent). Thus, racial profiling that was generally seen as unacceptable in terms of targeting young black men became more acceptable for targeting persons of Arab descent in the context of terrorism.

But was there a limit? How far would the American people be willing to go with their suspicion of Arabs and Arab Americans in the name of security? Although they seemed torn about the extent to which they viewed interviewing that targeted young Middle Eastern men as a violation of civil rights, and a majority said they would support it as a tactic for fighting terrorism, there were clear limits. *Newsweek* asked, "In response to the terrorist attacks, do you think the United States should put Arabs and Arab-Americans in this country under special surveillance, or would it be a mistake to target a nationality group as was done with the Japanese-

Americans after Pearl Harbor?" Only 30 percent of participants in this survey were willing to say that increased surveillance was permissible; 62 percent said it would be a mistake.[38] In the same survey, however, 35 percent of participants said that they would favor detaining "legal immigrants suspected of crimes indefinitely as a way to protect against terrorism," 43 percent said they would accept this if necessary, and only 19 percent said that it went too far. Again, Americans seemed very sensitive to the element of suspicion in these questions. As with free speech, issues of detention seemed to be more restrictive for those suspected of crimes when they "fit the profile" of possible terrorists. Even in June of 2002, a Fox News/Opinion Dynamics poll found that 54 percent of registered voters approved of "using racial profiling to screen Arab male airline passengers."[39]

There were elements of profiling that appeared to go too far, according to public opinion. When CBS/*New York Times* asked if allowing the U.S. government "to routinely question Middle Eastern men who have come to the United States in the past two years and are here legally, even if they are not suspected of any crime and there is no evidence against them" violates people's rights, 42 percent said it should be allowed and 54 percent said it was a violation.[40] But, when the same survey asked if "the United States government should be allowed to investigate religious groups that gather at mosques, churches or synagogues without evidence that someone in the group has broken the law," 75 percent said that such an act violated rights and only 22 percent said it should be allowed. Singling out religion, unlike race or ethnicity, seemed to push participants too far in terms of profiling suspected terrorists. In June of 2002, *Newsweek* found that profiling by race, ethnicity, or religion was accepted by half of survey participants but that only 14 percent were willing to say they strongly favored it. Echoing earlier findings, detaining people solely because of religion was not acceptable to 76 percent of participants in that poll a year after the terrorist attacks.[41] Thus, while in the immediate aftermath of September 11, security was enough of a concern to warrant racial profiling, a blank check for suspicion was not going to be issued by the American people.

If profiling by race was acceptable at times, what about legal status? Was there a difference in how citizens and noncitizens should be treated by the government? Did citizens and noncitizens have different rights? In November 2001, *Newsweek* asked whether the Bill of Rights applied to noncitizens living in the United States just as it did for citizens; 51 percent of survey participants said it applied only to U.S. citizens.[42] The NPR/Kaiser/Kennedy School study from late November 2001 echoed these sentiments, with 56 percent saying that "non-citizens living legally in or visiting the United States" should not have the same rights as citizens.[43] Interestingly, in the face of the judicial system, participants reversed their interpretation. When asked, "When it comes to non-citizens who are legally in the United States, should they have the same legal rights if they are arrested as U.S. citizens have if they are arrested for the same thing or should they have fewer rights?" Seventy percent said they should have the same rights. But, reflect-

ing the theme from the free-speech discussion above, when those participants who said noncitizens should have the same rights were asked if they
felt the same way if noncitizens were being charged with terrorism, 46
percent were willing to say that they should have fewer rights. Being a
noncitizen, even if you were legally in the United States, did not provide you
with the same legal status as citizens in the eyes of the American people after
September 11. Even one year later, *Newsweek* found that 56 percent of
Americans strongly favored or were willing to accept "giving government
the power to detain legal immigrants suspected of crimes indefinitely,
without review by a judge" but 52 percent said this was going to far when
the suspects were American citizens.[44] Civil liberties that were not absolute
even for American citizens were clearly not afforded to noncitizens. Security
trumped rights for those legally in the United States if they were not
"Americans." Still, as the data regarding racial profiling suggests, even those
citizens who "resembled" terrorists were not secure in their freedom from
suspicion.

How Far Is Too Far?

The American people were unsure about their civil liberties after September
11 and remained unsure one year later. They were concerned about civil
liberties and anticipated restrictions, but they were unwilling to tread on
privacy or free speech in cases that did not involve suspected terrorists or
their supporters. They were concerned about the rights of citizens but
unwilling to completely protect noncitizens in the same manner. They saw
profiling of religious groups as distasteful but were willing to consider race
and ethnicity as factors in targeting suspected terrorists. What exactly were
Americans willing to accept in the name of security? What went too far?
Would the government be trusted to be the arbiter of this decision or would
it fall prey to the temptation to trade civil liberties for security?

In November of 2001 the NPR/Kaiser/Kennedy School study asked about
Americans' trust in government with the following question: "How much of
the time do you trust the federal government in Washington to do what is
right—just about always, most of the time, only some of the time, or none of
the time?" The results were mixed: 58 percent of respondents said that they
trusted the government "just about always" (14 percent) or "most of the
time" (45 percent), while 41 percent were less trusting and answered "only
some of the time" (36 percent) or "none of the time" (5 percent).[45] Would
this trust carry over into a belief that government would protect their safety
and their civil liberties? CNN/Gallup/*USA Today* found in asking whether
"the Bush administration has gone too far, been about right or not gone far
enough in restricting people's civil liberties in order to fight terrorism," that
60 percent felt the government was doing the right thing and only 10 percent
thought it had gone too far.[46] *Newsweek* found the same results: 72 percent
of participants in their late November survey thought the Bush administration was just about right in what it had done to deal with terrorism and civil

liberties. In fact, their question asked if the administration's proposals for the future were going too far and only 11 percent were willing to say yes.[47] When *Newsweek* asked the same question in June of 2002, fewer Americans were willing to say the Bush administration was doing about right (57 percent), but not because they were concerned it had gone too far. In fact, the shift in sentiment reflected a feeling that the administration had not gone far enough (24 percent).[48]

But what exactly were Americans thinking about in terms of the government's actions to protect citizens and challenges to civil liberties? As mentioned earlier, Fox News/Opinion Dynamics found in their poll that Americans were willing to allow racial profiling but they opposed allowing the government to listen in on private telephone conversations or to read private e-mail. In November of 2001 the Zogby poll reported that Americans were willing to allow their personal belongings to be searched randomly when they were in a public place, but only a bare majority suggested that random searches of their mail were okay.[49]

In July 2002, Zogby found that Americans were no longer ambivalent about searches of their mail; 62 percent now opposed it. They were also less sanguine about their belongings being searched in public places: 48 percent said they favored this while 49 percent said they did not, and 3 percent were unsure. As in the fall of 2001, a majority still opposed monitoring of private telephone conversations. *Newsweek* found that the majority of Americans in the summer of 2002 favored or were willing to accept increased delays and security checks at airports in an effort to improve safety, and they also thought identification checks at the workplace and public buildings were a good idea. They didn't favor random identification checks on the street or in terms of roadblocks but the majority were at least willing to accept them (only 42 percent said they went too far). Americans gave the green light to monitoring access to books and information that might be used by terrorists through public libraries but they rejected allowing the government to listen in on private conversations.[50]

A Delicate Balance: Civil Liberties and Security

This review of public opinion data from the year following the September 11 attacks reveals the ambivalence Americans feel about the tradeoff between security and civil liberties. Overall, the American people cherish their civil liberties, especially in terms of their privacy and speech not related to terrorism. But, at the same time, they are willing to compromise when circumstances dictate.

In the immediate months after September 11 Americans were demanding action on terrorism and security and considered them top priorities for the Bush administration. By the summer of 2002 their priorities changed to show more of a balance between terrorism and domestic issues. However, terrorism and security remained highly salient one year later. Initially, Americans believed that their civil liberties would be compromised in the tradeoff between security and liberty and they were willing to make this trade; by summer 2002 they were less willing to think that they needed to make this sacrifice and less willing to do so.

Overall, Americans were not willing to give up their privacy, particularly in terms of government monitoring their phone conversations or e-mail correspondence. They were, however, willing to agree that the privacy between suspected terrorists and their council was violable.

Free speech remained an important civil liberty in the wake of September 11, but even this bastion of democracy was not impenetrable. Americans agreed that restricting free speech could be dangerous but at the same time were willing to do it when terrorism and support for terrorism were the topics of discussion.

In the aftermath of September 11, racial profiling of those who shared characteristics with the hijackers was generally seen as permissible by many Americans, especially when these people were suspects for potential terrorism. Not all profiling would be seen as necessary, however.

Finally, noncitizens clearly do not have the same rights in the eyes of the American people as citizens. Particularly for those suspected of terrorism, Americans were willing to say noncitizens had fewer rights than citizens. However, even American citizens suspected of terrorism could not count on public opinion to defend their rights.

Overall, the tradeoff between security and civil liberties is a difficult and complex one for the American public to make. They are generally willing to allow public checks of their identity and to accept delays at airports, but Americans are more guarded about their privacy and their communications. Americans are willing to pay a price for security but not if that price is total abandonment of the civil liberties they hold dear.

Notes

1. George W. Bush, "Address to a Joint Session of Congress and the American People," September 20, 2001. Available at http://www.whitehouse.gov/news/releases/2001/09/20010920–8.html (accessed September 29, 2002).
2. The Federalists supported the ratification of the constitution written at the Constitutional Convention in Philadelphia in 1787. A series of essays published by federalists Alexander Hamilton, James Madison, and John Jay under the pseudonym *Publius* appeared in New York newspapers From October 1787 to March 1788. There the authors defended the Constitution and the need for an effective national government. The anti-Federalists published essays under various pseudonyms including *Cato, Brutus, and John DeWitt,* which criticized what they saw as a dangerous consolidation of power at the national level.
3. Ralph Ketcham, ed., *The Anti-federalist Papers and the Constitutional Convention Debates* (New York: Mentor, 1986), 189.
4. John Dewitt, "Essay II," in *The Anti-federalist Papers and the Constitutional Convention Debates,* Rapoh Ketcham, ed. (New York: Mentor, 1986), 189.
5. Alexander Hamilton, James Madison, and John Jay, *The Federalist Papers,* Clinton Rossiter, ed. (New York: Mentor Books, 1999).
6. Alexander Hamilton, *Federalist #84,* in Hamilton, Madison, and Jay, *The Federalist Papers.*

7. *Griswold v. Connecticut,* 381 U.S. 479 (1965); *Roe v. Wade,* 410 U.S. 113 (1973).
8. Michael Linfield, *Freedom under Fire: U.S. Civil Liberties in Times of War* (Boston, MA: South End Press, 1990). Linfield provides an overview of violations of civil liberties from the Revolutionary War through Vietnam. The discussion here reviews only the most notable acts by government to restrict civil liberties. Readers are encouraged to consult Linfield's text for more details. For additional reading see: Mark E. Neely, Jr., *The Fate of Liberty: Abraham Lincoln and Civil Liberties* (New York: Oxford University Press, 1991) and William H. Rehnquist, *All the Laws but One: Civil Liberties in Wartime* (New York: Alfred A. Knopf, 1998).
9. U.S. Constitution, Art. I, Sec. 9.
10. Linfield, *Freedom Under Fire: U.S. Civil Liberties in Times of War.*
11. Any interpretation of public opinion polls must pay special attention to what pollsters call the margin of error or what statisticians call sampling error. All public opinion polls are based upon samples of a larger population, in this case the American public. This means that results from samples are reflective of, but not necessarily identical to, the results we would get if we were to poll the entire American public. Statistical theory allows us to determine how accurate a representation of the population we can get from our sample and, therefore, allows pollsters to be confident that a relatively small sample can yield highly accurate results. The margin of error reported by pollsters indicates how "off" their results may be. A margin of error of +/- 3 percent denotes the fact that if we were to ask everyone in the population the same question we asked our sample, we would expect the result to be within 3 percentage points above or below the results our sample yielded. This explains why, in a poll that asks, for example, if citizens favor security or civil liberties protections, with a 3 percent margin of error, reporters will note that a split of 51 percent for security to 49 percent for civil liberties is a statistical "dead heat." What they are saying is that the sample results show 51 percent in favor of security while 49 percent favor civil liberties protections but that our interpretation of what this may mean for the larger population of all Americans is that security could be favored by anywhere from 48 percent to 54 percent and civil liberties from 46 percent to 52 percent. Therefore, we cannot distinguish the percentages statistically; they overlap and chances are that the percentages favoring one option or another could be within that margin. We cannot say for sure which is greater or that they are not the same. In general, a poll that includes 1,000 *randomly chosen* people will have a margin of error of +/- 3 percent. Smaller samples have higher margins of error. This is why statisticians call this margin "sampling error." However, small samples of even 500 can give us good confidence in our results; a sample of this size will produce a margin of error of +/- 4.5 percent. For an overall introduction to public opinion polling and additional information about sampling error accessible to those without statistical training, see Herbert Asher, *Polling and the Public: What Every Citizen Should Know,* 5th ed. (Washington DC: CQ Press, 2001).
12. Humphrey Taylor, "Harris Report #44 September 5, 2001," *Harris Poll Interactive,* September 5, 2001. Available at http://www.harrisinteractive.com/harris_poll/index.asp?PID=255 (accessed November 3, 2002).
13. National Public Radio (NPR)/Kaiser Family Foundation/Kennedy School of Government Civil Liberties Study, October 30–November 12, 2001. Available at http://www.npr.org/programs/specials/poll/civil_liberties_static_results_1.html

(accessed on October 20, 2002). The question asked respondents: "What do you think are the two most important issues for the government to address?" Response options included (in descending order of percentage response): September 11/war on terrorism, the economy (nonspecific), the war on Afghanistan, education, healthcare (not Medicare), taxes, foreign policy (unspecified), immigration, social security, federal surplus/budget/deficit, peace/world peace/ peace in middle east, honesty in government/other government, race/civil rights, moral/religious values, Medicare, programs for poor/poverty, crime/violence, drugs, other, don't know.

14. Pew Research Center for the People and the Press, "One Year Later: New Yorkers More Troubled, Washingtonians More on Edge," released September 5, 2002. Available at http://people-ress.org/reports/display.php3?PageID=632 (accessed on November 3, 2002).

15. Pew Research "One Year Later." The remaining respondents either refused to answer, said they did not know, or suggested that neither should be Bush's priority.

16. Paul Weyrich, "Bush Must Ensure Civil Liberties and Not Casualties of Terror War," *Insight on the News* 11, no. 39 (October 22, 2001).

17. Bruce Shapiro, "All in the Name of Security: The Administration Is Using September 11 to Curtail Our Civil Liberties," *The Nation* 273, no. 12 (October 22, 2001).

18. NPR/Kaiser Family Foundation/Kennedy School of Government Civil Liberties Study, November 20–25, 2001. Available at http://nationaljournal.com/members/polltrack (accessed July 29, 2002). Unless specified otherwise, poll data are drawn from *National Journal*'s "polltrack" section.

19. CBS/*New York Times* poll conducted December 7–10, 2001. The survey found that 52 percent of Republicans, 35 percent of Democrats, and 42 percent of independents were worried that the government would fail to act, while 34 percent of Republicans, 53 percent of Democrats, and 45 percent of independents were more concerned that government would restrict civil liberties. The balance of respondents for each category either answered that they were worried about both, neither, or that they did not know.

20. CNN/Gallup/*USA Today* poll conducted January 25–27, 2002.

21. CNN/Gallup/*USA Today* poll conducted June 21–23, 2002.

22. And yet, it is important to note that in June, a Fox News poll showed that 63 percent of registered voters favored expanding law enforcement powers even if civil liberties were compromised in the process. Fox News/Opinion Dynamics poll conducted June 4–5, 2002.

23. CBS News Poll conducted April 15–18, 2002.

24. *Newsweek* poll conducted June 27–28, 2002.

25. NPR/Kaiser /Kennedy School Civil Liberties Study, October 30–November 12, 2001.

26. CBS/*New York Times* poll conducted December 7–10, 2001.

27. Fox News/Opinion Dynamics poll conducted November 28–29, 2001. The question appeared in a series of options to an item in which the interviewer asked participants: "please tell me if you favor or oppose each of the following possible solutions that have been proposed as ways of dealing with terrorism:" This particular item asked about "Allowing the government to increase monitoring of private telephone and e-mail communications." Forty percent of participants favored the proposal while 52 percent opposed and 8 percent said they did not know.

28. CBS/*New York Times* poll conducted December 7–10, 2001. Question text: "Until now, in criminal cases of all kinds, conversations between attorneys and their clients who are in jail have been private. Now the government wants to be able to listen in on conversations between attorneys and their clients. Do you think this is a good idea or a bad idea?" Sixty-four percent said it was a bad idea, 30 percent said it was a good idea, and 6 percent said either that it depends or that they did not know.
29. ABC News/*Washington Post* poll conducted November 27, 2001.
30. NPR/Kaiser /Kennedy School Civil Liberties Study, October 30–November 12, 2001.
31. For a discussion, see John L. Sullivan, James Piereson, and George E. Marcus, *Political Tolerance and American Democracy* (Chicago: University of Chicago Press, 1982) and George E. Marcus, John Sullivan, Elizabeth Theiss-Morse, and Sandra L. Wood, *With Malice toward Some: How People Make Civil Liberties Judgments* (Cambridge: Cambridge University Press, 1995).
32. NPR/Kennedy School Civil Liberties Study, October 30–November 12, 2001. Each of these questions was asked of half of the survey respondents (605 people).
33. CBS/*New York Times* poll conducted December 7–10, 2001. Question text: "Do you think everyone should have the right to criticize the government, even if the criticism is damaging to our national interest?" Five percent of participants said that they did not know and 1 percent volunteered "sometimes."
34. CBS/*New York Times* poll conducted December 7–10, 2001. These results come from two separate questions asking about speech criticizing Bush. The first question asked: "These days, if someone disagrees with the president's decisions on military issues, do you think it's OK to criticize him publicly, or should people not publicly criticize the president on military issues?" Fifty-eight percent of respondents said it was okay to criticize, while 39 percent said it was not, and 3 percent said they did not know. The second question asked: "These days, if someone disagrees with the president's proposals on economic or other domestic issues, do you think it OK to criticize him publicly, or should people not criticize the president publicly on economic or domestic issues?" Seventy-three percent said it was ok to criticize, while 22 percent said it was not, and 5 percent said they did not know.
35. Fox News/Opinion Dynamics Poll November 28–29, 2001.
36. Twenty-three percent said they disapproved and 10 percent volunteered that they were not sure.
37. Sixty-one percent of participants in the CBS/*New York Times* poll from early December 2001 said that this was a good idea while 31 percent said it was a bad idea and 8 percent said they did not know. Very interestingly, Democrats were 20 percentage points less likely to think this was a good idea compared with Republicans (52 percent versus 72 percent).
38. *Newsweek* poll November 29–30, 2001.
39. Fox News/ Opinion Dynamics poll conducted June 4–5, 2002.
40. CBS/*New York Times* poll December 7–10, 2001. The remaining 4 percent said it depended or they did not know.
41. *Newsweek* poll June 27–28, 2002. These questions were included in a battery of questions that were introduced with the following statement: "We'd like your opinion of some things that have been done—or might be done—to improve security and protect against terrorism in the United States. For each one, tell me if you strongly favor it, are willing to accept it if necessary or think it goes too

far." Responses to "using race, religion, or ethnicity as a factor in determining who is a suspected terrorist" were: 14 percent strongly favor, 34 percent willing to accept, 48 percent goes to far, and 4 percent don't know. Responses to "detaining people at airports solely because of their religion" were: 6 percent strongly favor, 15 percent willing to accept, 76 percent goes too far, and 3 percent don't know.

42. *Newsweek* poll November 29–30, 2001.
43. NPR/Kaiser/Kennedy School Civil Liberties Study, November 20–25, 2001.
44. *Newsweek* poll June 27–28, 2002. These questions originate from the same battery described in note 41 about racial profiling.
45. NPR/Kaiser /Kennedy School of Government Civil Liberties Study, October 30–November 12, 2001.
46. CNN/Gallup/*USA Today* poll conducted November 26–27, 2001. Twenty-six percent of participants felt the Bush administration had not gone far enough in restricting civil liberties, and 4 percent had no opinion.
47. *Newsweek* poll November 29–30, 2001.
48. *Newsweek* poll June 27–28, 2002.
49. Zogby poll November 27–29, 2001. The questions asked: "Would you favor allowing your purse, handbag, briefcase, backpack or packages to be searched at random anywhere (such as while shopping, entering and exiting pubic buildings, etc.)?" to which 62 percent of participants responded in favor, 36 percent said oppose, and 2 percent said unsure; "Would you favor allowing your mail to be searched at random?" to which 53 percent of participants responded favor, 46 percent said oppose, and 2 percent replied unsure.
50. *Newsweek* poll conducted June 27–28, 2002.

Chapter 10

The Possibility of Dissent in the Age of Terrorism:

A First Amendment Problem and a Proposal for Reform

Daniel P. Tokaji

It is perhaps unsurprising that in the immediate aftermath of the September 11 attacks, the nation witnessed a dearth of public dissent. The horrifying assaults upon citadels of American economic and military strength, combined with the anguish of seeing so many innocent people killed, created an apparent national unity not witnessed in decades.

Somewhat more surprising than the initial wave of post–September 11 unity is how little dissent accompanied public policy debates in the months that followed, despite growing reasons to question American policy both at home and abroad. A broad consensus of public opinion, to be sure, supported military intervention in Afghanistan, the initial phase of the so-called War Against Terror. But with the Taliban vanquished and the Al-Qaeda network disrupted if not destroyed, a number of difficult policy questions have emerged. Who exactly *are* our enemies in the War on Terror? How long can this war be expected to persist? How will we know when it ends? Is it appropriate for the United States preemptively to strike Iraq or other nations, based on the mere possibility of future terrorist acts?

Equally vital questions lie before us on the domestic front, some of which are being explored in the other chapters to this volume. For example, as our temporal distance from September 11 increases, will Americans be willing to tolerate the incursions upon our privacy and other civil liberties that John Ashcroft's Justice Department insists are necessary? Is it appropriate for the government to deport noncitizens based on mere suspicion of ties to groups that the government has deemed terrorist organizations? To what extent must the traditional wall of separation between foreign intelligence-gathering activities (traditionally conducted by the CIA) and domestic law enforcement activities (traditionally conducted by the FBI) be abrogated in order to ensure domestic security?[1] And while attention is focused on the War on Terror, must we to push to the back burner domestic issues, such as a faltering economy and the torrent of corporate scandals that came to light as the nation was reeling from September 11? To what extent does responsibility for these crises lie with the federal government, including the legislators from both major parties who received large contributions from those linked to the wave of corporate malfeasance?

This chapter endeavors not to answer these questions but instead to inquire into the reasons for our impoverished public discourse regarding them. My thesis is that the relative scarcity of public dissent over American foreign and domestic policy in the early stages of this age of terrorism reflects a deeper problem in American democracy, one that challenges conventional First Amendment doctrine. More specifically, I argue that the dearth of dissent in the wake of September 11—and the accompanying disinterest in politics on the part of the American public—is a product of the inadequacy of opportunities for citizen participation in the life of democracy. Despite the proliferation of outlets for communication, such as cable stations and Internet sites, we lack the sort of "robust, uninhibited and wide-open" public debate that Justice Brennan's opinion in *New York Times v. Sullivan*[2] envisioned. Perhaps the best evidence of the poor condition of our political discourse is the abysmal rate of voter turnout, especially among people of color. Equally telling is the silence of our government in response to the question "What can I do for my country?," which many Americans found themselves asking in the days after September 11. The absence of a coherent answer to this question suggests that our political and legal institutions have failed to create the opportunities for citizen participation that post–September 11 democracy demands.

At least partly to blame for our impoverished discourse, I argue, are the inadequacies of contemporary First Amendment doctrine. That doctrine is designed to prevent state officials from intentionally suppressing disfavored messages or ideas and is quite well-suited to accomplish this end.[3] Indeed, it is largely because of the doctrine's strength in this regard that post–September 11 America has, for the most part, been spared McCarthy-style tactics aimed at silencing dissenting voices.[4] While this *laissez faire* approach may prevent government from actively suppressing speech, it is not sufficient to ensure a robust marketplace of competing ideas. The inadequacies of this *laissez faire* approach to speech become especially apparent, where private rather than governmental entities limit channels for dissemination of dissenting viewpoints and where economic inequalities limit speakers' abilities to make themselves heard. Put another way, existing free speech doctrine is designed to safeguard "negative equality," by which I mean the state's affirmative suppression of unpopular views; but is not designed to advance "positive equality" by increasing the opportunities for all citizens to participate in public discourse.[5]

This chapter argues that the scarcity of dissent in the wake of September 11 reflects a serious First Amendment problem, the solution to which must include promotion of positive equality and, more specifically, the creation of pathways though which citizens of limited means may participate in the life of democracy. One such reform would be the creation of a more robust program of national service that includes opportunities for advocacy of political issues. In explaining why the government should play a role in stimulating political activism on the part of its citizens, I turn to what might seem unlikely sources: Dr. Martin Luther King's "Letter from Birmingham City Jail"[6] and the philosophy of dissent that he borrows from Henry David Thoreau's classic essay "Civil Disobedience."[7] Both men wrote about the centrality of dissent in times of great moral crisis, and our existing national service legislation expressly cites King's "life and teachings" as a source of inspiration.[8] Yet the modest national service program that currently exists fails to adequately embody his vision of citizen activism, including its importance both to the individual's moral life and to a healthy democratic discourse. An enhanced federally funded program that included an advocacy component would, I argue, serve both these ends. It would encourage participation by those who until now have not been engaged citizens and would promote a more vibrant democracy.

The first part of the chapter offers a sketch of post–September 11 American democracy, from the immediate response of the federal government to the November 2002 elections, highlighting the absence of public dissent on major issues of foreign and domestic policy. The second part examines this problem in the light cast by the writings of King and Thoreau, explaining how their conception of dissent bears upon the present condition of American public discourse. The third part connects the condition of public discourse to existing First Amendment doctrine, specifically to its limited ability to further the ideal of a democracy in which all citizens might participate as equals. I close by suggesting one way in which the government might encourage citizen activism: through development of an enhanced national service program that would allow participants to engage in expressive activities, including advocacy in opposition to government policies. By fostering rather than frustrating meaningful dissent, such a program would help fulfill the vision of a democracy that at once facilitates the moral development of the individual and plants the seeds for its own regeneration.

Public Discourse in the Wake of September 11

I start with a sketch of the condition of public discourse during the period following the September 11 attacks, up to and including the 2002 elections. My goal here is not to provide a comprehensive account of the events that took place in this period, but simply to give some flavor of the national response to September 11, with a special eye toward the impact of these events on citizen engagement and participation. Notwithstanding the inherent difficulties of proving a negative, I also aim to show the impoverishment of public discourse regarding the grave questions of foreign and domestic policy facing the nation.

Three days after the September 11 attacks, with only a single dissenting vote, the United States Congress voted to authorize the president to use force in retaliation for the attacks.[9] As the United States military prepared its response, many Americans wondered what they might do to serve their country.[10] President Bush's address to a joint session of Congress, delivered nine days after the attacks, expressly acknowledged this sentiment and sought to answer this question:

> I ask you to live your lives and hug your children. I know many citizens have fears tonight and I ask you to be calm and resolute, even in the face of the continuing threat. I ask you to uphold the values of America and remember why so many have come here. . . . We're in a fight for our principles and our first responsibility is to live by them. No one should be singled out for unfair treatment or unkind words because of their ethnic background or religious faith. . . . I ask you to continue to support the victims of the tragedy with your contributions. Those who want to give can go to a central source of information . . . to find the names of groups providing direct help in New York, Pennsylvania and Virginia. The FBI agents who are now at work in this investigation may need your cooperation. And I ask you to give it. I ask for your patience with the delays and inconveniences that may accompany tighter scrutiny. And for your patience in what will be a long struggle. . . . I ask your continued participation and confidence in the American economy. Terrorists attacked a symbol of American prosperity. They did not touch its source. . . . And finally, please continue praying for the victims of terror and their families, for those in uniform and for our great country. Prayer has comforted us in sorrow and will help strengthen us for the journey ahead.

As noble and comforting as the president's words may have been, they offered precious little in the way of advice to those seeking concrete ways by which they might serve their country. There was, for example, no call for sacrifice on the part of the citizenry at large. While providing an avenue by which concerned people might provide aid to those directly affected, there was little suggestion of what else Americans might do to turn their patriotism towards a more lasting constructive purpose.

It is, to be sure, unfair to criticize the president too severely for failing to offer more concrete suggestions in the immediate aftermath of the attack, just as it would have been unrealistic to expect any serious opposition to the immediate military response. More disconcerting were the developments that unfolded in the following weeks and months.

On October 26, 2001, the president signed into law the USA PATRIOT Act, which confers unprecedented "antiterrorism" powers upon the federal government. The USA PATRIOT broadens the circumstances in which executive detention is permitted, allows government to deny aliens permission to enter the country based on their expressive activities, increases the government's power to conduct surveillance, and increases the intelligence-gathering powers of the CIA and FBI.[11] The bill passed in the Senate with just a single dissenting vote, that of Wisconsin Democrat Russ Feingold. It was enacted despite the absence of any debate in committee or Senate markup, but was instead the product of private discussions between the Bush administration and key legislators that occurred almost entirely behind closed doors.[12]

The expeditious and secretive enactment of the USA PATRIOT Act stands in marked contrast to the consideration afforded to another bill, which might have provided a better answer to the question of what concerned citizens might do for their country. In November 2001, Senators Evan Bayh (D-IN), John McCain (R-AZ), and others introduced a bill, the "Call to Service Act of 2001," which would have dramatically expanded the scope of service programs created by the National and Community Service Act of 1990 and expanded by the National and Community Service Trust Act of 1993.[13] The National Service Corps created by these acts, commonly known as "Americorps," was intended to be a "sort of domestic Peace Corps."[14] Its broad mandate is to provide service opportunities, principally for young people, through the nonprofit sector.[15] The law specifically cites the life and work of Dr. Martin Luther King, Jr., as a guiding inspiration, stating that "service opportunities shall consist of activities reflecting the life and teachings of Martin Luther King, Jr., such as cooperation and understanding among racial and ethnic groups, nonviolent conflict resolution, equal economic and educational opportunities, and social justice."[16] The Bayh-McCain bill was intended to expand the service opportunities available, so that national service would be an option for every young person.[17] The act would have expanded Americorps from its present size of 50,000 to 250,000 by the year 2010, with 50 percent of the increase to be targeted for "Homeland Security."[18] It would also have removed the cap on the proportion of Americorps funds (currently set at one-third) that could be directed toward national nonprofits and would have increased incentives to participate by making education awards for Americorps participants nontaxable.

The president subsequently proposed a somewhat less expansive version of national service reform, featuring it in his January 29, 2002 State of the Union address. In this address, President Bush asked that all Americans give at least two years or 4,000 hours of service over the course of their lives.[19] Enhancement of our existing national service program garnered the support not only of liberals but also of some conservatives. William Bennett, for example, vigorously supported the Bush administration's proposal to allow "Americorps members . . . to build the administrative, technological and financial capacities of nonprofits, rather than simply to provide beneficial services to individuals."[20] Nevertheless, House conservatives prevented the bill from moving forward, citing their opposition to government-financed volunteer programs.[21]

In the midst of these unsuccessful efforts to provide outlets for public-minded Americans to serve their country emerged allegations of gross misconduct on the part of decidedly *non*-public-minded executives. About a month after being warned by one of Enron's vice presidents that the company might be nothing more than "an elaborate accounting hoax," and after disposing of some of his own stock, Enron Chair Kenneth Lay used the forum of an online chat to urge employees to purchase shares of the company.[22] Months before the company's collapse, the *Washington Post* had cited Mr. Lay's "[l]ong-standing ties of friendship, politics and ideology" linking him to the president, characterizing Mr. Lay as "one of Bush's most important political supporters."[23] But Enron did not limit it largess to Mr. Bush, donating $6 million to members of Congress since 1989, including contributions to half the members of the House and three-quarters of Senators.[24] It also lavished campaign contributions upon state legislators from Texas to Michigan and from California to New York.[25] Collapses of WorldCom, Tyco, and other large corporations followed the Enron collapse, resulting in a crisis of public trust in corporations. Even as some of the executives immediately responsible for these scandals were investigated and prosecuted, questions emerged about the necessity of systemic reforms to protect the public interest from runaway corporate greed.[26]

As the 2002 elections approached, the next phase of the War on Terror overshadowed such revelations of corporate malfeasance. With the Taliban government driven from power, the Bush administration focused its sights upon Iraq as the next enemy in the ongoing War on Terror. Only sparse cries of dissent from the American people found their way into the mainstream media. As one activist from a Chicago-based antiwar group called "Voices in the Wilderness" noted, "We haven't been hearing much about the grass roots. . . . But a lot's been happening under the radar."[27]

Despite the absence of evidence linking the regime of Saddam Hussein and the Al-Qaeda terrorist network, and the novelty of approving military force for a preemptive strike, the House and Senate approved the use of military force after only a few days of debate.[28] While the final vote (in contrast to the passage of the initial use of force resolution and the USA PATRIOT Act) did not approach unanimity, both houses voted to approve the resolution by lopsided margins.[29] Some attributed the introduction and speedy passage of these resolutions to political jockeying in the November 2002 elections—namely, the Republicans' desire to turn attention away from corporate scandals and toward the War on Terror, and the Democrats' desire to put the use-of-force resolutions behind them so that electorate might refocus attention on the country's economic woes.[30] Even after passage of these resolutions, however, Democrats generally evinced a reluctance to address the impact of the corporate accountability scandals on the national economy, perhaps because they might be viewed as equally complicit in allowing these episodes to occur.

The surge of patriotism evident after the September 11 attacks did not appreciably increase participation in the political process.[31] According to one estimate, turnout in the 2002 primary elections dipped as low as 17 percent of eligible voters.[32] Voter turnout remained well below 50 percent in the November 2000 national elections, with turnout among African Americans and Latinos especially depressed.[33] The show of patriotism and flag-waving so conspicuous immediately after the September 11 attacks thus appears to have generated little if any increased interest in democratic participation. And through their failure to vote at all, people of color have demonstrated an increasing disillusionment with the political process. To the extent that some hoped that September 11 might lead to a renewal of democracy, those hopes have yet to be realized.

The Necessity of Dissent

The preceding sketch illustrates the vital issues of foreign and domestic policy that demand the citizenry's attention, engagement, and participation. It is also meant to suggest that the nation is as ill-equipped for the demands of a post–September 11 democracy as we were for the attacks themselves. By this, I mean that our public institutions have failed to foster the citizen engagement and participation that is essential for democracy to function. This is evident in the scarcity of public dissent over the initial decision to use military force, the enactment of the USA PATRIOT Act, the resolutions authorizing the use of force against Iraq, and the structural economic issues like corporate accountability. Public engagement and participation in the debate over profound issues of national and international significance is nowhere near what it should be. Notwithstanding the plethora of instantaneous news and combustible commentary available everywhere from FoxNews to MSNBC.com, the citizenry—and especially people of color—are not engaged in the critical issues that we confront, a fact most clearly evinced by the abysmal turnout in post–September 11 elections.

What accounts for the conspicuous lack of citizen engagement in the grave issues of foreign and domestic policy generated by the September 11 attacks? Answering this question requires an analysis of two different forms of equality in the realm of speech, for which I use the shorthand "negative equality" and "positive equality." My claim is that the dearth of public dissent stems not so much from denials of negative equality (such as official suppression of disfavored viewpoints) but from the failure to promote positive equality (such as the creation of mechanisms by which citizens might participate in public discourse). A brief definition of these terms, developed more extensively below, may be useful. The term "negative equality" refers to the idea that government should not restrict speech based upon its underlying message or ideas; that it should act in an evenhanded fashion when making decisions such as what speech to prohibit, what speech to permit, and what speech to fund. The term "positive equality" refers to the idea that government should affirmatively promote a robust public debate in which a wide range of divergent viewpoints are expressed; that it should encourage a public discourse in which all citizens may participate as equals.

In explaining the importance of both negative and positive equality, I turn to two seminal essays explaining the necessity of dissent in times of crisis. Henry David Thoreau's "Civil Disobedience" depicts dissent as a moral obligation, taking the position that the individual has a responsibility to speak out—and even to disobey the law—in opposition to an unjust system of government. Martin Luther King, Jr.'s "Letter from Birmingham City Jail" turns Thoreau's philosophy of civil disobedience toward political strategy, explaining its use as a tactic by which to end racial segregation. For both, dissent is an individual moral obligation as well as a step toward the elimination of existing injustices. King and Thoreau's writings thus explain the necessity of dissent to the health of the individual and to democracy. They also bring into focus the inadequacy of existing institutions, manifest in the scarcity of dissent in post–September 11 public discourse, in terms of their failure to promote positive speech equality.

King wrote "Letter from Birmingham City Jail" in April 1963 while serving a sentence for participation in civil rights demonstrations, the same set of demonstrations that would, six years later, give rise to the Supreme Court's decision in *Shuttlesworth v. Birmingham*. King's open letter was addressed to eight prominent white clergymen who had criticized the Birmingham demonstrations as "unwise and untimely" and urged that the struggle for integration be allowed to proceed through the judicial system. The letter attempts to explain the reasons for adopting direct action tactics, such as public demonstrations and marches, that contravened local laws.

King's letter serves as a powerful affirmation of a radical form of dissent, civil disobedience, both to the individual confronted with serious injustice and to a healthy democracy. King begins his justification of the demonstrators' illegal actions by distinguishing between just and unjust laws, characterizing segregation as a form of the latter (p. 293). He further explains that laws such as Birmingham's permit statute may be "just on their face and unjust in its application," insofar as it is used to "preserve segregation and deny citizens the First Amendment privilege of peaceful assembly" (p. 295). While the clergy to whom the letter was responding viewed the "tension" caused by his demonstrations as a bad thing, King explains that such tension is vital in order to tear down an unjust system. He unfavorably contrasts the "negative peace"—the absence of public dissent urged by the white clergy— with the "positive peace which is the presence of justice" (p. 295). The need to advance such a positive peace, according to King, justified peaceful demonstrations that violated the laws of the City of Birmingham. Indeed, violation of the law constituted a critical part of the demonstrations' expressive impact, since it focused attention on conditions that would otherwise have gone unnoticed and unrepaired. Breaking the city's laws served as a powerful means by which to expose the unfairness of the system of racial segregation that Birmingham typified and thereby bring about the demolition of this unjust system.

Such demonstrations did not, however, merely serve the instrumental purpose of promoting a more just society; they also served a vital expressive function for the African Americans who were expressing their dissent: "The Negro has many pent-up resentments and latent frustrations. He has to get them out" (p. 297). This statement captures the duality of dissent: its importance both to the individual and to the objective of achieving societal change. Dissent fulfills a "vital urge" of the individual, providing a "creative outlet" for those long subject to oppression. It also serves the systemic interest of developing a more just democracy, which King describes as the "cosmic urgency toward the promised land of racial justice." These two purposes come together, insofar as individuals' participation in a collective effort to improve existing conditions is seen as a moral imperative. In using the term "imperative," I mean to suggest a Kantian moral aspect to King's defense of civil disobedience, something that is most directly suggested by his assertion that "there is no greater treason than to do the right deed for the wrong reason" (p. 301). Dissent not only serves a collective instrumental purpose, moving us toward a more just society, but also fulfills the individual's moral need to speak out against injustice.

In expressing the duality of dissent, its necessity both to the individual and to society, King self-consciously borrows from Thoreau's essay "Civil Disobedience." As Thoreau describes in this essay, he had refused to pay his poll tax as an act of dissent against American foreign and domestic policy—specifically, the then-ongoing war on Mexico and the institution of slavery—and willingly went to jail for his refusal to obey the laws of the Commonwealth of Massachusetts. Thoreau explains his actions as a "duty," just as King expresses the moral imperative of publicly expressing opposition to a system that is unjust to its very core. As Thoreau puts it, "[slavery's] very Constitution is evil" (p. 93), and he later complains of the "sanction which the Constitution gives to slavery," (p. 102). King's idea that there exists not only a moral right but also a moral obligation to express dissent when faced with an unjust system is drawn directly from Thoreau.

For both King and Thoreau, then, civil disobedience at once promotes the instrumental objective of creating a more just society and the individual's moral obligation to speak out against existing injustice. Moreover, both envision a democracy that not only tolerates but also encourages dissent, and thereby facilitates its own regeneration. In Thoreau's words:

> I please myself with imagining a state at last which can afford to be just to all men, and to treat the individual with respect as a neighbor; which even would not think it inconsistent with its own repose if a few were to live aloof from it, not meddling with it nor embraced by it, who fulfilled the duties of neighbors and fellow-men. A State which bore this kind of fruit, and suffered it to drop off as fast as it ripened, would prepare the way for a still more perfect and glorious State, which I have also imagined, but not yet anywhere seen (p. 104).

By "pleas[ing]" himself through imagining a more just state, Thoreau (like King) suggests that civil disobedience serves the needs of the individual. At the same time, the metaphor of a fruit dropping off the tree "as fast as it ripened" suggests the creation a "more perfect" state, one that would contain the seeds of renewal—that would not inhibit but instead encourage the sort of healthy tension that King understood as necessary to remedy existing injustice. Both King and Thoreau are of course most directly concerned with promoting racial equality, in Thoreau's case the abolition of slavery and in King's case the abolition of segregation. Yet implicit in both of their essays is also an ideal of how democracy should work. Part of this vision is, of course, the negative egalitarian idea that the government should allow speakers of various points of view to express themselves. It is not, however, sufficient that the state simply keep its hands off speakers seeking to express their own moral convictions; the state also has an affirmative obligation to "be just to all men" (p. 104). Both imagine a more perfect state, one that provides an outlet for individuals to express dissent and thereby contains the seeds of its own renewal.

As the preceding sketch of post–September 11 discourse suggests, our democracy is still a long way from this vision. Citizen engagement and participation are at historic lows, and dissent, if not affirmatively suppressed, is certainly not encouraged. The question thus to be asked is: Can we imagine something better? And might it be argued that the imperative for creation of something better lies in the Constitution itself?

A First Amendment Problem

My answer to both of these questions is an emphatic "yes." Not only is it possible for us to imagine a better democratic system, one that does not simply tolerate but actually encourages dissent, but it may also be argued that the Constitution *commands* the development of such a system. Examination of our impoverished post–September 11 public discourse in the light cast by free speech cases reveals a gap between First Amendment theory and what the doctrine actually accomplishes. While theoretical justifications for the First Amendment focus on both negative and positive equality, the legal doctrines that have developed are much more effective at securing the former than the latter. The gap between theory and doctrine calls for revisitation of our conventional understanding of what the First Amendment requires— though it may ultimately be the political branches rather than the courts that bear principal responsibility for effectuating positive egalitarian values in this area.

I start with First Amendment theory. The philosophical justification for civil disobedience offered by King and Thoreau bears a striking resemblance to the two theories most commonly offered to explain the centrality of the First Amendment: first, to promote both the individual's interest in self-expression; and, second, to advance the societal interest in a rich and enlightened public discourse, one that gives space to dissenting view-points.[34] The First Amendment should therefore, at least in theory, promote both negative and positive equality, both the right of each individual to be treated as an equal moral being and the right of the polity to receive information from a wide variety of perspectives.

Examination of First Amendment *doctrine,* however, reveals that this doctrine is much more effective at securing negative equality than positive equality. The doctrine is designed to guard against government action taken to suppress unpopular speakers but not to ensure that a multiplicity of viewpoints will actually be aired. And the doctrine is effective at accomplishing this end. This is evidenced by our present-day public discourse, the impoverished condition of which cannot readily be attributed to denials of negative equality, such as the official suppression of disfavored viewpoints. That is not to say, of course, that there is no danger of negative equality being denied in the age of terrorism. There have, of course, been some official attempts to intimidate those who question American foreign policy,[35] and history suggests that the federal government may ultimately use parts of the USA PATRIOT Act to squelch dissent.[36] Yet to this point, evidence of official attempts to suppress unpopular viewpoints is relatively scarce.[37] The shortage of post–September 11 dissent does not, for example, arise from the government denying dissenters permission to speak in public places or imprisoning those who seek to protest government policies.

This should come as little surprise since settled First Amendment doctrine provides effective means by which to safeguard negative equality and, more specifically, to prevent the government from singling out dissenting speakers for unfavorable treatment. One of the most prominent affirmations of this equality principle is set forth in Justice Thurgood Marshall's opinion for the United States Supreme Court in *Police Department v. Mosley*: "[A]bove all else, the First Amendment means that government has no power to restrict expression because of its message, its ideas, its subject matter or its content."[38] In *Mosley*, the Court struck down a Chicago ordinance that treated labor-related speech differently from speech on other subjects. In so doing, the Court recognized that, while the government may regulate such activities as picketing in a content- and viewpoint-neutral manner, it may not single out expression on particular subjects for either favored or disfavored treatment. As Harvard Law School professor Laurence Tribe has explained, *Mosley* stands for the "basic requirement that the government may not aim at the communicative impact of expressive conduct without triggering . . . exactly and usually fatal scrutiny."[39]

The negative equality principle underlies Justice Scalia's opinion for the Court in *R.A.V. v. City of St. Paul*. Building on the rule against content-discrimination set forth in *Mosley*, the *R.A.V.* Court affirmed that: "The First Amendment generally prevents government from proscribing speech, or even expressive conduct, because of disapproval of the ideas expressed."[40] The *R.A.V.* Court applied this principle to strike down a city ordinance that targeted expression designed to provoke race-based anger or resentment, such as burning crosses on someone's front lawn. Even though the Minnesota Supreme Court has construed the law to cover only "fighting words," a category of speech that may be banned outright without violating the First Amendment, the U.S. Supreme Court still held this law unconstitutional. The greater power to prohibit a category of expressive conduct outright did not include the lesser power to prohibit speech *selectively* based on its content or viewpoint. Thus, the City of St. Paul might criminalize fighting words generally but could not single out one category of fighting words based on content or viewpoint. Put simply, the government must act evenhandedly when regulating speech and not based on hostility toward disfavored ideas or messages. Cases like *Mosley* and *R.A.V.* stand for the negative egalitarian principle that when government makes determinations about whether to prohibit speech (or, conversely, to permit or facilitate private speech), it may not generally base its decisions based on the ideas or messages to be expressed.

This ideal of negative equality is also apparent in a line of cases, most of them concerning expression in public fora, that limit the exercise of official discretion in granting or denying permission to speak. Supreme Court precedent provides for a searching review of schemes, vesting broad discretion in official decisionmakers to decide who may speak. Among the earliest examples is *Thornhill v. Alabama,* where the Court considered a state law that made it a crime to picket a place of business "without just cause," which had been applied against union-affiliated picketers. The lack of specificity in this law made it too susceptible to "harsh and discriminatory enforcement by local prosecuting officials against particular groups deemed to merit their displeasure."[41] So too, in *Shuttlesworth v. Birmingham,* the Supreme Court considered a law authorizing denial of a parade permit based on such amorphous criteria as "public welfare" and "morals."[42] Finding these criteria insufficiently definite, and therefore susceptible to discriminatory enforcement against disfavored speakers, the Court invalidated the convictions of civil rights demonstrators arrested for failing to obtain the required permit. More recently, in *Forsyth County v. Nationalist Movement,* the Court considered a county ordinance giving local officials to adjust permit fees based upon the hostility likely to be engendered by the speech at issue. In acting on a facial challenge to the law brought by a white supremacist group, the Court found that such a law created the unacceptable risk that official discretion would be used to suppress unpopular points of view.[43]

The principle of negative equality is thus embodied not only in the prohibition against laws *expressly* targeting certain points of view, but also in the requirement that government set clear standards when it requires permission to speak. In his opinion for the Court in *City of Lakewood v. Plain Dealer,* Justice Brennan explained how the requirement of clear standards serves the objective of evenhandedness: "Without these guideposts, post hoc rationalizations by the licensing official and the use of shifting or illegitimate criteria are far too easy, making it difficult for courts to determine in any particular instance whether the licensor is permitting favorable, and suppressing unfavorable expression."[44] This objective underlies not only the requirement of precision, *Lakewood* notes, but also the special features of free speech doctrine, broadening the circumstances in which vague or overbroad laws may be challenged on their face, even by speakers whose conduct could legitimately be banned by a properly drawn statute. The doctrine applied in cases such as *Thornhill, Shuttlesworth,* and *Forsyth County* advances the negative equality principle articulated in *Mosley*—namely, the idea that the First Amendment "above all else" means that government may not restrict speech based on its messages or ideas. The doctrine thereby provides a bulwark against government acting to suppress dissenting points of view, either overtly or covertly.

Even when government is subsidizing rather than restricting speech, there are limits upon its authority to discriminate based on speakers' viewpoints. Two recent cases elucidate these limitations. The first is *Rosenberger v. Rector and Visitors of the University of Virginia,* which struck down a state university's system guidelines for funding on-campus expressive activities by student groups—specifically, the university's prohibition against funding for "religious organization[s]." The Court held this restriction to be impermissible viewpoint discrimination, even though the "forum" created by the university's funding scheme was "one of [the state's] own creation."[45] The second case is *Legal Services Corporation v. Velazquez,* striking down a federal regulation prohibiting government-funded legal services programs from representing indigent clients in challenges to existing welfare laws.[46] As in *Rosenberger,* the Court held such a restriction on government-funded organizations to be impermissible viewpoint discrimination. Under these cases, the critical question is whether the government's funding is "designed to facilitate private speech" (as in *Rosenberger* and *L.S.O. v. Velasquez*), in which case viewpoint discrimination is forbidden, or, alternatively, to "promote a governmental message" (as in *Rust v. Sullivan*[47]), in which case viewpoint discrimination is allowed. Like the doctrines of vagueness and overbreadth, the Supreme Court's recent decisions concerning viewpoint discrimination in the area of government funding are designed to guard against government targeting disfavored points of view.

Time will tell whether the Supreme Court will consistently apply First Amendment doctrine protecting negative equality when the government raises the specter of "terrorism." One area of special concern is the broad discretion vested in the United States attorney general to designate certain organizations as "terrorist" and to put a federal prohibition upon making monetary contributions to such organizations, a power that lends itself to the targeting of organizations espousing views unpopular with the United States government.[48] The Supreme Court's settled doctrine frowning on unfettered discretion in the speech context would seem to call such broad powers into serious question. Nevertheless, at least one federal circuit court has upheld the statute, giving the secretary of state broad discretion to declare organizations "terrorist" and thereby to prohibit giving material support to those groups.[49]

There are thus deeply important questions still open about whether the Court will apply the rigorous constitutional safeguards for negative equality, when the countervailing interest advanced by the government is to combat terrorism. It is uncertain whether the courts will choose to use the powerful tools available under existing doctrine to safeguard negative equality.

When it comes to *positive* equality, on the other hand, existing constitutional doctrine provides the judiciary with precious few tools in the first place. At best, First Amendment doctrines regarding overbreadth and vagueness provide a blunt tool by which to ensure that a variety of different perspectives will actually be aired. They do an even worse job of encouraging all citizens, especially those of limited means, to actually participate in democratic discourse. Responsibility for promoting opportunities for democratic participation is generally entrusted to the other branches of government. And even where the other branches of government *have* acted to promote positive equality, the Court has not always recognized a legitimate constitutional interest.

The best example of this tendency may be the Court's consideration of First Amendment challenges to campaign finance legislation, most famously its decision in *Buckley v. Valeo*.[50] In *Buckley,* the Court struck down under the First Amendment federal legislation limiting campaign expenditures. The legislation infringed on negative equality, insofar as it treated expenditures on behalf of candidates differently from other expenditures; put another way, it discriminated based on content, in specially targeting expenditures for speech relating to candidates for federal office. As the Court put it: "Advocacy of the election or defeat of candidates for federal office is no less entitled to protection under the First Amendment than the discussion of political policy generally or advocacy of the passage or defeat of legislation."[51] One of the countervailing interests advanced in support of the legislation was "equalizing the relative ability of individuals and groups to influence the outcome of elections."[52] The *Buckley* Court soundly rejected this positive egalitarian interest as a legitimate reason for limiting campaign expenditures, emphatically stating that "the concept that government may restrict the speech of some elements of society in order to enhance the relative voice of others is wholly foreign to the First Amendment. . . . "[53]

Curiously, the *Buckley* Court went on to acknowledge the positive equality principle, noting that the First Amendment was designed to "secure 'the widest possible dissemination of information from diverse and antagonistic sources.'"[54] One might well argue that a limitation on campaign expenditures actually advances this interest, insofar as it helps promote the discourse surrounding political campaigns from being dominated by the voices of the wealthy, thereby promoting the expression of views from a diversity of sources. Yet the *Buckley* Court disallows such a justification for limitations on campaign expenditures, thereby privileging the interest in negative equality over the interest in positive equality.

The Court has not, however, uniformly discounted positive equality as a legitimate justification for government action in the realm of speech. In *Red Lion Broadcasting v. F.C.C.,* for example, the Court upheld the so-called "fairness doctrine," requiring broadcasters to allow the expression of opposing points of view.[55] In doing so, the Court recognized the positive equality interest in facilitating the expression of divergent viewpoints. On the other hand, in *Miami Herald v. Tornillo,* the Court refused to allow a comparable right of reply in the print media, concluding that considerations justifying the fairness doctrine (including the limited "space" available on the public airwaves) did not apply with respect to newspapers—where, at least as a theoretical matter, there is no limitation on the publication of divergent points of view.

All of these cases, it bears emphasizing, pertain to what government *may* do to promote positive equality and not to what it *must* do. The Court has never said, for example, that the First Amendment requires the F.C.C. to encourage the expression of divergent viewpoints by adopting the fairness doctrine, or something like it. It has never said that the National Endowment of the Arts is required to fund artistic expression. It has not required universities like the University of Virginia to fund the expression of student organizations, as it chose to do in *Rosenberger*. Nor has it ever required that the government adopt campaign finance reform legislation to counteract the corrosive influence of accumulated wealth on the political process and to ensure that all citizens have an equal opportunity to influence elections.[56] It may well be that, outside the approval of such legislation or regulations, the promotion of positive equality simply lies beyond the capacity of courts. After all, First Amendment doctrine is well-suited to deal with government suppression of dissenting viewpoints (whether overt or covert) but not to require government to develop opportunities for citizens to participate in democracy. This includes situations—as is the case with the unequal system of financing political campaigns and limited access the broadcast media—in which the actions of private rather than public entities threaten to diminish the availability of dissenting viewpoints.

One recent example of this problem is the response to remarks made by Bill Maher, formerly the host of the television show *Politically Incorrect,* shortly after the September 11 attacks. After Mr. Maher asserted that the September 11 hijackers were not cowardly but that it was cowardly to launch guided missiles at distant targets, some of the shows sponsors abruptly pulled their advertising.[57] Another example is the November 11, 2001 report issued by the American Council of Trustees and Alumni (ACTA), an organization founded by Dr. Lynn Cheney and Senator Joseph Lieberman (D-CT). This organization listed statements and names of academics that questioned or criticized aspects of the initial phase of the War on Terror. In explaining why this was deemed necessary, the ACTA report asserted that college and university faculty had been the "weak link" in the response to the September 11 attacks.

It is easy to see how such private action might prevent dissenting viewpoints from being heard. Under settled case authority, private action by advertisers or advocacy organizations aimed at squeezing out dissenting speech does not provide the basis for any judicial intervention. Nor is there any plausible theory upon which the First Amendment can be read to require the political branches of government to intervene. To the contrary, if government were to venture into this era—by, for example, prohibiting advertisers from pulling their commercials in response to the expression of controversial views or by limiting the ability of groups like the ACTA to publish statements and "name names"—it would violate the First Amendment rights of those private actors under settled doctrine.

Existing First Amendment doctrine therefore provides very limited means by which to ensure that dissenting voices will actually be heard. This helps explain the increasing disengagement of the American public, even in this post–September 11 democracy that demands the active participation of the citizenry. Of course, the need for such participation in times of great moral crisis is nothing new, nor is the need to take extraordinary steps to air dissenting views. It was, after all, the need to call attention to the systemic injustices around them – to make those injustices visible to society at large— that propelled both King and Thoreau to engage in their acts of civil disobedience. Disobedience of the law provided the means by which to advance positive equality, by calling public attention to dissenting voices.

Does this mean that promotion of positive equality simply lies beyond the reach of the law? Is disobedience of the law the *only* means by which dissenters may focus public attention on systemic injustices? I think not. In considering why not, it is helpful to revisit the two commonly advanced theories of the First Amendment,[58] theories that correspond roughly (though not precisely) to the values of positive and negative equality that I have described above. One theory is atomistic, focusing on the rights of the individual. It views the First Amendment's fundamental purpose as the protection of a sphere of individual liberty, having at its root the ideal of each person as an "equal sovereign citizen" whose expression is worthy of protection.[59] The other view is systemic, viewing the First Amendment's fundamental purpose as the promotion of a vibrant democracy in which a variety of divergent perspectives are available. It is rooted in the "very foundations of the self-governing process,"[60] more specifically in the idea that a wide range of antagonistic views must be aired for the democratic process properly to function. Neither theory is complete unto itself. It can scarcely be questioned that the First Amendment advances both the individual's interest in autonomy and society's interest in a well-functioning democracy.

As a general matter, the atomistic view tends toward an emphasis on negative equality, while the systemic view tends toward an emphasis on positive equality. These theories only "roughly" correspond to the two equality norms here identified, however, because preservation of negative equality is vital to the systemic theory of the First Amendment as well as to the atomistic theory. For example, as cases like *Thornhill* and *Shuttlesworth* exemplify, negative equality is essential to a fair democratic process. Where government is left free to deny speakers espousing dissenting viewpoints permission to speak, it not only infringes upon their interest in individual autonomy, but it also threatens to disrupt the functioning of the democratic process, which demands that such dissenting perspectives be aired. Another example is the principle defined in *Rosenberger* and *L.S.O. v. Velazquez,* which limited government's ability to discriminate based on viewpoint once it makes the decision to fund private speech. The First Amendment, as it has consistently been interpreted, does not obligate the government to fund student organizations or legal services for the indigent. But once it chooses to do so, the First Amendment imposes negative egalitarian limits on the conditions the government may place on funded speech. The rule laid down in these cases does not simply advance the atomistic interest in individual autonomy; it also advances the systemic interest in a rich and varied public discourse in which all citizens might participate.

To say that negative equality is a necessary condition for a well-functioning democracy is not, however, to say that it is a sufficient condition. Take, for example, the positive egalitarian interest mentioned in *New York Times v. Sullivan* and quoted in *Buckley v. Valeo*—namely, that of promoting the "widest possible dissemination of information from diverse and antagonistic sources" and ensuring the "unfettered interchange of ideas for bringing about political and social changes desired by the people."[61] This ideal cannot be achieved simply by requiring that government keep its hands off speech, nor by requiring that, when the government regulates speech, it avoid targeting disfavored ideas or messages. It also requires that government take steps to promote the dissemination of divergent perspectives and encourage participation on the part of people espousing a diverse spectrum of views, including voices of dissent. It may well be beyond the capacity of courts to *require* that other branches of government take affirmative action to promote such broad participation. It nevertheless bears contemplation whether there are steps that the political branches of government *should* take to promote the positive egalitarian ideal of "the widest possible dissemination of information from diverse and antagonistic sources." It is to this question that I now turn.

Creating Channels for Dissent

A healthy democracy requires the availability of channels for dissent, so that issues of social importance can be debated and "antagonistic" voices disseminated. The present condition of our democracy recalls Thoreau's disconsolate recognition, while jailed for failing to pay his poll tax in protest of the State's support for the institution of slavery, that imprisonment was "the best use it could put me to" and that the State "had never thought to avail itself of my services in some other way" (pp. 96–97). Equally troubling is our government's failure to answer the frequently asked post–September 11 question, "What can I do for my country?," with anything better than a shrug-of-the-shoulders suggestion that we invest in the economy.

It is possible to imagine something better. I take Thoreau's suggestion of a "more perfect and glorious State" to point toward a system that would provide avenues for dissent, through which citizens might participate in the renewal of their democracy. One means by which to pursue this objective would be the creation of a more robust system of national service, one containing an advocacy component that would allow participants to articulate their own vision of justice—including dissent against existing institutions of government. I do not, of course, assert that the First Amendment could be construed to obtain judicial relief *requiring* the government to subsidize advocacy, much less advocacy on behalf of dissenters. Put another way, I am not arguing that it would be appropriate for courts to require that an advocacy component be included within national service legislation. But to the extent that the government subsidizes some speech activities through national service, there is a compelling argument that it must do so evenhand-edly and, more specifically, that it may not refuse funding based on the viewpoint espoused.

To see how enhancement of existing national service legislation might promote positive equality and, more broadly, advance the King-Thoreau vision of a more just state, it is helpful to start with the provisions of the existing national service law. The National and Community Service Act of 1990 provided federal funding for some service activities. This legislation was significantly expanded through legislation adopted in 1993, largely at former President Clinton's urging. The 1993 legislation created the Americorps program, providing opportunities for young people to engage in voluntary national service and receive assistance with college tuition or educational loans in return. These opportunities are provided both through government-sponsored entities and through the nonprofit sector.

Although the Americorps program was controversial at the time of its enactment, conservatives and liberals have embraced the program. Among the supporters is William Bennett, who cogently explains his support for expansion of Americorps as follows:

> Expanding a government program to promote voluntary action does, of course, seem counterintuitive. But since our nation's beginnings, the relation-ship between the state and civil society often has been positive and mutually supportive. Government has often acted as a catalyst for civic association; it can act as such again.[62]

Bennett therefore urges not only increased funding of Americorps but changes in law that would allow participants to "build the administrative, technological and financial capacities of nonprofits, rather than simply to provide beneficial services to institutions."[63] As Bennett expresses it, Americorps might provide a mechanism for developing non-governmental entities, through which individuals might join in collective action.

What Bennett and other supporters of Americorps do not squarely address is the extent to which federal monies can or should be used to support *advocacy* on the part of nonprofit organizations. Existing law does not preclude federal monies from being used for expressive activities, including those that criticize the institutions of government. Instead, the act provides that "nothing in this section shall be construed to prevent partici-pants from engaging in advocacy activities undertaken at their own initia-tive."[64] The act does provide that federal assistance may not be used for "religious instruction," to "assist, promote, or deter union organizing," or to finance elections.[65] Beyond these few content-based restrictions, the law does not restrict the ability of nonprofit organizations to use federal monies for expressive activities. As one commentator has observed, the act provides for a highly decentralized structure that "imposes few if any limiting constraints" on permissible activities. This characteristic of the program advances the objective of positive equality by providing additional resources that nonprofits may use to engage in expressive activities.

As previously mentioned, the as-yet unpassed Bayh-McCain bill would provide for a 500 percent increase in the size of Americorps and would lift the existing one-third cap on funding to national nonprofits. So long as new restrictions are not placed on advocacy activities, this proposal has the possibility to significantly expand opportunities for dissent by increasing the resources available to the nonprofit sector. In addition to promoting a more robust and varied democratic debate, the proposed amendments to Americorps would enhance the opportunity of individuals to participate in public discourse. Significantly, the proposal would expand opportunities for those of varied ideological predilections. The act increases funding for "homeland defense," thereby providing opportunities for young people interested in promoting this end. Yet it would not seem to preclude the speech activities from engaging in a variety of expressive activities including, for example, both opposition to and support for expansion of the nascent War on Terror. Interested young people would have the opportunity to participate in the activities of nonprofits espousing views that they tend to share. So, for example, those seeking to engage in advocacy in opposition to war in Iraq or elsewhere in the Middle East might receive funding for their work through the program.

It might seem strange to suggest that the government should play a role in fostering dissent against its own policies. But the idea of government funding the speech of nonprofit organizations, including speech that seeks to challenge the government's own actions, is not as revolutionary as it might initially sound. This was, after all, one of the purposes served by federally funded legal services. Federal monies for legal services have long been used to fund litigation challenging the actions of the federal government—and, indeed, providing indigent persons with the means by which to challenge government action was one of the core objectives of the legal services program.[66] Under *L.S.O. v. Velazquez,* moreover, the federal government is prohibited from imposing viewpoint-discriminatory conditions upon entities that receive federal legal services funds. While there is no enforceable constitutional requirement that Congress fund legal services for the indigent, to the extent that it chooses to do so, there is a limit on its ability to prevent entities receiving those monies from engaging in dissenting speech.

So too, there is no enforceable constitutional requirement that Congress advance positive equality through adoption of a national service program containing an advocacy component. While these are content-based restrictions upon the use of funds, they appear tailored to avoid viewpoint-based restriction upon the uses of government funds—which would likely be deemed unconstitutional under *Rosenberger* and *L.S.O. v. Velazquez.* If, for example, Congress were to allow Americorps funding to nonprofits that support the war in Iraq but prohibit it to groups that oppose that war, such a restriction would almost certainly violate the rule against viewpoint discrimination laid down in these cases.

Expansion of the national service program is only one example of how the ideal of positive equality in the realm of expansion might be advanced. Increasing the amount of funding for the nonprofit sector would enable individuals to participate in service activities that would include an advocacy component. It would thereby further King and Thoreau's vision of a more just state, one that contains the seeds of its own renewal. Legislation along the lines of that contained in the Bayh-McCain bill would not only provide a better answer to the question "What can I do for my country?" but would also expand the channels for expression of dissenting viewpoints.

Conclusion

The premise of this chapter is that the response to September 11 presents a serious First Amendment challenge, one that our existing institutions and doctrine are inadequate to meet. Its argument is that the political branches of government can and should do more to promote citizen engagement in the life of our democracy, and that enhancement of the existing national service program to include an advocacy component would be a step in the right direction. Such a component should allow funding for a wide range of viewpoints, including advocacy in opposition to actions of the national government. This would serve vital free speech interests, including both the individual's interest in self-expression and society's interest in a robust public discourse that includes antagonistic viewpoints. I do not of course mean to suggest that this proposal would be a panacea for the serious problems of citizen disengagement that plagues post–September 11 democracy. Expansion of the national service program to allow increased government support for nonprofit speech is, however, one way in which the government might seek to promote *New York Times v. Sullivan*'s vision of an "unfettered interchange of ideas for bringing about political and social changes desired by the people," a constitutional ideal that may not be not completely realizable but to which we can and should aspire.

Notes

1. For a discussion of the civil liberties questions raised by the federal government's actions subsequent to the September 11 attacks, see David Cole and James X. Dempsey, *Terrorism and the Constitution: Sacrificing Civil Liberties in the Name of National Security* (New York: The New Press, 2002).
2. *New York Times v. Sullivan*, 376 U.S. 254 (1964).
3. See Daniel P. Tokaji, "First Amendment Equal Protection: On Discretion, Inequality and Participation," *Michigan Law Review* 101 (forthcoming, 2003).
4. A noteworthy exception appears to be the PATRIOT Act's broad definition of support for any "terrorist organization," which arguably encompasses a pro-

scription òn support for wholly innocent activities. See Cole and Dempsey, *Terrorism and the Constitution,* pp. 153–55.

5. My use of the terms "positive equality" and "negative equality" is similar to that employed by Kenneth W. Simons in "Equality as a Comparative Right," *Boston University Law Review* 65 (1985): 422 and n. 74 (using "negative equality" to describe prohibition against discrimination on particular grounds and "positive equality" as mandate that benefits granted to one "must be granted to all"). Others have used the terms "positive equality" and "negative equality" quite differently from how they are used here. See, e.g., Hannah Arendt, *The Human Condition* (Chicago: University of Chicago Press, 1958), pp. 212–15 (using "negative equality" to describe sameness and "positive equality" to describe individuation); Erin Rahne Kidwell, "The Paths of the Law: Historical Consciousness, Creative Democracy, and Judicial Review," *Albany Law Review* 62 (1998): 139 (using the term "positive equality" to describe the need to be treated like others and the term "negative equality" to describe the need to be treated as an individual); Marie A. Failinger, "Equality Versus the Right to Choose Associates: A Critique of Hannah Arendt's View of the Supreme Court's Dilemma," *University of Pittsburgh Law Review* 49 (1987): 176 (describing Arendt's conception of positive and negative equality).

6. Martin Luther King, Jr., "Letter from Birmingham City Jail" (1963), in *The Essential Writings and Speeches of Martin Luther King, Jr.,* ed. James M. Washington (San Francisco: Harper Collins, 1986). Subsequent references to "Letter from Birmingham City Jail" are provided in parentheticals with the page number from this edition.

7. Henry David Thoreau, "Civil Disobedience" (1848), in *Walden and Other Writings,* ed. Joseph Wood Krutch (New York, Bantam Books, 1962). Subsequent references to "Civil Disobedience" are in parentheticals with the page number from this edition.

8. *National And Community Service Grant Program: Investment For Quality And Innovation,* 42 U.S.C. § 12653(s)(1).

9. The dissenter was Congresswoman Barbara Lee.

10. See William J. Clinton, "Faith in the USA Flourishes as Citizen Service Grows," *USA Today,* 20 June 2002, p. 23A ("One of the most gratifying responses to the tragedies of 9/11 was the sudden desire of millions of Americans to give something back to their country for the blessings of democracy and freedom.").

11. Cole and Dempsey, *Terrorism and the Constitution,* pp. 152–53.

12. Cole and Dempsey, *Terrorism and the Constitution,* p 151; Robert O'Harrow, Jr., "Six Weeks in Autumn," *Washington Post Magazine,* 27 October 2002, pp. 6–11, 17–22.

13. Both acts are codified at *National and Community Service,* 42 U.S.C. § 12501 *et seq.*

14. Daniel E. Witte, "Getting a Grip on National Service: Key Organizational Features and Strategic Characteristics of the National Service Corps (Americorps)," *B.Y.U. Law Review* (1998): 744 n.6 (quoting President William J. Clinton).

15. See Witte, "Getting a Grip on National Service," pp. 744–45.

16. *National And Community Service Grant Program: Investment For Quality And Innovation,* 42 U.S.C. § 12653(s)(1).

17. See *Call To Service Act Of 2001,* 107th Cong., 1st Sess., S. 1792.

18. *Call To Service Act Of 2001,* Section 104.

19. George W. Bush, State of the Union address, January 29, 2002. Available at http://www.nationalservice.org/about/principles/foreward.html.

20. William J. Bennett, "More Firepower for the 'Armies of Compassion,'" *Los Angeles Times,* 18 August 2002, p. M5.

21. George Weeks, "Opposition to Service Act Short-Sighted," *Detroit News,* 10 September 2002, p. 9A.

22. Richard A. Oppel, Jr., "Despite Warning, Enron Chief Urged Buying of Shares," *New York Times,* 19 January 2002, p. A1.

23. Peter Behr, "Enron's Political Power Rises; Chairman Worked Closely with Bush," *Washington Post,* 9 March 2001, p. E01.

24. Peter Vibig, "The Great Enron Disappearing Act," *New York Times Upfront,* 11 March 2002, p. 12.

25. Leslie Wayne, "Enron, Preaching Deregulation, Worked the Statehouse Circuit," *New York Times,* 9 February 2002, p. B1.

26. Kurt Eichenwald, "Even if Heads Roll, Mistrust Will Live On," *New York Times,* 6 October 2002, sec. 3, p. 1.

27. Johanna Neuman, "Military Action May Get Peace Movement Rolling," *Los Angeles Times,* 2 September 2002, at p. A8.

28. See Diana Abu-Jaber, "Express Yourself," *Washington Post,* 27 October 2002, p. B7 ("Our government appears to be disturbingly free of dissent at this volatile moment; even our media seem docile and one-note; opposition voices are rare and marginalized").

29. "House Vote on Iraq Resolution" and "Senate Vote on Iraq Resolution," *New York Times,* 12 October 2002, p. A11.

30. Frank Rich, "The Jack Welch War Plan," *New York Times,* 28 September 2002.

31. Thomas E. Patterson, "Disappearing Act: The Downturn in Voting Continues, Despite a Patriotic Fever after 9/11, and Much More Than Citizen Apathy Is to Blame," *Boston Globe,* 25 August 2002, p. D1 ("Many of this year's primary elections had record low turnout rates").

32. "The Torricelli Factor," *USA Today,* 2 October 2002, p. 19A.

33. Leonel Sanchez, "Latinos Lose Momentum at Polls in California; Turnout Tumbles from Peak in 1998 Election," *San Diego Union-Tribune,* 12 November 2002, p. B-1; Mark Z. Barabak, "Negative Campaign Repelled Some Voters: A Times Exit Poll Finds Alienation of Latinos and African Americans Also Kept Turnout Low," *Los Angeles Times,* 11 November 2002, pt. 2, p.1; Jim Yardley, "Campaign Season: Looking for Alternatives to California Candidates," *New York Times,* 13 October 2002, p. 24.

34. See *First National Bank of Boston v. Bellotti,* 435 U.S. 765, pp. 804–807 (1978) (explaining that the values served by First Amendment include both 1) "self-expression, self-realization, and self-fulfillment" and 2) protection of "the interchange of ideas"). For an example of the individual autonomy–based theory of free speech, see Charles Fried, "The New First Amendment Jurisprudence: A Threat to Liberty," *University of Chicago Law Review* 59 (1992): 225. For an example of the public discourse based theory of free speech, see Owen Fiss, "Free Speech and Social Structure," *Iowa Law Review* 71 (1986): 1405.

35. Bill Carter and Felicity Barringer, "A Nation Challenged: Speech and Expression; In Patriotic Time, Dissent Is Muting," *New York Times,* 28 September 2001, p. A1.

36. See Cole and Dempsey, *Terrorism and the Constitution,* pp. 151–68. Among the most worrisome provisions of the USA PATRIOT Act are those that expand

"guilt by association" to make innocent associations with organizations defined as "terrorist" a ground for deportation. Ibid., pp. 153–55.

37. But see Carter and Barringer, "A Nation Challenged" (citing examples of suppression of dissenting viewpoints in the days after September 11).

38. *Police Department v. Mosley,* 408 U.S. 92, 95–96 (1972). See also Kenneth L. Karst, "Equality as a Central Principle in the First Amendment," *University of Chicago Law Review 59* (1975): 20 ("the principle of equal liberty lies at the heart of the first amendment's protections against governmental regulation of the content of speech").

39. Laurence H. Tribe, *American Constitutional Law.* 2d. ed., § 12–18, (Mineola, NY: Foundation Press, 1988) p. 941.

40. 505 U.S. 377, p. 382 (1992).

41. *Thornhill v. Alabama,* 310 U.S. 88, pp. 97–98 (1940).

42. *Shuttlesworth v. Birmingham,* 394 U.S. 147, p. 154 (1969).

43. *Forsyth County v. Nationalist Movement,* 505 U.S. 123, pp. 129, 133 (1992).

44. *City of Lakewood v. Plain Dealer,* 486 U.S. 750, p. 758 (1988).

45. *Rosenberger v. Rector and Visitors of the University of Virginia,* 515 U.S. 819, p. 829 (1995).

46. *Legal Services Corporation v. Velazquez,* 531 U.S. p. 533, 536–37 (2001).

47. *Rust v. Sullivan,* 500 U.S. 173, p. 193 (1991) (rejecting a challenge to federal regulations forbidding government-funded health care providers from discussing abortion, on the ground that the government had the ability to determine what speech it would and would not support).

48. See Cole and Dempsey, *Terrorism and the Constitution,* pp. 141, 228–229 n. 20.

49. *Humanitarian Law Project v. Reno,* 205 F.3d 1130, pp. 1136–37 (9th Cir. 2000).

50. *Buckley v. Valeo,* 424 U.S. 1 (1976).

51. Ibid., p. 48.

52. Ibid.

53. Ibid.

54. Ibid (quoting *New York Times v. Sullivan,* p. 266).

55. *Red Lion Broadcasting v. F.C.C.,* 395 U.S. 367 (1969).

56. For an argument that the inequalities in the present system of funding campaigns violates equal protection, see Jamin Raskin and John Bonifaz, "The Constitutional Imperative and Practical Importance of Democratically Financed Elections," *Columbia Law Review 94* (1994): 1160.

57. Carter and Barringer, "A Nation Challenged."

58. I discuss these theories at greater length in Tokaji, "First Amendment Equal Protection."

59. Fried, "The New First Amendment Jurisprudence," p. 233.

60. Alexander Meiklejohn, *Free Speech and Its Relation to Self-Government* (New York: Harper, 1948), p. 26.

61. *Buckley v. Valeo,* 424 U.S., p. 49 (quoting *New York Times v. Sullivan,* 376 U.S, pp. 266, 269).

62. William J. Bennett, "More Firepower for the Armies of Compassion," *Los Angeles Times,* 18 August 2002, p. M5.

63. Ibid.

64. *National and Community Service Grant Program Administrative Provisions,* 42 U.S.C. § 12584(a)(5).

65. *National and Community Service Grant Program Administrative Provisions,* 42 U.S.C. § 12634.

66. See, e.g., Richard Abel, "Law Without Politics: Legal Aid Under Advanced Capitalism," *UCLA Law Review* 32 (February 1985): 528 (describing inception of legal aid as an instance of the state having "created and funded the institutional structure that gives the subordinate partner [the poor] legal representation through which to assert legal claims against the dominant member [the state]").

Chapter 11

The Way Forward:

Locke or Hobbes?

John W. Wells

As important as the questions surrounding America's public policy response to 9/11 are, perhaps the most important concern is the extent to which the nation's political culture has been altered. In other words, have the events of September 11, 2001, resulted in a dramatic shift in the nation's democratic sense of itself and will the nation's institutions be permanently altered by the experience of terrorism on American soil? While it is too soon to tell with any definitive certitude what the long-term impact may be, preliminary conclusions can be reached. Even before the planes hit the towers in New York, American-styled liberalism was in transition. The attacks themselves have added to the changes that were already taking place. The impact of those changes on the nation's political culture is the focus of this final chapter.

American Political Culture and Civil Liberties

The United States has been fortunate. Throughout its long history the geographic realities of friendly borders and two vast oceans have served to protect the country from most foreign threats. These arrangements have allowed democracy to take root in a few important ways. First, the presence of the frontier and its legacy has made America the land of second chances.[1] Immigrants from across the world have come to American shores to seek a better life, free, at least presumably, from the ancient prejudices of Europe. While such a view of America is clearly optimistic, there has been a kernel of truth in the description. Far more than in Europe, the mass of citizens in America have availed themselves of the opportunity to experiment with new forms of living. Alexis de Tocqueville observed that with this spirit, Americans are born free.[2] He was impressed by the fact that Americans had the space, both in terms of physical geography and in social relations as well, to develop in unique ways. From jazz to the philosophical movement of Pragmatism, the emphasis on innovation and experimentation has permeated the American experience.

In his famous address of 1890, historian Frederick Jackson Turner credited the frontier with this spirit of innovation.[3] The frontier served as a safety valve for the young republic, channeling what might otherwise have been revolutionary and disrupting sentiments westward. The assumption behind this idea was that the ready availability of new land provided at least the possibility of breaking free from social conventions that, due to over-crowded cities and more contracted space, were considered inviolable in Europe. Departing from the age-old notions of divine right and the eternal chain of being, the vast newness and openness of the unsettled country afforded a unique opportunity for the human race to recreate itself and live anew its infancy, replaying options that were already exhausted in Europe.[4] With the possibility of moving westward and finding new ways to live, Americans tended to view personal identity as less fixed and more negotiable.[5] Such a view of personal identity lends itself to greater possibilities of tolerance and diversity.

Perhaps the quintessential American expression of this kind of impulse was Thomas Jefferson's dismissal of religion as the fundamental definition of anyone's identity. Realizing that the absolute truth claims of the Old World had contributed to the unfortunate wars over religion, he embraced the plurality of religious expression by stating that a man's religious beliefs were his own affair.[6] Such views, as well as the universal declarations of broad freedoms found in the Declaration of Independence, are much more difficult to envision in the absence of a largely unsettled continent full of possibilities.

With a philosophical worldview tending toward self-creation, the new country's political culture helped to foster a citizenry open to the emergence of democracy and pluralism. To be sure, the potential for diversity and tolerance was not always in evidence. Racial strife and intolerance toward immigrants are central elements of the American narrative. In addition, there have been many significant and regrettable moments when Americans abandoned their faith in toleration and resorted to centralized efforts to impose conformity. The Alien and Sedition Acts during John Adams's administration, restrictions of civil liberties under Abraham Lincoln, the suppression of dissent during World War I, and the McCarthy period all demonstrate the difficulties of maintaining a popular consensus around issues of civil liberty. Despite such historical realities, however, there has persisted a widespread acceptance, at least in theory, of the rights of free expression and personal liberty. What is important to realize, however, is that the ideals of recreation and diversity were present from the beginning, and while they have periodically been interrupted, they have persisted as defining features of the American experience.

Thus, the frontier initially provided the historical context for the development of a political culture of tolerance and plurality. Turner's thesis, however, expressly raised concerns regarding the political ramifications of the disappearance of the frontier. Most certainly, the century-old republic was altered by the changing geographic realities, but the effects of the frontier lingered long after the prospect of cheap land and inexhaustible resources had passed into history. Ironically, the ideas most closely associated with the frontier, openness and diversity, became more readily apparent when the actual frontier disappeared. This was due to the fact that while Americans could no longer point to the physical reality of the frontier, it persisted as an ideological construct. Americans felt freer than other nationalities and continued to live their lives against the backdrop of a frontier that existed in rhetoric if not in fact.[7] The frontier nation existed apart from the rest of the world, isolated by geography but also in attitude. Even when the rest of the world erupted into savage fighting during the two world wars, the United States remained largely unscathed, as enemy bombs fell no closer than Hawaii. The frontier was, despite American involvement in the wars, still a healthy part of the nation's self-conception.

The events of 9/11 have raised the question as to whether Turner's concerns are again relevant. The arrival of terrorism on America's shores may very well be the moment that the country experienced the limits of the frontier. Just as the physical frontier gave way to the frontier as ideological construct, the reality that isolation is effectively at an end may mean the end of American exceptionalism. The world has arrived in America and suddenly the luxury of space seems to have been dramatically protracted. The disappearance of this frontier construct, existing as it has ideally if not in geographic reality, poses the very real prospect of a new kind of America, one that may come to share the more Hobbesian concerns that have traditionally characterized other polities. Americans may sense that pluralism and diversity, aided as they have been by the sense that there is room enough for everyone, are no longer as easily accommodated in a land that has reached its limits. The sense of being in the world, a part of the global system with its attendant difficulties of securing national defense, may undermine the cultural ethos of openness that has existed as a remnant of the frontier experience.

In addition to the social possibilities of self-creation provided by the frontier, American political culture has been positively shaped by the isolation afforded by geography. Largely freed from the imminent threat of war, democratic ideas have taken deep root. Machiavellian dictates of centralizing authority in the face of external threats have played a much smaller role in the United States than in Continental polities. Although Americans have often reacted in the same spirit as other nations when feelings of vulnerability have surfaced, they have tended to view such moments as temporary. The expectation has always been that the norm is isolation and protection from the problems of the world. Even during the cold war, many Americans hoped for a return to older more traditional notions of an America separated from the unsavory affairs of Europe and the rest of the world. It is the latter feature of the nation's historic sense of itself—its relative isolation from the nasty disputes that have plagued much of the rest of the world—that may have been most affected by the events of September 2001.

For those concerned about civil liberties, the historical record provides a rather bleak account of the nation's reaction during times of crisis, when the sense of isolation has given way to feelings of vulnerability. In the immediate aftermath of the first world war the efforts by Attorney General A. Mitchell Palmer resulted in the first Red Scare. At Palmer's urging, police powers were expanded and the country was gripped by an ugly return of nativism.[8] During the early days of the cold war, the belief that the Soviets were undermining American democracy from within was widespread. A kind of national paranoia spread throughout the country, fanned by the likes of Senator Joseph McCarthy (R-WI) and the John Birch Society. In the aftermath of both instances, however, there was a revival of the frontier idea and a concomitant return to self-expression and diversity.

While the United States never fully escaped the nativism of the immediate post-war culture, the 1920s emerged as a time of cultural ferment and experimentation. Women's rights and the rise of bohemian culture were elements of a decade that saw Americans wishing to turn away from the world and revisit the frontier values of self-creation.[9] The 1960s was a decade marked by an even more explicit return to the frontier idea. Beginning with John Kennedy's explicit use of the word "frontier" as the title of his new economic program, the decade will be remembered as a time of student protest, citizen activism, and the contesting of heretofore accepted social mores. The fallout from the 1960s continues to stir debate, but the strong fact remains that by revisiting the frontier idea, the country emerged from that decade more diverse than when it entered it.

Thus, periods when Americans sensed that their safety was an issue are generally marked as times when civil liberties came under assault. The optimistic news is, however, that in the twentieth century, both periods characterized by such fears were followed by the return of the frontier construct. It is important to remember, however, that despite the fact that this pattern was in evidence in the past, there are no guarantees that the current period of concern over national security will be followed by a time of embracing the ideological construct of the frontier. History offers few guarantees that the future will replicate the past. It remains to be seen if the frontier idea of self-creation and a willingness to embrace pluralism and diversity will survive intact in light of the War on Terror.

The immediate objection to the idea that the events of September 11 delivered a potentially fatal blow to the nation's sense of isolation is the contention that the United States has already surrendered the idea of isolation. According to this line of thought, American independence was largely achieved as a result of the geopolitical realities of great power politics. Because of England's military and economic hegemony in the late eighteenth century, nations such as France rallied to the aid of the fledgling American colonies in their struggle for separation from Britain. A broad reading of American history could point to the Spanish-American War as well as the persistent engagement of the United States in world affairs throughout the twentieth century. While this historical narrative is in many respects compelling, it neglects the fact that Americans always had the sense that their country was somehow separated from the world and could chose to participate or not. Isolationist sentiment has been a strong and consistent theme running throughout the course of American history. The fundamental difference now is that the sense that the world is somehow "out there," separated from America, has been undermined by the reality of foreign-sponsored domestic terror.

The terrorist attacks have accentuated the darker side of globalization, a process that has largely been hailed by American elites as representing a new opportunity for the country.[10] Globalization, a process that is having a profound cultural and economic impact on the entire planet, continues to progress at a seemingly unstoppable pace. Critics charge that the process should better be referred to as "Americanization."[11] In other words, the United States finds itself the purveyor of the world's popular culture. It has become the world's storyteller and commodity retailer. And yet, this Americanization of the world, with its concomitant technological innovations in the areas of transportation and communication, is not simply altering the indigenous identities of peoples around the world. The process may, in fact, be altering the very necessary background for America's democratic culture by drawing the country further into the world. The sense that all is well and the troubles of the rest of the planet do not affect the United States adversely may very well be giving way to the reality of a new world order that observes no permanent boundaries. By being perceived as the primary force behind globalization, the United States has become the de facto target of frustration for groups resisting the rise of the global market. The periodic attacks on overseas McDonalds restaurants and the efforts by even modern countries like France to limit the number of American movies shown in French theaters speak to this reality.[12]

In light of globalization, 9/11 confirmed what has already taken place. In other words, the terrorist attacks dramatized the fact that the country cannot pretend to be above the affairs of a world that has been altered through American popular culture. America must now confront the reality of a world brought closer together and that includes the arrival of some of the more unsavory practices that have heretofore not been seen in the United States. Such a realization was dramatically burned into the national mindset in September 2001. The communication and transportation revolutions have been in place for years, and America's presence in a rapidly globalizing structure was already a fait accompli before 9/11. What is different, however, is the widespread popular perception of the country's placement in the world. The United States is not merely reorganizing the world in its image—the world has arrived on American shores as well. The relationship, it turns out, is not unilateral; it is symbiotic and the option of isolation is no longer available.

Americans have not been entirely blind to the gradual immersion of the country into the affairs of the world. In fact, much of the politics of the last fifty years can be viewed as an attempt to deal with the new reality. As

Francis Fitzgerald points out, national politics has, especially in the past two decades, been concerned with trying to find a way to reinstate an older feeling of impregnability.[13] In the 1980s this desire took the form of an unbridled faith in the power of technology to bring about a de facto isolation. The Strategic Defense Initiative, far from being the quixotic fascination of a cold war president, actually reflected the nation's longstanding political culture quite well.

The debate over "Star Wars" therefore represented a latent awareness on the part of the American people that their feelings of being above the world's problems were already becoming outdated. Nothing could have crystallized such dormant insecurities as quickly as a surprise attack. This was the true significance of the terrorist strike. The glacially rising perception of vulnerability was confirmed in the starkest of terms when the New York skyline was so dramatically scarred. Now, however, with no frontier and no sense of isolation from the world to comfort Americans who would like to see the United States safely ensconced away from world affairs, the nation's reaction may depart from historical precedent and accept a more permanent place for the national security state. The question that remains open two years after the terrorist attacks is the extent to which the country's commitment to civil liberties was dependent upon the dual pillars of the frontier and the sense of isolation.

From Locke to Hobbes?

America's commitment to civil liberties stems not simply from the contingent factors of the nation's geography. John Locke's principles undergird American democracy.[14] Natural rights, the inviolability of individual property, and the emphasis on the rational consent of the governed continue to pour forth from the nation's founding more than two centuries after Thomas Jefferson officially penned them into the nation's philosophical DNA. Such views are not without their detractors, of course. Postmodernists have savaged the metaphysical assumptions of classical liberalism, dismissing natural rights as evidence of so much political mythology and word play.[15] While such criticisms have gained widespread currency in the Academy, popular language regarding the rights and responsibilities of citizens continues to hold primary sway throughout the country's political dialogue. The central question to be answered in the coming years is whether or not the persistence of this Lockean system depends upon a cultural background of security and the frontier construct. In other words, can the country's Lockean philosophy withstand the evolution of its political culture? Will restraining the power of the police and limiting the intrusion of the state be viewed as luxuries that can no longer be afforded?

John Locke's "state of nature" posits the idea of a more or less civil individual, minding his own business, and conducting his affairs without the need of Thomas Hobbes's Leviathan state. Thus, the Lockean system is dependent upon a shared sense that the world is a more or less benevolent place and dangers, while present, are generally of only minimal importance. Critics of Locke have accused him of reading seventeenth-century man back into the state of nature and thus distorting the true Augustinian nature of human beings.[16] Without descending into that debate, it is clear that Locke's "natural man" is a benign entity, endowed with the capacity of spontaneous sociability.

One is struck by the largely pacific features of Locke's ideal citizen. War and conflict seem to be distant and the state has only limited roles that it need perform.

> But though this be a state of liberty, yet it is not a state of licence; though man in that state have an uncontrollable liberty to dispose of his person or possessions, yet he has not liberty to destroy himself, or so much as any creature in his possession, but where some nobler use than its bare preservation calls for it. The state of Nature has a law of Nature to govern it, which obliges every one, and reason, which is that law, teaches all mankind who will but consult it, that being all equal and independent, no one ought to harm another in his life, health, liberty or possessions. . . . And, being furnished with like faculties, sharing all in one community of Nature, there cannot be supposed any such subordination among us that may authorise us to destroy one another, as if we were made for one another's uses, as the inferior ranks of creatures are for ours. Every one as he is bound to preserve himself, and not to quit his station wilfully, so by the like reason, when his own preservation comes not in competition, ought he as much as he can to preserve the rest of mankind, and not unless it be to do justice on an offender, take away or impair the life, or what tends to the preservation of the life, the liberty, health, limb, or goods of another.[17]

In no other country has Locke's view of reality had more resonance than the United States. The tolerance that has been fostered by the ready availability of land and the safety from external threats has come nearer to approximating Locke's ideal in the United States than anywhere else.[18] Americans have been consistently suspicious of government centralization and more jealous of their individual liberties than virtually any other state.[19] Such feelings do not occur in a vacuum. They are formed by benefit of the nation's political culture—a culture profoundly affected by such variables as the sense of safety and the construct of the frontier. If the background assumptions accompanying this view are no longer valid, what is likely to take its place?

The chances that the United States will completely abandon more than two centuries of liberal idealism are remote. What is more likely to occur is a retreat to the protoliberalism of Thomas Hobbes. Along with Locke, Hobbes is usually introduced to undergraduates early in their academic career. And, more often than not, Hobbes and Locke are juxtaposed against one another. Locke, the defender of individual liberty and small government, makes for an easy point of comparison to Hobbes, the pessimist who sees the state of nature as a war of all against all. While such easy contrasts between the two tend toward over-simplification, there is still much to be gleaned from such a discussion. Hobbes is decidedly less convinced that society could be left to its own devices.

> Again, men have no pleasure (but on the contrary a great deal of grief) in keeping company where there is no power able to overawe them all. For every man looketh that his companion should value him at the same rate he sets upon himself, and upon all signs of contempt or undervaluing naturally endeavours, as far as he dares (which amongst them that have no common power to keep them in quiet is far enough to make them destroy each other), to extort a greater value from his contemners, by damage; and from others, by the example.[20]

Without the overwhelming presence of the state to keep individuals from acting on their most negative inclinations, violence is the inevitable result, and the fear of violent death ultimately undermines any hope for the success of a liberal order. Further, Hobbes is clearly less sanguine than Locke regarding the prospects for spontaneous and benign sociability. Hobbes lists the factors that drive man toward unsociability: "So that in the nature of man, we find three principal causes of quarrel. First, competition; secondly, diffidence; thirdly, glory."[21] No, the state must be carefully designed using a mixture of mythological imagery and rational calculation. This is the Hobbes with whom most students of politics are familiar.

A more careful look at Hobbes's work, however, yields a slightly more nuanced picture. Without delving too deeply into the intricacies of his thought, it is clear that Hobbes truly should be viewed as a protoliberal. His seemingly unlimited state is actually limited. When the state speaks it is sovereign, but when the state is silent, the individual retains the right of self-determination in the private sphere. It is this private sphere that is so crucial to classical liberal discourse. The fact that Hobbes respects its inviolability is evidence of his being sympathetic with what flowered into the liberal project.

As Hobbes recognized, when the individual is in fear of violent death, little else matters. The rights and liberties commonly associated with free thought are simply not realizable without some guarantee that mortality will be kept at bay. In this sense, Hobbes represents a major voice in the drive toward establishing an order whereby individuals might be left alone to experiment with their lives and live free from onerous state regulation.[22] In addition, Hobbes's social contract is based upon the idea of rationality. The people give consent to a state that provides safety while they in return reduce their overtly expressive exercises of freedom.

Even with this more positive interpretation of the work of Hobbes, the sound of the argument still grates the ear of the civil libertarian. Why should the state restrict the rights of individuals in so draconian a manner? How can a free society flourish without some sort of publicly shared discourse whereby individuals are protected by well-established civil rights from government interference? These are obvious questions but they may very well be running counter to what has already taken place in American society—the destruction of a meaningful public realm.

At the time of the terrorist attacks, debates were already raging among political theorists concerning the health of American democracy. Sparked by the widely discussed study by Robert Putnam, many democratic theorists openly worried that the intermediary institutions of civil society were no longer robust and may, in fact, be leading to a kind of mass consciousness.[23] This concern is by no means new. Throughout the 1950s, theorists and social critics poured scorn on what they perceived to be a uniform culture where individual expression was no longer valued and the pressure to conform became paramount.[24] Thus, the retreat to the private realm, always the privileged sphere in liberal discourse, is largely complete. Public institutions are generally held in poor esteem while the intermediating groups of civil society continue to decline.[25] In other words, the citizenry has already largely surrendered the public realm and chosen to find fulfillment in the private. They have, therefore, already made the first major step toward adopting the Hobbesian view of liberalism; liberty is experienced in the private realm while the public realm becomes a place of security and state control. Much as in the earlier debate, the fear is that thinking in terms of the mass directs citizens away from their individual rights and makes them less tolerant of diversity. Of even more importance is the neo-Tocquevillian theme in the contemporary literature that the failure to socialize leads to a rising distrust.[26] When citizens are not engaging with one another in various civic organizations (e.g., churches and little league), it presumably becomes much easier to assume the worst about each other. If such fears are well founded then they clearly pose a threat to the Lockean assumptions of American society.

What the terrorist attacks have done is to simply reinforce the post–World War II mentality that safety must come first. In the decade following the conclusion of the war, Americans moved in large numbers to what some viewed as bland and sterile neighborhoods in the suburbs. From Levitt-town to California, many Americans retreated to a suburban utopia where they could collectively endeavor to lead private lives. More recently, gated communities have risen across the country, further adding to the sense of safety that so many of the residents crave.[27] In the case of the gated communities, residents are more than willing to surrender the right to determine even minute details of their home, such as the height of the mailbox or what flowers may hang from the front porch, in exchange for the feeling that they are somehow immune from crime.

All of this is to suggest that the movement toward a protoliberal Hobbesian society is already underway, spurned onward by such domestic factors as the fear of crime and deteriorating urban centers. What is important to note here, however, is that such a paradigm is not necessarily dystopic. Those who would charge that the country is on the verge of embracing a kind of Americanized fascism or a blind faith in the power of the central government to determine the lives of the citizens miss the point. The liberal Hobbesian paradigm continues to stress the importance of rights, especially the right to be left alone. In a mass consumer society such as the United States, the right to pursue private projects is paramount. Freedom is seen as the right to consume and to be expressive by benefit of participation in the market.

When U.S. Attorney General John Ashcroft announces the need to strengthen the government's powers in order to secure a safe haven for freedom, many Americans find that they have no real quarrel with such a program. They may very well be inclined to conclude that nothing will really change in their day-to-day affairs. The stress on freedom in the private realm has emerged as the prevailing way in which Americans view their liberty. The concerns of civil libertarians that public discourse will be affected seem largely out of place in the consumer republic. As the Lockean notion of political agency is replaced with the power of the credit card, and acquisition takes the place of active political participation, the protoliberalism of Hobbes's theoretical program emerge.

Conclusion

Traditional American political culture fostered a belief in the primacy of the individual and the need to restrict the power of the state. Such beliefs have been encouraged by the historical contingencies of the American experience. In particular, the frontier served as a safety valve affording Americans who wanted to experience life on their own terms the potential for doing so. With the passing of the frontier at the end of the nineteenth century, Americans turned to an idealized conception whereby expanded civil liberties provided the resources once made possible by the ready availability of cheap land.

In addition to the idealized frontier, the United States has been blessed by friendly borders and two vast oceans. Such favorable geographic factors have contributed to the belief that the country is somehow separated from the world and less in need of a strong centralized state to maintain security. With the terrorist attacks of September 11, 2001, however, both of these traditional assumptions have been thrown into stark relief against the backdrop of a world drawn closer together. The frontier mentality has always been closely tied to the feeling of security. With the advent of domestic terror and the fading sense of invulnerability, the question remains to what extent the frontier mentality of self-creation, free expression, and the right to dissent will flourish. One way to view the attacks is to see their effects as confirming a redefinition of freedom that was already taking place in America. This view of freedom accentuates the private realm and devalues the public; it does not portend a disappearance of the liberal order, but, rather, its evolution.

Despite the valid concerns of theorists and critics, the United States does not appear to be abandoning completely its commitment to civil liberties. In fact, as the time since 9/11 has elapsed, the belief that civil liberties must be protected has increased, and yet this is not the whole story.[28] Americans appear to be more willing to see those rights circumscribed, and they have elevated the value of stability. This is occurring as Americans come to the realization that the historical contingencies of geography and exceptionalism are giving way to the realities of America's place in the global community. The fact of globalism is not new, but the darker realities of it are only just now becoming apparent to much of the population.

Fear of the impending embrace of some sort of American-styled police state appears grossly overstated at the present time. This is due to the presence of a long history of feeling relatively secure. This experience has left the United States with a well-engrained political culture that ensures a skeptical public reaction whenever government officials talk of expanding police powers too dramatically. And yet, political cultures are not static. They do not exist in some perpetual state but rather change slowly depending upon historical circumstances. The 9/11 attacks loom quite large and appear to have set in motion forces that run counter, at least to some degree, to the nation's historic commitment to privacy and negative freedom.

Adding to the probability that civil liberties will continue to be circumscribed, though still existent, are the changes taking place in national life on an economic and social level. The continued penetration of mass consumer capitalism into every facet of the country's life has contributed to the much-lamented decline of the public square. As citizens have come to view themselves as consumers, private life has become increasingly important while the public realm has declined. Such freedoms as free speech, citizen activism, and certain Warren-era criminal rights appear to be on the losing side of contemporary trends away from the public realm. Paradoxically, it is the embrace of private life, with its attendant abandoning of the public realm, that may serve as the greatest barrier to full encroachment on civil liberties.

In summation, America is a land in transition. At the present time this movement is not characterized by an abandoning of civil liberties wholesale. What does appear to be occurring is the view of rights most closely associated with Hobbes's protoliberalism. Stability is the most important value. Without stability and safety all other rights and privileges are meaningless. Contemporary America seems particularly well suited to such a view of freedom in that citizenship has been devalued in favor of consumerism.

A word of caution is in order, however, given the possibility that terrorism takes an extended break from American shores. Should the fear of terrorism abate sufficiently, history suggests that the country will revive its commitment to civil liberties and reaffirm its Lockean heritage. At this point though, it is still unclear as to how complete the move from Locke to Hobbes will be.

Notes

1. Frederick Jackson Turner's famous thesis helped to structure much of the debate regarding American political culture for over a century. See Frederick

Jackson Turner, *The Frontier in American History* (New York: Dover Publications, 1996). See also Seymour Martin Lipset, *American Exceptionalism: A Double Edged Sword* (New York: W.W. Norton Press, 1996).

2. Alexis de Tocqueville, *Democracy in America,* ed. by Richard D. Heffner (New York: The New American Library, 1956).

3. Turner, *The Frontier in American History.*

4. See Hannah Arendt's discussion of natality in *On Revolution* (New York: Viking Press, 1963).

5. George Cotkin, *Existential America* (Baltimore, MD: Johns Hopkins University Press, 2003).

6. The most complete religious biography on Jefferson is Edwin Gaustad, *Sworn on the Altar of God: A Religious Biography of Thomas Jefferson* (Grand Rapids, MI: W.B. Eerdmans Publishing, 1996).

7. This might be termed the "existentializing" of the American frontier. While the physical reality of the frontier had disappeared, the frontier continued to exist as an attitude characteristic of American political culture.

8. See David J. Goldberg, *Discontented America: The United States in the 1920s* (Baltimore, MD: Johns Hopkins University Press, 1999). This was when the Ku Klux Klan reemerged on the national scene, driven more by a concern over the spread of communism and a fear of immigrants than by the earlier emphasis on terrorizing racial minorities.

9. Lynn Dumenil, *The Modern Temper: American Culture and Society in the 1920s* (New York: Hill and Wang Publishing, 1995).

10. Thomas L. Friedman, *The Lexus and the Olive Tree* (New York: Farrar, Straus, Giroux, 1999).

11. See Jerry Mander and Edward Goldsmith, *The Case Against the Global Economy: And for a Turn toward the Local* (San Francisco, CA: Sierra Club Books, 1996).

12. Benjamin Barber, *Jihad vs. McWorld: How Globalism and Tribalism Are Reshaping the World* (New York: Ballantine Books, 1996).

13. Frances FitzGerald, *Way Out There in the Blue: Reagan, Star Wars, and the End of the Cold War* (New York: Simon and Schuster, 2000).

14. See John Locke, *Second Treatise of Government,* ed. by C.B. Macpherson (Indianapolis, IN: Hackett Publishing Company, 1980).

15. See Richard Beardsworth, *Derrida and the Political* (New York: Routledge Press, 1996).

16. The argument over the true nature of human beings is at the heart of much of modern political theory. In order to break with earlier notions of human depravity, Locke devised a new political anthropology that suggested that in the state of nature human beings are actually benign. The consequences of such a view are immediately apparent. If human beings are essentially good, or at least not harmful to one another, then the need for a strong and powerful government is reduced.

17. Locke, *Second Treatise,* p. 9.

18. Obviously, the presence of systematic racism, the destruction of Native American cultures, etc., cannot be discounted; however, the fact remains that Americans, at least rhetorically, cherish the Lockean ideal.

19. See Mary Ann Glendon, *Rights Talk: The Impoverishment of Political Discourse* (New York: The Free Press, 1991).

20. Thomas Hobbes, *Leviathan* (New York: E.P. Dutton and Co., 1940), chapter 13.

21. Ibid.

22. David van Mill, *Liberty, Rationality, and Agency in Hobbes's Leviathan* (Albany, NY: State University of New York Press, 2001) provides the most convincing overview of the protoliberalism of Thomas Hobbes.
23. See Robert Putnam, *Bowling Alone: The Collapse and Revival of American Community* (New York: Touchstone Books, 2001). Putnam's work, stemming from a 1995 *Journal of Democracy* article, has become a central text in the ongoing discussion regarding the decline of American civil society.
24. See Kevin Mattson, *Intellectuals in Action: The Origins of the New Left and Radical Liberalism, 1945–1970* (University Park, PA: Pennsylvania State University Press, 2002) for a complete discussion of the left's critique of 1950s suburban culture.
25. See Mickey Kaus, *The End of Equality* (New York: BasicBooks, 1992).
26. See Adam B. Seligman, *The Problem of Trust* (Princeton, NJ: Princeton University Press, 1997). In addition, see also Francis Fukuyama, *Trust: Human Nature and the Reconstitution of Social Order* (New York: Touchstone Books, 1996).
27. Evan McKenzie, *Privatopia: Homeowner Associations and the Rise of Residential Private Government* (New Haven, CT: Yale University Press, 1996) provides much insight and analysis into the rise of gated communities.
28. See Susan Tabrizi's chapter in this volume.

About the Editors

David B. Cohen

David B. Cohen, Ph.D. University of South Carolina, M.A. University of Tennessee, Knoxville, B.A. University of Wisconsin-Madison, is currently an assistant professor of political science and honors adviser at The University of Akron. His research on executive politics and other topics has been published in *American Politics Quarterly*, *Congress & the Presidency*, *Presidential Studies Quarterly*, *PS: Political Science & Politics*, *Southeastern Political Review*, and *White House Studies*. His primary areas of interest are the American presidency, and the conduct and formulation of U.S. national and homeland security policy.

John W. Wells

John W. Wells, M.A., Ph.D. University of Tennessee, Knoxville, is currently an associate professor of political science at Carson Newman College. During his tenure he has devised a number of political theory courses and interdisciplinary team-taught classes. For three years he was the director of the honors program. He has received two commendations for his teaching and lecturing skills. In addition, he has served as a television commentator for a local Knoxville station. His research interests include the nature of contemporary American democracy, civil society, and political theology. He has published articles on the inter-relationship between democracy and religious fundamentalism as well as on the political significance of the Holocaust.

About the Contributors

Christopher P. Banks

Christopher P. Banks, Ph.D. University of Virginia, J.D. University of Dayton, B.A. University of Connecticut, is currently an associate professor in the Department of Political Science at The University of Akron.

John C. Blakeman

John C. Blakeman is currently an assistant professor of political science at the University of Wisconsin–Stevens Point. He received his Ph.D. at the

University of Virginia, an M.S. from the London School of Economics, and a B.A. from Wake Forest University.

Alethia H. Cook

Alethia H. Cook is an instructor at The University of Akron as well as an academic advisor for the Department of Political Science. She received her M.A. in international relations from The University of Akron and is currently A.B.D. for her Ph.D. in public policy from Kent State University.

Chris J. Dolan

Chris J. Dolan, Ph.D. University of South Carolina, M.A. Northeastern University, B.A. Siena College, is an assistant professor of political science at the University of Central Florida.

Brian J. Gerber

Brian J. Gerber, Ph.D. State University of New York at Stony Brook, M.A. University of New Mexico, B.A. University of Wisconsin-Oshkosh, is an assistant professor of political science at Texas Tech University.

David J. Louscher

David J. Louscher, M.A., Ph. D. University of Wisconsin-Madison, M.A. American University, B.A. Morningside College, is chair of the political science department at The University of Akron.

L. Christian Marlin

Christian Marlin, J.D. Emory University, B.A. University of Central Florida, is a former adjunct professor of constitutional law at the University of Central Florida and currently serves as associate general counsel to Lennar Corporation.

Jerel A. Rosati

Jerel A. Rosati is a professor of political science and international studies at the University of South Carolina. He received his B.A. in political science at the University of California Los Angeles, his M.A. in political science at Arizona State University, and his Ph.D. in international relations at American University in Washington, D.C.

Edward R. Sharkey, Jr.

Edward R. Sharkey, Jr., Ph.D. Northern Arizona University, M.A. and B.A. University of Montana, is an assistant professor of political science at Columbia College in Columbia, South Carolina.

Otis H. Stephens, Jr.

Otis H. Stephens, Jr., is Distinguished Service Professor of political science and resident scholar of constitutional law in the College of Law at the University of Tennessee-Knoxville. He earned A.B. and M.A. degrees at the University of Georgia, a Ph.D. degree in political science at Johns Hopkins University, a J.D. degree at the University of Tennessee, and is a member of the Tennessee Bar.

Kendra B. Stewart

Kendra B. Stewart, Ph.D., M.P.A. University of South Carolina, B.A. University of Central Florida, serves on the faculty of Eastern Kentucky University as an assistant professor.

Susan J. Tabrizi

Susan J. Tabrizi, Ph.D., M.A. State University of New York at Stony Brook, M.A. University of South Carolina, B.A. Utica College of Syracuse University, is currently assistant professor of political science at Bucknell University.

Daniel P. Tokaji

Daniel P. Tokaji is a professor in the Moritz College of Law at The Ohio State University. Previously, he was a staff attorney at the American Civil Liberties Union Foundation of Southern California. He earned a J.D. from Yale Law School and graduated summa cum laude from Harvard College with an A.B. in English and American literature and philosophy.

Index

ABC *see* American Broadcast Company
ABC/*Washington Post* poll, 191
Adams, John, 2, 228
AEDPA, *see* Antiterrorism and Effective
  Death Penalty Act (1996)
Afghanistan, 45, 71, 78, 80, 89, 173,
  188, 192, 204
African Americans, 2000 voter participation
  and, 208–9
African National Congress, 107
Al Odah v. U.S. (2003), 77, 79
Al Qaeda, 71, 80, 82, 83, 89, 107, 159,
  192, 203, 208
Alejandre v. Republic of Cuba (1998),
  96, 99, 101
Alien and Seditions Acts, 2, 175, 228
Alien Tort Claims Act (ACTA), 91–2
Alliance, Ohio, 109
American Association of Airport Execu-
  tives, 161
American Broadcast Company (ABC), 167
American Civil Liberties Union (ACLU),
  125, 144, 159, 161
American Council on Trustees and Alumni
  (ACTA), 217
American Herald (Boston), 186
American Revolution, 10
Americorp, 207, 220
ANSER Institute for Homeland Secu-
  rity, 125
anthrax (*Bacillus anthracis*), 105, 117
anti-Americanism: Palmer, A. Mitchell and,
  2; Bush administration and, 3
anti-Federalists, 2, 29
Antiterrorism and Effective Death Penalty
  Act (1996), 30, 39, 40, 41, 95–6; award
  disposition and, 97–9
Arab Americans, 22, 160, 193
*Argentine Republic v. Amerada Hess
  Shipping Corp* (1989), 95
Articles of War, 74, 75
Ashcroft Doctrine, 45, 55
Ashcroft, John, 30, 45, 47, 48, 83, 158,
  169, 203, 236
Aum Shinrikyo, 107
Australia, 77
Aviation and Transportation Security
  Act, 147, 152
Aviation Transportation and Security
  Act, 157, 158
Baloch, Shakir Ali, 159
Banks, Christopher, 3
Bayh, Evan, 207
Beckett, Samuel, 126

Beirut, Lebanon, 179
Bennett, William, 207, 220
Berger v. New York (1967), 33
Berlin, Isaiah, 6
Bill of Rights, 9–10, 29, 180, 185, 186
Bin Laden, Osama, 89, 168
biological weapons: twentieth century use ·
  of, 107; civil liberties and, 108; planning
  responses to attack with, 117–18;
  reasons for use of, 108; terrorism and,
  4–5; unique problems of, 108–10
Biological Weapons Convention (BWC), 107
Birminghma, Alabama, 210
Black, Hugo, 177
Blakeman, John, 4
Boeing Company, The, 159
Boim v. Quranic Literacy Institute (2002),
  90, 93, 100
Bork, Robert Heron, 92
Bosnia, 179
Brandeis, Louis, 29
Brennan, Justice William, 204, 214
Brill, Stephen, 179
Brokaw, Tom, 105
Buckley v. Valeo (1976), 216
Bureau of Alcohol, Tobacco, and Firearms
  (ATF), 154
Bush administration: anti-Americanism and,
  3; civil rights contraction and, 162;
  creation of Department of Homeland
  Security, 153; ordering military tribunals
  and, 71; political orientation to
  homeland security and, 126; use of
  military tribunals and, 4
Bush, George H. W., Special Isotope
  Separation Project and, 22
Bush, George W., 3, 45, 73, 76, 131, 147,
  171, 188, 192
Cable News Network (CNN), 157
Call to Service Act (Bayh-McCain bill), 207
Canada, 115
Carnivore Diagnostic Tool (DCS-
  1000), 46, 51
Caute, David, 17–18
CBS News/*New York Times* poll,
  189, 191–194
Center for Constitutional Rights, 159
Center for Law and the Public's Health
  (Georgetown University and Johns
  Hopkins University), 110
*Center for National Security Studies v.
  U.S. Department of Justice* (2003),
  49–50, 72, 159
Centers for Disease Control and Prevention
  (CDC), 106, 110, 113